"This guy can really write!"

—ALMA GUILLERMOPRIETO, author of *Dancing with Cuba*

"In Mexico City, trends, fashions, youth lifestyles—punks, emos, and hipsters, like hippies and Beats long before—arrive from the U.S. and are adopted and mutate until they are as Mexican as anything. Unlike in the U.S., they never really go away. Daniel Hernandez is our guide into this labyrinth of urban tribes, this vast twenty-first-century urban survival laboratory. He writes about his experience as he lived it, with daring curiosity, bursts of stunning poetry, charming earnestness, penetrating intelligence, always without clichés. The reader witnesses Hernandez's transformation, too, from down-and-delirious gringo outsider into totally down-and-delirious *chilango*."

—FRANCISCO GOLDMAN, author of *The Art of Political Murder*

"Daniel Hernandez writes with forthright generosity of spirit and intelligent acuity. Told from the perspective of a fascinated outsider gradually becoming a knowing insider, *Down and Delirious in Mexico City* takes us into a teeming, complex, vast, dark city of wonders, its people and places, cultures and rituals, food and drink, history and present. Concise, pithy, honest, and clear-eyed, Hernandez is a trustworthy, infallible guide through one of the most amazing cities on earth."

—KATE CHRISTENSEN, author of *The Great Man* and *Trouble*

"Daniel Hernandez takes on Mexico City, and the results are simply brilliant. A reader couldn't ask for a more compassionate, more daring, or more honest guide to the world's most maddening megacity. The beauty and terror, the dynamism and precariousness of life in *El Defectuoso* is vividly portrayed on every page of this important book."

—DANIEL ALARCÓN, author of *Lost City Radio*

"Guided by his passions, Daniel Hernandez let himself become engulfed by Mexico City's complexity and contradictions. He got very deeply into el D.F. very quickly. His marvelous *Down and Delirious in Mexico City* is essential reading for anyone who cares about this confusing and misunderstood megalopolis, and particularly what it means to be young here."

—DAVID LIDA, author of *First Stop in the New World: Mexico City, the Capital of the 21st Century*

"Daniel Hernandez navigates the beautiful chaos of Mexico City with a reporter's tenacity, an adventurer's daring, and an open heart that allows him to discover the history that lives inside him. His lush, eyewitness portrayals take you inside the crush of crowds that pop up all over Mexico City—at soccer stadiums, religious pilgrimages, art happenings and always the dance floor. A gorgeously done book."

—LAURIE OCHOA, co-founder and editor of *Slake: Los Angeles*

"This is Mexico City as seen from its quaking mosh pit, a ferocious ancient-modern swirl of passion, bodies, style, and release. Hernandez is a Mexican gringo on an urban pilgrim's quest, pulled between fearlessness and introspection, the street and the keyboard, the North and the South. *Let's Go Mexico City* this isn't, and we're all the better for it."

—JOSH KUN, University of Southern California

"Pitch-perfect and incandescent. Hernandez's shape-shifting abilities take us from emo to punk to neo-Aztec; from new age to old school to trans-*everything*, then back again only to find ourselves transmuted into something else. If Hernandez started off as a visitor, as many great writers who have written about Mexico did—from Artaud, Kerouac and Burroughs to Bolaño—he adopts and is adopted by this city and is now truly a *chilango* insider. His narrative of grit, glitter, and glory is not only a must *re*-read, it is an invitation to live."

—GABRIELA JAUREGUI, author of *Controlled Decay*

"Legions of writers have made the pilgrimage to the Aztec capital—from Breton to Lowry, from Lawrence to Burroughs—but few stayed long enough or wandered far enough from the expat-friendly circuit in this most iconic capital of the Global South. Daniel Hernandez crisscrosses *la capital* and transcends borders that have held others back—from the coruscating decadence of the party city to the outlying barrios where people survive by their wits amid the bewildering violence of Mexico in the age of the narco. As a young Mexican-American author, Hernandez is both on intimate terms with and alienated from the city, a kinetic point of view that reveals to us a post-postmodern place that is melancholy and loving, frightening, and inspiring—this most indispensable city of ghosts and the forever young."

—RUBÉN MARTÍNEZ, Fletcher Jones Chair in Literature and Writing, Loyola Marymount University, and author of *Crossing Over: A Mexican Family on the Migrant Trail*

Down & Delirious in Mexico City

THE AZTEC METROPOLIS IN THE TWENTY-FIRST CENTURY

DANIEL HERNANDEZ

Scribner

New York London Toronto Sydney

SCRIBNER

A Division of Simon & Schuster, Inc.
1230 Avenue of the Americas
New York, NY 10020

First Scribner trade paperback edition February 2011

SCRIBNER and design are registered trademarks of The Gale Group, Inc.,
used under license by Simon & Schuster, Inc., the publisher of this work.

For information about special discounts for bulk purchases, please contact
Simon & Schuster Special Sales at 1-866-506-1949 or
business@simonandschuster.com.

The Simon & Schuster Speakers Bureau can bring authors to your
live event. For more information or to book an event contact the
Simon & Schuster Speakers Bureau at 1-866-248-3049 or
visit our website at www.simonspeakers.com.

Book design by Ellen R. Sasahara

Manufactured in the United States of America

1   3   5   7   9   10   8   6   4   2

Library of Congress Control Number: 2010044455

ISBN 978-1-4165-7703-4
ISBN 978-1-4516-1018-5 (ebook)

For my brothers and sisters

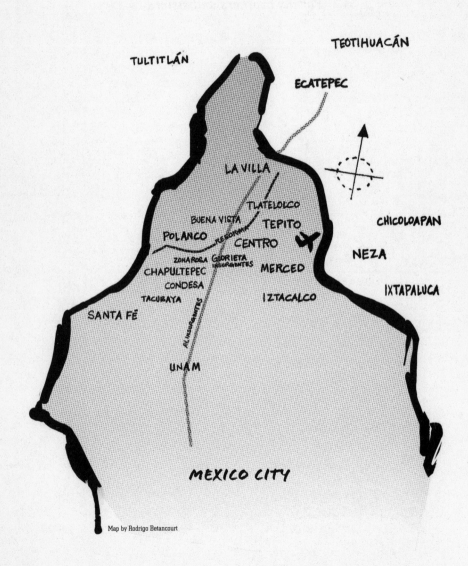

TEOTIHUACÁN

TULTITLÁN

ECATEPEC

LA VILLA

TLATELOLCO

BUENA VISTA
TEPITO

POLANCO
REFORMA
CENTRO

ZONA ROSA GLORIETA
INSURGENTES

CHAPULTEPEC
MERCED

CONDESA

TACUBAYA
IZTACALCO

SANTA FÉ

AV. INSURGENTES

CHICOLOAPAN

NEZA

IXTAPALUCA

UNAM

MEXICO CITY

Map by Rodrigo Betancourt

Contents

A Note to the Reader: Getting Down   ix

Part I | ASSIMILATIONS

1 Guadalupe's Test   3

2 Points of Arrival   16

3 *La Banda*   32

Part II | TENSIONS

4 Fashion & Facsimile   51

5 The Warriors   66

6 The Lake of Fire   94

7 Kidnapped   105

8 The Delinquent Is Us   119

Part III | TAKING CHANCES

9 A Feathered Serpent in Burberry Shades   133

10 Negotiating Saints   146

11 Originals of Punk   162

12 Attack of the Sweat Lodge   181

13 Death by Decadence   198

Part IV | MUTATIONS

14 At Home   211

15 The Seven Muses of Mexico City   230

Notes on the Chapters   247
Acknowledgments   267
Postscript   271

| A Note to the Reader: Getting Down

What are you? Consumer or participant?

—Epigram for the day, November 16, in the 2008
calendar of the Mexico City goth club El Under

When the Pumas scored the day's first goal on a Sunday in late fall 2007, we had just arrived at the Estadio Olímpico to take a standing position in the student section. It was a clear, gorgeous afternoon. I had been in Mexico City for only a few weeks. Behind the stadium's swooping southern rim you could see the green mountains to the south, each covered in a carpet of pine trees, and above the range, the gleaming blue sky. The Pumas, the professional football team at the national university, were playing the Jaguares from Chiapas, and Naomi, my guide that day, had warned me that the Jaguares were a formidable foe. I was told to prepare myself for a long, hard-fought game. What I didn't understand was that *hard-fought* was more a reference to the fans than the action on the field.

We didn't actually see the first goal happen. You might say we *felt* it happen. I was standing with Karen, Naomi's sister, when a shattering roar echoed throughout the stadium, and in an instant I felt a half dozen people falling on top of me. Diving, ferociously, first into the air and then down upon anyone who might be in the rows below. The Pumas had scored, and members of La Rebel, as the student section of fans is called, responded by doing what they've done for years anytime their team scores. They rioted. I ducked and leaned to the left and tried to grab Karen's shoulders. But she had slipped under the weight of the people on top of her, and some guy's elbow was jammed into her cheek. I could see her complaining desperately to an ear nearest her mouth, but I couldn't make out what she was saying. The roar was deafening. Arms, heads, rear ends, legs, clamoring in every direction. When the tangle of bodies cleared up, I half-expected Karen to be weeping and ready to leave. Instead, she bounced to her feet, let out a wild *"Woo-hoo!!!"* and squeezed through her neighbors to rejoin her friend Happy, who was standing on the concrete passageway before us. Where was Noami? Somehow she'd wound up in the section below, several rows down. Naomi turned and waved brightly. It was still too loud to talk but we all made reassuring eye contact with each other.

Welcome to La Rebel. Welcome to Mexico City. What fun.

Two things stand out here, I'm thinking, almost three years later. Life in Mexico City is a contact sport. It might be scary at first, unforgiving, violent, but to really grasp it, you gotta get in, release all inhibitions, all cultural blinders. You have to get down and play.

Since relocating to Mexico's capital city, I've attended parties, rallies, marches, meetings, sporting events, and spiritual rites. I've checked out markets, festivals, cantinas, and all-day outdoor concerts. I've read and collected what must be thousands of articles, clippings, and flyers. I've gone wherever the city—and chance— took me.

Mexico City is young. Within the Federal District (known as the D.F., for Distrito Federal), one in three residents is between the ages of fifteen and twenty-nine. The average age overall is twenty-seven. I fit right into the category, moving here days before my twenty-seventh birthday. These young people were Mexico's future. Eager to better understand where the country might be headed, and where I might fit in it all, I began researching Mexico City's youth movements and subcultures. I consulted academic sources, magazines, self-published histories, and vintage media. I interviewed dozens upon dozens of people. I took hundreds of photographs, recorded hours of audio, and wrote hundreds of pages of notes.

The result is this book, a collection of reported essays, personal and subjective, covering roughly the period between 2007 and 2010. It is not meant as a definitive "portrait" or "guide" to the Mexican capital. It is also not meant as a proper catalog of the young "urban tribes" of Mexico City. Some tribes are discussed at length, some barely. My documentary approach consisted of observing, listening, and participating wherever possible, wherever an invitation occurred naturally.

The stories narrated in these chapters are all true. It is a truth as far as I noted, recorded, recalled, and photographed it. In a few instances, the names of some of the people who appear in these pages have been changed, where circumstances warranted privacy. The Internet, print journalism, and the work of other writers was central to putting the tales together. The book contains occasional quotations from Web pages and social media sources, and echoes of entries from my personal blog, Intersections.

Finally, I should note that while I use the term *urban tribe* and its subcategories, in general young people in Mexico City reject identifying themselves in such terminologies—*goth, rasta,* etc.—even if they otherwise appear fully immersed in a specific subculture. I made every effort then to distinguish subjects in the book by noting their unique characteristics. Yet I also allowed myself to make generalizing references to *emos, hipsters,* and so on when the text calls for it. Though these terms may rarely be used for self-identification in Mexico City or anywhere else, they are widely imposed by young people upon one another. My usage of them here reflects the social reality.

Throughout this process, I also had to consider my own place in the cultural and geographic landscape of the D.F. This book is ultimately the story of how I found it.

—D.H., Mexico City, July 2010

El apocalipsis no es una metáfora es un lugar lleno de belleza y llevamos años ahi. La publicidad nos engaña.

    —PONCE

The apocalypse is not a metaphor, it is a place full of beauty and we have been there for years. The media mislead us.

    —PONCE

Part I | ASSIMILATIONS

1 | Guadalupe's Test

A crowd of candles at La Villa. (Photo by the author.)

At 10:00 p.m. on December 11, 2007, we enter the procession at the Zócalo, the vast public square and thumping heart of historic downtown Mexico City. The towers of the cathedral rise over the square like baroque apparitions. Beneath them, thousands of people are gathering before they set off for the basilica to the north by foot or by bicycle. Fleets of bike taxis cluster under Christmas lights draped upon the walls of the brown buildings that border the square. The bikes are fitted for a party, decorated with balloons and strings of lights, boom boxes held aloft, playing reggaeton and holiday songs. Nearly everyone is carrying a portrait-size replica of the holy image of the Virgen de Guadalupe. The image is heavy on their backs, a burden carried with an apparently absolute clarity of faith. Bundled into a sweater and scarf, I circle the square to take in the surroundings, feeling both excitement and intimidation for the hike ahead. It is a carnival of a scene, but clearly serious business.

Since her miraculous appearance before an indigenous peasant in 1531, the Empress of Mexico, as Guadalupe is sometimes known, has drawn pilgrims to a holy hill in the north of the Federal District, and so we are going. There, at the place they call La Villa, the sacred image hangs on permanent display in a large and modern basilica built in the early 1970s—the original viceregal basilica having sunk unevenly over the centuries into the soft former lake bed below. The pilgrims arrive from all corners of the republic and beyond for the midnight dawn of her feast day, December 12, to bow and pray before the "private flag of Mexicans." As they have for years, pilgrims travel—some for days—to La Villa, entirely on foot. Some are true believers but most are only nominally so. For many, the attraction of the ritual of December 12 is its sheer spectacle. The most ardent believers are easy to spot because they enter La Villa inching along on their knees.

The trek is a minor sacrifice relative to the occasion: the anniversary of the olive-skinned Virgen's appearance before the converted native man Juan Diego, ten years after the fall of the Aztecs to the Spanish conquistadors. Never mind the credible doubt cast on the authenticity of the Guadalupe miracle by the rigors of modern science, or that she appeared on a hill that had been sacred ground where the Aztecs had venerated Tonantzin, the mother goddess. The annual observance of this event is a rite unlike any other in

4

Mexico or in the entire Americas. La Villa feels in some ways like the Mecca of the Western Hemisphere. The shimmering garment is these pilgrims' Black Stone, a talisman that demands from its faithful, one night a year, a total disregard for the health of their feet and knees and for the general boundaries of personal space.

I decide to check out the pilgrimage with a group of adventurous American and European expats and friends. Some of us might be here for the aspect of amateur anthropology, but I felt a desire—secret, personal—to deliver myself to Mexico and Mexico City's patroness, La Morenita, as they affectionately say. Participating in this rite so soon after moving here would, I think, ensure without question my admission into the ranks of true countrymen. This is my first real test, my welcoming. Not as a Catholic, but as a *paisano*.

"Cafecito, cafecito," the voices call from the sidewalks. *"Pan, tortas."*

We march north on Calle República de Brasil, from the Zócalo. Families from the street's crumbling brown buildings stand on the crowd's edge handing out food and drinks in the chilly night to the passing pedestrians and cyclists. Coffee, bottled water, fresh unpeeled oranges, tacos, *tortas*. Children dart in and out of the parade. *"Aguas, aguas, aguas!"* There are fruit juices and Guadalupe rearview-mirror ornaments and CDs with Guadalupe-themed tracks. It is a storied custom, far more wanton gift-giving and random acts of Christian charity than in a whole month of manufactured Christmas cheer. After a few blocks, I begin to politely decline more gifts, as my backpack can fit no more. Police stand by their cruisers, with their flashing and whirling siren signals. Everyone is talking and singing and playing music and laughing and eating, huddling close in the chill. We cross Paseo de la Reforma. The crowds continue to swell. More food and drink rain upon us from the sidewalks. My crew of expatriates begins to break apart in the flow. Then from behind I hear a voice: *"Hey, güero! ¿De donde son?"*

I stop and turn, a natural response when you are brown-skinned and someone calls you "white boy." I guess he smells foreignness on me.

He is a smiling guy who introduces himself as Christian. He wears a wavy amber Afro and carries a long, sturdy branch he uses as a walking stick, like some kind of rebel highlands shaman. I tell him I am from the United States, and before I know it, Christian pulls me toward his group and places before my face a ceramic pipe filled with marijuana, asking with another smile, *"¿Fumas?"*

I have lost my foreigner friends in the surge of people. *Might as well.*

My exhaled smoke dissolves into the cold air. As we walk onward, Christian introduces me to his friends: Ulises ("But they call me Gozu"), Porku, and a shaggy-haired guy who seems old enough to be their father, who went by El Cochinito, or Little Pig. The others are no older than twenty or twenty-one. They carry backpacks filled with basic provisions, and a tent. They smile a lot. They are walking to La Villa from their pueblo at the edge of the Distrito Federal, "near the tollbooth" on the road to Cuernavaca. That's twelve hours to the south by foot.

"We're going to see the Virgen and then we're going to camp out, a little farther away from the people, and stay all night smoking and drinking," Christian announces proudly. The rest of the crew nods and smiles. It goes without saying that I am invited.

"*Órale*," I say.

The flow of pilgrims has now completely taken over the wide avenue Calzada de Guadalupe, on a direct angle toward La Villa. It is crowded yet weirdly orderly—everyone focused on the destination, upon Guadalupe. My new friends cluster around me. One of them passes me a bottle of processed juice mixed with tequila, "to warm you up," and we trudge on, passing long streams of backed-up traffic, hotels, and an illuminated Walmart—like some intruder from another civilization. Our movements on the march up the Calzada de Guadalupe become slower and slower as the ranks of the pilgrims multiply.

"Once we get closer to the basilica," Gozu warns with a gleeful smile, "we'll barely be able to move." So sincere and forthright is his enthusiasm for the prospect of potential death by crushing, so earnest is his determination to march by my side, I don't know how to respond. I feel suddenly that I have found a band of brothers. No standoffish getting-to-know-you interval, no competitive head-to-toe scanning. They are like expressions of a Mexican stereotype that has almost zero self-consciousness: the free and happy young person. But a task is at hand, and I must concentrate. I puff on their pipe again, and the drug's mind-altering properties crawl into my bloodstream and piggyback upon my brain waves. My heart begins to race. I begin sharing in my friends' determined jubilation. I add my laughter to theirs. I begin to think that maybe a faint trickle of something new is rising from my pit, something unfamiliar. Faith.

"Why are you doing this?" I ask Porku.

The Virgen de Guadalupe, upon a bandanna, is wrapped over his forehead. "We have to," he says with a wide grin. "It's faith. You don't question it."

I try to understand. The faith we're talking about here is not Roman Catholic, it is in one another, in brotherhood, in the ritual. And in intoxication.

I pass the pipe back to Christian and Porku but they resist, their faces displaying scorn at the idea of my taking only two hits. "More," they say. "Smoke more. You smoke." So I smoke. More and more, which pleases the band tremendously, until I say I can puff no more, and they look into my glassy eyes and agree, laughing and smiling. *Anything for la Virgencita*, I think to myself.

I ask them why people along the pilgrimage path become so generous.

"It comes from their heart," Porku responds immediately.

"They see these dudes walking," adds Gozu excitedly, his skin the color of dark wood, his hair tucked under a backward cap, "and they go, 'Look, here they come walking. We must give them something.'"

It is such a simple and logical idea, but I can't help laughing. "We're almost there!" Gozu squeals. "Careful, because they'll steal from your pockets."

"Even at La Villa?" I ask.

He only shrugs. Doubt your faith in fellow man but never in La Virgen.

It is almost midnight, and we are now within a kilometer or two of the Basílica de Nuestra Señora de Guadalupe. I know this because up ahead I see the bright double arches of a McDonald's restaurant, a sure signpost in many places in the developing world that you're approaching a significant cultural or historic site. By now the pilgrimage has gridlocked. People are packed so tightly that instead of walking we shuffle our feet ahead a few paces, wait for a minute or so, still and silent, then shuffle ahead a bit more when space permits. Everyone is concentrating.

"Hold on to my backpack," Christian tells me over his shoulder. It is becoming difficult to keep up. He stands behind Gozu, close, his chest against his friend's backpack, his hands holding on to Gozu's arms from behind, just above the elbows. "You all right?"

I hear Christian ask Gozu, who just nods, his focus fixed on the mass of people ahead.

I watch as Christian gently squeezes his friend's arms, to let him know that he is right behind him, a reassurance. It is a completely sexless gesture, an expression of unfiltered affection between friends, a common display in Mexico, I learn. Best girl friends hold hands on the street, best guy friends stroll locked arm-to-neck. Maybe it is the weed blooming inside my heart, because seeing this sort of affection so intimately, so close, makes me experience a cascade of nostalgia—and also a misplaced pinch of embarrassment.

I turn away, alarmed at myself, wondering if I should have felt shame for spying on this moment between Christian and Gozu. But the crew from the Cuernavaca tollbooth don't let me slip too far back. They are resolved to have me hang out with them this night. Just like that, after a few words of introduction. It was a summons as heartfelt as one received from a relative or a lifelong friend, only these are complete strangers. Confronted with this band of brotherly potheads from the deep south of D.F. on one of the holiest nights on the Mexican calendar, I feel right in this moment an intense urge to celebrate and reaffirm the bonds I've had in my life such as these, among the brothers you choose. I have not felt this way in so long I am wondering if the sensation is artificial—considering the *mota*.

We press on. Minutes pass when there is nowhere to move, nothing to do. So people simply stand, their gaze ahead. No one speaks, but the hum of the masses penetrates the skin. "Once we get closer," Porku says, "we'll raise the Virgen over our heads, so she can see that we've made it."

I hope quietly that the Virgen will take notice, because by now the pilgrimage has taken on an epic quality. Success and even survival is in doubt. We are still a hundred yards or so from the basilica, and I sense an anxiety rising in the crowd. I catch sight of a fainting over my left shoulder, a woman who crumples onto a bench and is laid flat on her back, exhaling heavily. "An ambulance over here," a kid with spikes in his hair calls listlessly to a uniformed monitor nearby. A few people watch with curiosity but must move on with the flow. More faintings follow. The pathway ramps upward, more police are visible, and my crew of friends grow excited. We suddenly begin moving faster, indicating that we are nearing the complex. We have made it. Almost.

The modernist basilica structure looms above us, a round, towering thing with a swooping bronze rooftop like a droplet of emerald liquid. Once we finally make it inside the compound's gates, under the brilliant glow of white floodlights, the lack of a proper crowd-control mechanism becomes wildly apparent. Police in helmets and shields and the Catholic scouts—earnest young men and women in khaki shorts and bright sashes tied around their necks, high school age—lock arms, forming lines surrounding the basilica. Every few minutes, they open a break in the line to allow a few hundred people to move—or rush frantically—across the concrete plaza to the steps of the shrine. As they hold back the line, more and more people are pressing in from the street. We are caught in a compressor of bodies, staring directly into the eyes of the scouts who are preventing us from moving forward. This creates some tension.

"Please! Let us through!" people scream.

"They're letting people in over there!"

"Don't push! Don't push!"

"Have some consideration!"

People around me begin panicking. I am panicking. Our huddle

resolves to simply run the scouts over, but the attempt is unsuc-
cessful. My crew of new friends presses to the front of the pack,
pleading, saying that it is just five of us and would they please let
us pass? More near-faintings, more chaos. It would be impossible
to complete the final leg of the pilgrimage across the vast plaza on
one's knees, per the custom. *Was it past midnight yet? Would we
make it in? Can you see her inside?* We are all tightly gripping one
another's backpacks and jackets. Porku, near the front of our huddle, senses a moment of distraction in the guards' line. He quickly
makes sure we are held together and, mustering his last morsels of
energy, rams through the scouts' arms, yanking the rest of us ahead.
A break! Commotion! Air! We break free and run toward the basilica, grateful to the Virgen for her intervention. We run under the
glow of the lights, across the plaza, up the steps, to face the multitudes pressed together inside the shrine. We are in awe, laughing at
our fortune, basking in our faith, just under the covered entrance
to the basilica, which is packed with people and human breath and
perspiration. Waiting to keep moving inward, the crew begin talking about preparing for the night ahead of warmth and drink and
weed, in a tent, among friends. People are already pressing in from
behind, eager to enter the basilica. We again form a human chain
with our jackets and bags. "Hold on, hold on!" Christian yells over
his shoulder.

But we have another barrier to contend with. A severely outmatched Catholic scout, a girl of about twenty in a crisp red shirt,
pleads helplessly to the crowd pushing to get inside, "Please no
pushing, no running!"

"We're inside the basilica!" another scout scolds.

But it is hopeless. Inside the basilica there doesn't seem to be
enough oxygen to go around for everyone, let alone any personal
space. Chanting from the altar choir fills the vast tent of the shrine's

interior. The smell of potent incense heightens the delirium. I can't see anything but the upper surfaces of the basilica's interior swooping walls of polished wooden panels and modern chandeliers showering pale yellow light downward. It feels like an overdone late-disco-era penthouse.

My *banda* keeps double-checking on itself. Christian hangs on to Gozu, and Gozu hangs on to Porku, and Porku hangs on to El Cochinito. I hold on at the back as best I can until—to my great horror—my knees begin to give. It has been three hours of walking and standing, in the cold, surrounded by a sea of millions. I feel dizzy. There is chanting and incense and the human hum, but I can't see what is happening beyond the mass of people. We are stuck behind an intimidating stucco pillar. I cannot see the Virgen de Guadalupe. Gridlock. My limbs check in with my brain and inform it that they can no longer go on. Calling to Christian and Porku, I say, "I can't go in there. I'll wait for you right here, against this wall."

The guys glance at each other, and at me—quick looks of panic and the awareness of imminent loss. Voices and ears are all around us. No time to discuss or reassure one another, not a second. Bodies pressing forward. They have to keep moving. All of us know, in those short seconds as we are swept with the crowd farther into the church, that we will probably never see each other again. I immediately feel that I have made a terrible mistake.

My friends disappear into the masses inside the shrine and I work my way backward, to a corner near a doorway, searching for air. I watch a poor guy attempt to enter the basilica on his knees, clutching a framed portrait of the Virgen and a few wilting red roses. He seems frightened and, with his shaved head and heavy glasses, looks vaguely like a fellow Mexican American, just as in-over-his-head as I am.

Nearing collapse, I anchor myself against the cold stone wall. It has taken us hours to get here, to reach her, Mexico's patron saint and Holy Mother. And now I am alone, inside her basilica, stuck behind a brown pillar near the entrance, not even able to see the Virgen's image from where I am standing. Defeated, I don't know what to do next. My friends are gone. I have failed them. I have failed in light of the faith I was developing in the bonds with the brothers you choose, in the face of a tradition that binds all Mexicans. I have failed myself. I struggle my way back outside and breathe the crisp night air, crestfallen. More crowds are coming in, but I am in a no-man's-land between the lines of police and basilica attendants and the shrine itself. I wander the plaza in a daze. If I could just have held on a bit longer, stayed brave, I would already have been hanging out with my new band of brothers on the other side of the basilica. By now, outside on a patch of grass or concrete somewhere, we'd be pitching a tent, smoking pot, drinking, and talking about our devotion to Guadalupe. Or whatever.

I reach into my backpack for one of the charity oranges handed to me earlier, open its skin with my fingernails, and started munching on the icy flesh. The orange just reminds me of my lost friends, Porku, Christian, Gozu, and El Cochinito, the guys from the tollbooth to Cuernavaca. I become afraid I am already beginning to forget their faces. I make my way around to the rear of the shrine, hoping to see my friends. Instead I am ushered out of the complex by guards and told I will be unable to reenter the gates.

I wander the crowded streets of La Villa neighborhood, my depression turning into despair. *What time is it? Two a.m.? Three?* Thousands of people stand anywhere they can, eating and playing music to Guadalupe, while thousands more are sleeping on sidewalks, in bushes, in doorways, near street stalls, piled together under blankets and sheets, framed Guadalupe images clutched close to their hearts. I come across several clusters of kids standing around smoking pot, praying each time that someone will look up and call my name, *"Güero!"* and say, "There you are!" But no. Nothing.

The next day, December 12, my knees are in agony. My feet are blistered. I feel chastened. A *real* Mexican, I scold myself, would have seen the pilgrimage all the way through. I demonstrated to my new friends and the Virgen herself that as a culturally weakened Chicano—a *pocho*—my faith is still incomplete, that on my journey toward becoming Mexican I still have a long way to go. In the afternoon I board the metro and return to the basilica hoping for a miracle. I hadn't even had a proper conversation with them, but the crew from the tollbooth to Cuernavaca represent to me the sort of connection that you never want to lose in Mexico: young people who bring you in, no questions asked, absorb you into their family on the spot. But I had not exchanged phone numbers, e-mail addresses, or social-networking names with a single one of my new friends. The only possibility of reuniting with them is a chance sighting, perhaps of the boys packing up their tent or heading back down the hill to the south end of the Valley of Mexico.

The pathways to the basilica are less crowded. Some pilgrims are still headed in the direction of La Villa on foot. Well-wishers still stand along the path bearing gifts, water, and food. The sun is hot. Trash is piled up high anywhere it has landed, plastic bags filled with greasy napkins and chicken bones, rolled-up used diapers, cores and skins of eaten fruit, artifacts from the night before. I enter La Villa's plaza freely and search the crowds for a sign of the guys. The wide stone esplanade is alight with provincial dance groups in full regional costumes paying homage to the Virgen with drumming and song. Pilgrims stand around taking pictures and enjoying snacks. Constant song and prayer and incense emanate from the basilica. Faith is lifting the air.

The sun begins to set over Mexico City in the vaguely disorienting slant of late fall, like a concave mirror image of itself, burning orange and pink, clouds soaring monumentally. I wander up the stone steps of the hill of Tepeyac, behind the colonial and modern basilicas and the chapels of La Villa, among trees and fountains, still holding out hope that I will find my friends. But I see only strangers lounging upon the stone steps and terraces. Some hold statues of Guadalupe in their arms, as if the things are living creatures. Some take tourist photos before panoramas depicting the manger scene and Juan Diego's encounter with Guadalupe, thirty pesos a shot. I join the many tired pilgrims who lean against the terrace's volcanic brown ledges to rest. At La Villa, to the Virgen de Guadalupe, the sinner is indistinct from the saint, the native *paisano* cannot be told apart from the foreign *pocho*. With the other pilgrims, I silently watch the city simmer below us in the wide yellow heat.

2 | Points of Arrival

(Illustration by Sergio Hernandez.)

A nd this is the house where La Malinche lived," Victor says, pointing to a plain colonial structure on Calle República de Cuba, in the Centro. The building doesn't seem like much: pink walls, brown wooden doors that appear indifferent to their age, shuttered windows. On a wall high above the sidewalk, a tile marker with blue cursive script indicates that "according to tradition" the house once belonged to a woman named Doña Marina. Also known by her Indian name Malinalli Ténepatl, Marina served infamously as Hernán Cortés's translator and mistress during his conquest of the Aztec Empire.

"*Uff*," I respond, and frown. Among some Mexicans in the United States, La Malinche is reviled as a traitor, the Judas Iscariot of the New World. By grunting I think I am doing my duty.

But Victor, an artist with whom I have struck up a fast friendship, recoils. "You Chicanos need to get over the *conquista*," he says. "La Malinche was amazing. She was incredibly smart and beautiful and knew many languages. She is one of the only women historical figures we have from the period."

I am strolling with Victor after lunch. It is a warm and drizzly day, mid-July 2002, just a few weeks into my first visit to Mexico City. From the moment I land, nearly every human interaction and every street corner turned offers an eye-widening lesson. The onslaught of information and sensations leaves me fatigued. Almost anything I say is analyzed, mocked, or critiqued in relation to my being a sort of native foreigner—a Mexican born in the United States, Mexican but not quite. Victor's reproach shocks my brain. As far as I know, to be accused of *malinchismo*, the undue love and devotion for the foreigner, for the American or the European, is slanderous in Mexico. I mean, that's what I *had been taught* back in California. Mexico, Victor says to me carefully on that street, is a fusion of two civilizations, the Spanish and the indigenous. *We are both, half and half,* he says. It is *mestizaje,* the joining, and we are mere by-products of that merging. That's just history.

Victor is bright, friendly, and generous. I am having lunch a couple times a week at El Generalito, the restaurant he operates with his partner, Juan Carlos. After the meal, the coffee, and the conversation, they rarely bring me a check.

"The Conquest happened," Victor says with a firm finality on Calle República de Cuba. "Five hundred years ago."

As Victor and I walk away from the house of La Malinche, I am aware that I have been "schooled." I thought I knew so much about being Mexican, but evidently I do not. I have just finished college, but the realization strikes me that I know so little. Moving on to lighter topics, Victor and I keep walking through the Centro Histórico, the city's ancient downtown, raindrops patting our backs.

Before this trip, my understanding of Mexican history, culture, and identity was forged in two narrow environments: the far northwest tip of Mexico and the far southwest tip of the United States, in Tijuana and San Diego in the 1980s and 1990s. These are the "borderlands" that the two branches of my family have called home for generations. As I walk with Victor, I reach back into my memory that afternoon and think about the little things you hear growing up in a Mexican American border community, where Spanish-language newscasts are played in living rooms and English-language newspapers gather on kitchen tables: soccer scores, the Mexican president announcing this or defending that, that red-green-and-white sash across his breast, gossip from the Tijuana society pages, the word *Aztec* echoing up and down the vocabulary. I remember occasional mentions of a massive capital city, far, far away, and its high urban myths.

It is the biggest city in the world, the legends go, whistled through teeth. *The pollution is so bad they have phone booths that sell oxygen.* The crime, the smog, the corruption—in San Diego and Tijuana in those days, Mexico City was a place you'd never want to visit on purpose unless you absolutely had to. But for every child these stories scare away, there are those who find them alluring. I sought out and soaked up history wherever I could. Mexican history is not given much attention in the U.S. public school system, even in California. Most of what I picked up, informally, in passing, was

18

presented in black and white. The Aztecs were great and glorious. The Spanish were evil conquerors. The United States stole half of Mexico. La Malinche sold out. There were enemies and there were victims. There was pre-Hispanic Mexico and postcolonial Mexico. All the things that have happened since then, particularly all the bad and tragic things, are to be read as indicators of the evil of the original sin, the arrival of Cortés to the Valley of Mexico, the fall of the Mexica people, and the destruction of the grand imperial city of Tenochtitlan.

Mexico's history, like any nation's history, is not a tale of black and white, but a parade of gray. The Conquest, the Colonial period, the Inquisition, Independence, the Reformation, the Porfirian period, the Revolution, the era of modernization and authoritarian rule under the Institutional Revolutionary Party—all markers in a story of multiplying layers, where *mestizaje* is not only a state of ethnic mixing but of historical mixing as well. From a young age, figuring out where I fit into that story became my objective.

In college, the question took on a new urgency. One day a roommate brought a friend over to our apartment. The friend was a young, redheaded, blue-eyed native of Mexico City, dressed like a gutter punk, who was "hanging around" California. I told the young Mexican girl my parents were Mexican and that I was born in San Diego, that we're from Tijuana. "But you're not *really* Mexican," the girl responded.

I was not? Until then I had always been under the impression that the world perceived me as Mexican, like it or not. I *felt* Mexican—stuck between a dominant American culture that shunned the "Mexican" within its society, and contemporary Mexicans back in Mexico who found it so easy to dismiss our mixed heritage as somehow unrelated to theirs. Around that time films such as *Amores Perros* and *Y Tu Mamá También* were opening up radically new conceptions of Mexican life for people north of the border. The same should have been true in the opposite direction. But no. As a Mexican American, born in gringo territory, I was still excluded from the national narrative in Mexico. Would we forever be banished to a state of ambivalence, or could we be two things at once? To answer this question, I knew I had to go to Mexico and find out for myself. *One summer there,* I thought naively, *is all I need.*

In late spring 2002, after I graduate from Berkeley, I am offered a dream job, as a reporter on the downtown metro desk of the *Los Angeles Times.* The editors want me to start right away, but I ask for the summer off. I want to see more of Mexico. I book a one-way flight to Mexico City, from Tijuana. I pack a large rectangular suitcase with clothes, a clunky laptop, and a $6 rubber wristwatch from Walmart (cheap—so as not to attract attention to myself, my mother instructs me). The irony is not lost on me: While millions of Mexicans are migrating northward, I go south. It is an act of rebellion. My parents, who left Tijuana and settled in San Diego in 1976, shake their heads in disapproval.

"They'll steal your socks without taking off your shoes," Dad warns.

"What is he going to do down there?" perplexed cousins in Tijuana and San Diego ask my parents.

"We don't know," they say. *"Está loco."*

I am determined to make my own assessment. Before I leave, I poke around the Internet looking for work to sustain me while there, finding the *News,* Mexico City's English-language newspaper. An editor has an opening on the paper's online news desk. Could I start on Monday? My sighing parents try to offer measured guidance. Dad, a middle-school counselor by day and a boxing trainer by night, makes a connection with friends of friends in the Mexican boxing circuit. I would stay with the Uruzquieta family, they determine. Over the telephone, the adults confer. I can stay as long as I wish, so long as I keep my appointed space neat, respect the household, and contribute money for groceries. It is happening, an open-ended summer in Mexico.

Don Alfredo Uruzquieta, a trainer in a Mexican barrio, just like my dad, meets me in the terminal at the Benito Juárez International Airport. I am told he would be holding a sign bearing his name, not mine, for safety's sake. I am dragging my suitcase along the gray stone floor, already dizzy from my first encounter with the high-altitude air. I find the sign—URUZQUIETA—and approach with a smile. Don Alfredo shakes my hand unenthusiastically and looks at me with an arching glance. Tall, potbellied, he has a curled-up Pancho Villa mustache and reeds of graying hair falling away from the top of his shiny head. He wears brown trousers and a leather belt and boots, a stained white work T, and car keys attached to a chain. I thank him for agreeing to take me in for the summer and deliver *saludos*—the customary greeting—from my parents. Don Alfredo grunts at me to follow in his direction, out of the terminal. He begins telling me about his house, his family, the neighborhood, but I detect a casual suspicion from him the entire ride out of the airport. I am shaking my head, silent, in delirium. We are riding on swooping speedy overpasses crowded with traffic that seems to have no use for lanes. Cars and trucks flow with the instinct of blood cells. I see the tops of concrete houses, enormous billboards. It is a landscape of scratchy urban flatness, then rolling hillsides of structures that disappear into a white horizon of

21

haze—the smog. I am overwhelmed by the smell of the city, like charred maize doused in crude oil. You cannot escape it. My senses are in shock. I am twenty-one years old and have never been inside Mexico farther than Tijuana and Ensenada.

The hour of my arrival is midafternoon, lunchtime, so Don Alfredo drives me to the Central de Abastos, a vast open-air whole-sale market described as the largest in the world. On maps, the market is a wide stain on the urban grid, like a lake. The afternoon is not sunny, more like blazing pale gray, and hot. Don Alfredo wants me to try *barbacoa,* goat wrapped in banana leaves and slow-roasted in a ditch in the ground. I have never seen such a thing in my life. We sit under a rain tarp overlooking a pit in the dirt, at a rickety table adorned with vats of fresh salsas, and diced tomatoes, onions, cabbage, and lime. No plastic wrappings or warning labels separate me from my food. I eat carefully, watching Don Alfredo eat and chew and grunt and swallow, a hunter gorging on his kill. Around me, the sights and smells of the market overwhelm my ability to process. There are tarps and stands and stalls, vendors, children, Indian women selling toys and candy, guys pushing loaded dollies, trucks driving large goods in and out, men engaged in deals and negotiations. The air sits on top of me and presses against my back. Beads of sweat collect on the crown of my nose. It is the first time in my life I feel truly dizzy. The feeling, days and weeks later, never fully goes away.

We drive into the Colonia Zapata Vela, in the eastern borough of Iztacalco, not far from the airport and under the pathway of the landing jets, to a narrow concrete street lined with two- and three-story houses. Each is constructed and decorated according to the whims of its owner. Power lines, public and pirated, dive across the air, linking building to building, an electrical spiderweb. Kids and cars fill the pavement. Small makeshift shops operate from garages and anywhere else, kernels of ingenuity popping through the stresses of the urban skin. I smile. It looks and feels like places I know in Tijuana.

At Don Alfredo's home, I meet his wife, Doña Sabina, and his son, Alfredo, and Alfredo's wife, Silvia, and two small children, Carolina and Job. They have a comfortable and modest house, wedged between other houses with brightly painted exteriors. Inside I enter a warm space of tiled floors and wooden furniture, where plastic covers the crocheted white cloth over the dining table. Two bedrooms and a bath are upstairs, and a garden on the roof, where another cousin, Sebastián, lives in tiny work quarters. That night there is a birthday party at the next-door neighbor's house. I join the entire Uruzquieta family as guests. Strings of pink balloons are hoisted over the street outside, a favor between neighbors. Greetings and hugs and the customary hello, a kiss, cheek to cheek. We dine on homemade *pozole* stew. There is music, games, children by the armful running around playing. Full, exhausted, overwhelmed, I settle into my room, a cool, airless cube at the end of the ground-floor driveway. The window does not catch sunlight and faces the open outdoor toilet. Only a bed and a wooden stool fill the space. As he shows me around, Alfredo Jr. informs me that spirits sometimes haunt the room. This is where I open my laptop, my Scribe notepads, and begin writing.

I spend just ten weeks in Mexico in summer 2002, but the experience recalibrates my life. For the first time I feel as though I am living purely on the commands of my instincts, survivalist and nihilist equally. To get to the *News*'s offices, where I sit and translate news items from the papers, from Spanish into English, I ride the metro every weekday morning from Iztacalco to Salto del Agua,

Salto del Agua to Balderas, Balderas to Juárez, my defense anten-
nae high and alert. I read whatever book I can maintain control
of in the crowded cars, dodging vendors, commuters in business
suits, blind beggars, and *niños de la calle*—children of the street—
who perform by laying their bare backs upon shards of glass on the
floor of each car. Pesos fly their way if only out of disgust.

The Uruzquietas are tremendously considerate during the time
I stay in their house. They correct my Spanish when it needs cor-
recting and explain the ticks of big-city life. A relative who drives
a taxi offers to take me to the major central landmarks for a decent
price. I see the Zócalo, the Palacio Nacional, the Palacio de Bellas
Artes, the Árbol de la Noche Triste (the "Tree of the Sad Night" is
where Cortés stopped to weep after suffering deep losses in battle
against the Aztecs), and the Plaza de las Tres Culturas, a square sit-
uated between pre-Colombian ruins, a colonial church, and modern apartment buildings, in Tlatelolco, just north of downtown.

I always thought I had a good sense of direction, but here I am
never quite able to tell north from south, east from west, even in
the brightest daylight of the Distrito Federal. At every corner, it is
impossible not to notice how *brown* it is, whether because of the
pollution, or the ubiquitous *tezontle* volcanic stone, or some other
kind of blanketing pigment that rises organically from the earth. I
wonder if some sort of Aztec fairy dust has sprinkled everything in
the color of dirt, bark, and leather. The city heaves. The city attacks.
The city is sinking. The weight of 20 million people and 4 million
cars and skyscrapers and tunnels and elevated highways presses the
ground year after year into what was once a vast bed of interlock-
ing lakes, a sinking that is accelerated by depleting groundwater.
Buildings in the old center lean this way or that in the soft earth.
Steps are added at the bottom of outdoor staircases to level the
land for pedestrians. Asphalt streets tumble along in uneven waves.

What was once a landscape of water is now a landscape of concrete, blinking lights, and tubing. It is literally starving for water. It is a city in perpetual delirium. Backward when it should be forward, upside down when it wishes to be right side up. It is running in circles, pricking at its own skin, possessed.

I do my best to fit in. But the signals the city gives me in response are not computing. I go to work, commute back and forth between Centro and Iztacalco, then head out and meet people and make friends, locals and foreigners. Some of those I meet understand me as a fellow Mexican subject, like them. Others do not.

"But you're so Mexican," a friend remarks to me one night, as we party our way to the Estadio Azteca with a pack of friends to see Lenny Kravitz in concert. By looking at me, and listening to me speak, he seems unable to conceptualize me as an American. The dissonance in his logic is internal: I'm an incidental fan of Lenny Kravitz just as he is—what other confirmation of my Mexicanness would you need?

But for every moment like this, another arrives, reminding me that in Mexico I can be perceived as American almost at first glance. One weekday night, at a dinner party at a friend's, I go out to get fresh beers with one of the guests, a native guy with an aristocratic air. Handing me a pack of Bud Light dismissively, he huffs, "Here. Because I know this is what you guys drink." I stammer and laugh, assuming he is joking. Then I realize he is not. He is mocking stereotypes of the United States at my expense.

I am determined to adapt. I fall in with a company of young American and British expats who had done more or less just what I have: moved to Mexico City on escapade. We venture to the relatively safe central neighborhoods where most foreigners or cosmopolitan-leaning Mexicans congregate, the Roma, the Zona Rosa, the Centro, and to the ground zero of cool in Mexico City, the Condesa. Night after night, my varying crew of expats and Mexicans, dedicated to delirium, teach me the ways of the D.F. underground. We hit house parties for those in the know, DJ parties in old cantinas, make excursions to places packed with kitsch and tourists but are made categorically "cool" by our periodic presence. We are foreigners, Mexicans who love hanging out with foreigners, and Mexicans who otherwise don't prefer foreigners' company but also don't mind it.

"We are *chilangos*! Who cares?!" the Mexicans holler above the noise in the bars and parties.

I take note. A *chilango* is not strictly a native Mexico City resident—that's a *capitalino,* those born and raised—but a sort of native intruder, a Mexican from "the provinces" who has made the D.F. his home and adopts all the most disagreeable characteristics of those caught in the city's frenzy. It is a slur that is morphing into a badge of honor. I wonder if the term is flexible enough to include me, too.

Results remain inconclusive. I party on. My friends take me to observe the decadent rituals of the most committed *fresas,* the slang term for middle- and upper-class children of privilege, the "strawberries." More parties, more drinking. The Uruzquietas regard my adventures with guarded empathy. "If you stay out past ten p.m.," Doña Sabina warns one evening over dinner, before I'm heading out the door, "don't come home. Find somewhere to stay where you are at." The metro shuts down at midnight and cabs off the street are not to be trusted.

We gather at El Jacalito and Bullpen, bars on Medellín Street in the Roma district, the sort of places that are sprinkled with addicts and the people who work as their suppliers. Brawls are a threat as constant and banal as a backed-up toilet in the dingy restrooms. Raggedy salsa bands play till dawn. The walls in the Bullpen are covered with murals depicting rastas, hippies, cholos, transvestites, vaqueros, and a red-skinned devil. The subjects of the murals are drinking, fighting, fucking, and shooting up. Each night brings its risks and rewards. Once, a barkeep at Jacalito known as La Chimuela slips and falls on the beer-sticky floor while serving. La Chimuela—the nickname indicates disfigured teeth—rips open her left forearm in a splash of bottles. It looks as if she is bleeding buckets. She is rushed to a hospital. Two hours later, La Chimuela is back at El Jacalito, happily serving beers, her arm wrapped in bandages.

Along the way, I meet Leti, seven years or so older than me, who decides to take me under her wing. Leti is Mexican, but my knowledge of what shapes her life is almost nonexistent. I know nothing except that she lives far from the Roma, and that she'd like to study gastronomy. Leti has short, spiky black hair and light freckles, clear blue eyes, and wears jangly metal bracelets all the way up to her elbows. I never learn her last name. She is a punk-rock Mexico City mystery, keeping me close by, hardly ever saying a word.

"Here," she says one night in El Jacalito, handing me a tiny, folded-up piece of white paper, and indicating the men's room. Cocaine. Everywhere, in everyone's pockets. On its way north from Colombia to America, it stops in the Aztec metropolis, fueling a million nihilistic bouts of rage, lust, and vanity on any given night. I was raised to view recreational drug use negatively, but four years at Berkeley have clouded my value systems. I find myself rationalizing. I see participating as a way to merge into Mexico City, for good or ill. I see no moral quandary on my plate, no endless narco war on the horizon. I see only the gathering of the senses. For the first time, I sample the devil's dust. It seems so casually *Mexico City* to do so, part of the "local experience," as a professional traveler might put it. Leti feeds me the powder as though it's breakfast cereal. And then we dance.

After the bars, we cobble together a spontaneous group and find our way to some stylish art deco building in the Condesa, across from the Roma. Both neighborhoods are still in the early stages of their eventual gentrification. We stumble up several landings of stairs and into someone's apartment, where we indulge on a sump-tuous spread of canned beer, cigarettes, and coke. I want to please Leti. I want to fit in. She coos to me in raspy Spanish. This is how it goes until the glare of sunrise catches the silhouette of the fifty-five-story Torre Mayor, then under construction, its unfinished top exposed in shredded angles of steel.

Late at night, or sometimes in the morning, my head pounding, I return to the Colonia Zapata Vela, just a few miles to the east of Condesa and Roma but a world away from the scenes of organized hedonism. After a month or so with the family who first welcomed me to Mexico, I make a few connections and move into an triangle-shaped closet in a bachelor pad on loud and crowded Avenida Cuauhtémoc, between the Roma and Doctores neighborhoods, a few corners away from metro Hospital General. The roommates are two Scots and a model and musician from the city of Torreón, in the northeast near Monterrey. I am closer to the *News,* and also closer to achieving my *chilango*-fication.

I never pause to take notes about these first nights out in Mex-ico City. That would be uncool, and Leti and her friends seem to me in 2002 to be the epitome of cool. Their tastes and values are radically different from what I have just left. At Berkeley, the accepted standards at the time consisted of musical acts such as the Counting Crows, maybe some Mos Def, and anything popu-lar in the imagination of an idealized Berkeley of the late 1960s. In Mexico City the youth sound that I encounter is mostly electronic, a mashed-up, bass-heavy, dirty disco beat that I have never before heard. It sounds cooler than cool. My friends navigate the city effortlessly. I envy their confidence and sophistication. They hustle, they bargain, they drink, smoke, and do drugs. They wear mullets and fauxhawks back when mullets and fauxhawks are only just cutting-edge. Sexuality is fluid, negotiable, and often utilized as trap or trick on partners or potential mates. I am running with a band of true modern *hipsters* before the term enters the lexicon and the market, before the self-eating self-awareness of global cool fully kicks in. They engage life with a surrender, a sustained vitality. I am entranced and intimidated in equal measure.

I lose track of Leti eventually. I spend my last three weeks in Mexico that summer backpacking across the south, from Cancún to Oaxaca and Veracruz and Chiapas and back. By September, it becomes time to return to the "real world" and start a career. I return to California a different person from the one who had left.

Mexico City is a site of essential rediscovery. For the first time I begin to consider the possibility that living with a cultural bipolarity could be okay, on balance. It is the city's underlying lesson. My identity can remain unresolved. And if so, the possibility exists for me to walk in two worlds at once. And if I can walk in two worlds at once, I could walk in three, four, or forty. The journey, the searching, is itself the point of arrival. *Mestizaje* became a material truth operating inside me, inside all of us. So Mexico City, teeming with millions and millions, as surreal as Los Angeles, as majestic as New York, a mighty city all its own, became both my crossroads and my destination.

Before long, it beckons me back. Early on the morning of

November 1, 2007, my parents drive me from San Diego across the border to Tijuana's international airport. I take it as a welcome omen that it is the start of the Days of the Dead. A few hours later I am riding in an airport taxi along choked Viaducto to a house in Tacubaya, one of the oldest *colonias* in Mexico City. Mario, a blogger I know—raised in Mexico City, based in Barcelona—puts me in touch with two guys who have an extra room in a large, old art deco house on a private courtyard. One is a musician, the other a researcher and writer. It sounds perfect.

I know I am part of a wider movement. For a period in the middle of the '00s—around the time when the trendy L.A. clothing company American Apparel decides to launch not only a store in Mexico City but a magazine about it—twentysomethings of certain means from all over the world fall under the spell of the Mexican megacity. We leave jobs, college campuses, and home addresses where unemployment checks would still be sent. For the most part, it is not an exodus of much significance. We move to Mexico simply to breathe and live the culture, to pursue our writing, art, or photography, to capitalize on its cool.

I ready my survival arsenal. In a flurry of bureaucratic maneuvering and with the help of relatives in Tijuana, I leave California armed with a Mexican birth certificate and a Mexican identification card. My parents are Mexican. In accordance with the current binational diplomatic relations, I could be as well. "Mexican born on foreign soil." It sounds absurd, which is just the sort of tone I'm after.

The new roommates in Tacubaya, Diego and Pablo, greet me at the doorstep and lead me upstairs for a tour and a glass of tequila poured in a new way for me, just a quarter way up. A guitar and an upright piano are in the living room. Plants are perched territorially in corners. They show me my bedroom, tell me I can use its creaky wooden desk. The sensation—the feeling of temporary weightlessness that comes with moving, making a fresh start—reminds me of my arrival five years earlier at the Uruzquietas' home. This time, my stay doesn't have an end date.

3 | *La Banda*

They're D.F. kids, they're *banda*, and they're into the Ramones. (Photo by the author.)

When it is time for the weekly Chopo street market to shut down, the rains come. It is Saturday afternoon, 5:00 p.m., Aldama Street, around from the Buenavista rail station and above the Buenavista metro, northwest of downtown. During rainy season a shower strikes in the afternoon at roughly the same time, in more or the less the same way, every day. First it is a sprinkle, then a steady pattering, then a violent downpour so ruthless it seems almost self-aware. El Chopo, the historic street market that caters to Mexico City's alternative "urban tribes," is a village of pirates beneath the rainfall. It is one of those places in the world that creates its own set of unspoken rules and collective behavior, invisible to the casual eye. For thirty years, on Saturdays when there isn't much else to do, kids in Mexico City have been getting together here to buy and sell music and rock T-shirts. Mostly they just hang out. Do whatever you want to do, the mood seems to say, but respect the flow.

When the rain comes, the stalls shut down and the punk rockers scurry into the *cervecerías,* the neighborhood beer joints that dot the streets near the Chopo market. Most of them are cramped single rooms open wide to the street. They're already packed. All you can find in the beer joints are just a few chairs and a couple of refrigerators brimming with frosty *caguama* liters of Corona, Indio, and Victoria. The bottles are wide enough to fill a whole hand. Old women sit out front offering quesadillas, making the beer joint a "restaurant," but everyone in the room knows the place is really there for the purpose of being drunk in. It's standing room only.

Inside the *cervecería* there are couples making out, fingers strumming a guitar, a voice singing, mohawks twinned in earnest discussion, play and sound, muggy lighting. I am here alone again, trying to be inconspicuous, avoiding the aggressive gazes that regulars reserve for any newcomer. I bum a cigarette from a guy in a green military jacket. He flags me immediately as a nonlocal, by my accent.

"There are few Mexican people who keep a respect for others, for people from other countries," the guy tells me. "I suggest to you that if you do not have a Mexican tour guide, you get yourself a hotel room, maybe by around eight at night, and you stay there till morning."

My lecturer is a twentysomething Chopo regular in shades. I can tell that he's smart, and probably a little drunk. He is assuming that I am a tourist. "If you want to hang out until tomorrow, that's cool . . . but . . . your accent."

"Indicates that I'm not—?" I start asking.

"You just have to say, '*Cerveza, cerveza,*'" the guy says, mocking a gringo Spanish accent. "If a sharp person sees you talking in some other accent, they'll say, 'This *pendejo* I'll make him a *pendejo.*'"

An idiot.

"But my accent is—"

"Your accent is foreign," he interrupts.

"But I'm from California," I protest.

"Even if you're from Monterrey, I recognize the accent, dude." Monterrey is the big industrial city in the north, and it's also not anywhere near California. "Even if you're from Monterrey, I recognize that accent, and I'll go, 'This *güey,* charge him triple, *güey!*'"

I can't help but laugh. We laugh together.

"Mexicans don't trust other Mexicans," the guy sighs.

During my first stay in Mexico City with the Uruzquietas, Don Alfredo's nephew Sebastián guides me on excursions to the city center. Sebastián's usual look is baggy jeans and hemp jewelry. With dark brown skin and intensely curly and shiny black hair, he is a Mexico City native whose genetic code leans heavily toward *afromestizo,* the African-dominant racial mixture. He is walking ahead of me, moving like a cool and calm explorer of the urban obstacle course, a tropical gangster. He takes me for the first time to El Chopo.

"You can get good jeans there" is all he says by way of explanation.

Then as now in 2008, my initial fascination with the market is superficial. Mohawks, dreadlocks, all the outward sincere displays of "true music fans"—didn't all of this go out of style with the start of the new millennium? Don't irony and cynicism reign now? El Chopo is on its face a retro throwback. Just a few blocks long, one street wide, the once-a-week Tianguis Cultural del Chopo— *tianguis* is a Náhuatl word that survives in usage today, meaning "market"—is the permanent citadel of the Mexican counterculture. Or what's left of it. This is where a small band of romantic souls keep their idea of utopia or anarchy on perpetual repeat. The *choperos,* as the writer Carlos Monsiváis once put it, "find a provision of energy in the obsessions that so many others have retired." The landscape is jarring, definitely, coming across hordes of punks and rastas and skinheads, dressed almost too perfectly so, week after week. This quality of persistence is precisely what makes so many others dismiss El Chopo as a parody of itself, a thing of quaintness.

But something about the attitude of the regulars intrigues me. Ritual attendants at Chopo are usually suspicious of outsiders. They treat their market like it is an intangible jewel to be protected—as if they were hiding a secret they don't want you to know about. The day I meet the guy who tags me as a tourist and instructs me to get to a hotel and not emerge till morning, I hobble back to Tacubaya feeling both chastened and hopeful. *At least someone talked to me this time.* I have been going to El Chopo about a couple times a month since I moved here, trying to figure it out. Most times I am alone. I wander the stalls, browsing the tour T-shirts, pipes, jeans, hoodies, and vintage jackets. I look at HELLO MY NAME IS stickers, leather and hemp jewelry, skateboards, old rocker magazines, CDs, concert DVDs, Doc Martens boots, hip-hop mix-tapes, beanies, spray-can caps, studded wristbands—whatever a young Mexican kid needs to visually present himself as an "alternative" individual. It's all sold here. The punk, goth, skinhead, rockabilly, skater, hip-hop head, tagger, emo, or rasta, or any mix-and-match combination of the above, is at home. Carrying an item bought at El Chopo implies its own kind of currency. The *tianguis* has a value beyond its obvious function of commerce.

One afternoon I meet a woman in plain motherly clothing standing at the back of the market resting against a chain-link fence, behind the area where bands play and hard-core "anarco-punks" sell patches and vegan tacos. The woman's little son is nearby. A conversation bubbles up between us. "I met my husband here," she tells me, "way back in 1982."

I don't know this at the time, but the woman is referring to a different physical location. For its first several years after starting in fall 1980, I'd later find out, El Chopo took place at the Museo Universitario El Chopo, a museum affiliated with the UNAM, the national university, which is how the *tianguis* got its name. But El Chopo is El Chopo wherever it's held, and over the years it's been held at many places before finding its home here on Aldama Street. It is not just a street market, it is a happening.

The woman and I watch a group of kids in *lucha libre* wrestling masks mosh incoherently to the sounds of an indie band playing before us, in the shadows of a few nondescript apartment towers and a huge electrical generator plant. The moshing kids can't be more than fifteen or sixteen years old. They wear masks, they tell me later, because their favorite band, Los Elásticos, wear masks.

The Chopo mom is silent. She sighs. "It used to be a lot more punk."

The first iteration of the Tianguis Cultural del Chopo happened on October 4, 1980. That's a month before I was born—or in rock-n-roll terms, aeons ago. It did not have a name at first. The *tianguis* came together in response to a call from the director of the Chopo museum at the time, the author Ángeles Mastretta, for a "space for musicians, collectors, producers, and all the *banda* interested in rock, jazz, and related sounds to exchange, distribute, and sell records and everything related to music," according to a small volume on the history of the market, *Tianguis Cultural del Chopo: Una larga jornada.*

"Bartering was El Chopo's blood," writes the author of the history, an original *chopero* named Abraham Ríos. "Esoteric records appeared: the European progressives, the Mexican productions by Focus, the psychedelic H. P. Lovecrafts and Ultimate Spinach; the first Zappas, the Happy Trails of Quicksilver Messenger Service, Grape Jam, or Fever Tree."

A nerve had been struck. The spontaneous market grew and grew. It outgrew the museum and spilled out onto the streets. The local borough government and neighborhood toughs seeking to extort the rockers constantly threatened to kill the market, sometimes through direct violence. It moved several times, conjuring images of a chosen tribe of rockers wandering the desert of the unforgiving city. But El Chopo could not be contained. The *chavos,* the *banda,* had spoken.

"There was no place for *chavos* to get together at the time," says Javier Hernández Chelico, another Chopo OG. Hernández, gray-haired and wearing jeans and a vest, writes a weekly column on the market in the daily *La Jornada.* We meet one day near the anarco-punks. "They took control of a thing that was not theirs. There was no directive, no order. The *chavos* generated El Chopo."

The term *banda* pops up often in discussion on the Chopo community. Its meaning is simple yet elusive. Evoking youth, rock-n-roll, and resistance, *la banda* is the umbrella under which all subcultures are accepted. To be *banda* is to be part of the crew, the tribe. *Banda* is the ultimate compliment. But back then, forming part of the *banda* functioned also as a survival mechanism for the young people of Mexico. In the period when the foundations of El Chopo were being laid, the government didn't just frown upon alternative types, it killed them. The Institutional Revolutionary Party, or PRI, had ruled Mexico as a quasi-authoritarian state since the end of the Revolution, the so-called "perfect dictatorship." The PRI dominated all segments of government and society at large and regarded state violence as a fundamental tool of order and control. Three critical events, in 1968 and in 1971, laid the groundwork for a *banda* revolution to which El Chopo owes its existence. The bartering rockers who founded and still guard El Chopo were doing nothing short of standing up to a history stacked mightily against them.

In late July 1968, a series of innocent-looking brawls between rival street gangs and so-called *porro* student groups sparked an unprecedented popular movement for government reform—a movement that was ultimately defeated by the government with fatal force. The student brawls had violently been repressed by state riot police, who entered campuses and caused wider mayhem on the streets. The repression generated an indignant response from the university communities. Marches were staged. Manifestos were drafted. Far-left political groups, unions, and professionals of many kinds joined the movement. The PRI began feeling the heat.

The PRI—and its partner in paranoia and repression, the U.S. intelligence community—feared that if left unchecked, the movement that emerged in summer 1968 would grow and embarrass the country hosting the first Olympics staged in the developing world or, worse, could possibly herald a Cuban-style upheaval in Mexico, which was what some in the movement at the time actually wanted. It had to be stopped. Days before the opening of the

1968 Olympic Games in Mexico City, on October 2, government forces opened fire on hundreds of unarmed protesters who had gathered for another rally at the Plaza de las Tres Culturas in Tlatelolco. Shots rang out across the city that rainy night as the PRI, its police and its paramilitaries, sought to squelch once and for all a peaceful student movement that clamored for reform, accountability, and transparency in the government. The number killed at Tlatelolco may never be fully known. The government initiated a blackout campaign on the massacre that to this day is only beginning to be unmasked.

Tlatelolco was a turning point. It left a permanent scar on those who survived it and provided a key reference point of collective trauma for generations to come. The one-party state had declared open war on its sons and daughters. It was only the beginning of an epic struggle. From then on, as was happening in other Latin American pseudo-democracies, Mexico initiated a so-called Dirty War against dissidents. From university students in the cities to land-rights leaders in the countryside, activists of every stripe were arrested, persecuted, or simply "disappeared." Journalists were silenced or put on the PRI payroll. People from those generations still tell stories of being profiled, rounded up, roughed up, harassed, and intimidated as they raised their voices in protest against the regime.

A second mass attack on unarmed demonstrators followed on June 10, 1971. Demonstrators in D.F. attempted to march to the Zócalo from a collection of technical colleges in a northeast area of the city known as Casco de Santo Tomás, near metro San Cosme. A paramilitary group known as Los Halcones, or the Falcons, surrounded the students with clubs and guns. Many died in the violence that followed. Once again, we'll never know how many for sure. The news media by then operated as a complicit arm of the PRI, the party's willing censors and stenographers. The dailies reported the next day that a "conflict between students" had occurred at the Casco de Santo Tomás. President Luis Echeverría, who had been interior minister during Tlatelolco and therefore instrumental in its execution, once more succeeded in violently squelching dissent. The Jueves de Corpus massacre, as it was named because it occurred on the Corpus Christi feast day, would largely be forgotten.

Yet a concurrent revolution was also brewing. Rock-n-roll from the United States, Latin America, and Europe had been trickling into Mexico and infecting a receptive youth population with the potent ideal of liberation through music. Through television, film, foreign magazines, and foreigners traveling to Mexico to hunt for native psychotropic plants, young people in Mexico became acquainted with the rocky tide of the global counterculture, as Eric Zolov chronicles in his book *Refried Elvis*. In Mexico it came to be known as La Onda, the Wave. La Onda encapsulated the counter-culture's many faces: protest rock, folk rock, psychedelic rock, and a phenomenon Zolov refers to as La Onda Chicana, a reference to the infusion of a Mexican sensibility into the U.S. American rock idiom—think Carlos Santana.

On September 11, 1971, La Onda reached its climax at the Avándaro music festival, also known to this day as Mexico's Wood-stock. An estimated two hundred thousand people overwhelmed the woodsy resort area in the state of México, west of the Federal District, where the concert was held. The event was messy, disorga-nized, and didn't end till the next night. Bands with such names as Los Tequila, Peace and Love, Los Dug Dug's, and Three Souls in My Mind (who eventually became the legendary rockers El Tri) played while soldiers ominously stood guard on the outskirts. It was a watershed moment. There were no confrontations with authorities at Avándaro, but in the days that followed the one-party state swiftly condemned the festival. Photos emerged showing nudity, Mexican flags modified with the peace sign, and members of the *banda* happily dancing around with an American flag. "While the U.S. flag stood for imperialism at protests in 1968, at Avándaro in 1971 it symbolized solidarity with youth abroad and especially the Chicano fusion at the heart of the Mexican rock counterculture," Zolov writes. Yet, predictably, the images scandalized the regime, the press, and leftist intellectuals who saw Avándaro as a sign of looming cultural imperialism from the United States. From then on, rock concerts were severely repressed in Mexico. The PRI routinely refused permission for foreign bands to play on Mexican soil for years thereafter.

Young Mexican rockers retreated into *hoyos fonquis*—"funky holes," purposefully misspelled as it would be in graffiti—for underground gigs. The "holes" were held in dead urban spaces in mostly neglected barrios in the sprawling megalopolis. Police often raided the concerts, violently dispersing the youth. But La Onda persisted. "Several *hoyos fonquis* became famous," the Chopo history book recounts. "The Maya, the Salón Chicago, the Siempre lo Mismo, the Herradero, the gymnasium of Nueva Atzacoalco, and the 5 de Mayo." In spite of the state, Mexico City became a rock-n-roll kind of town. By the start of the 1980s, sunlight beckoned. More and more new rockers were seemingly sprouting from the cracks in the Mexico City concrete. New movements such as punk and heavy metal had arrived. The *banda* had to keep making rock-n-roll. El Chopo gave La Onda a site, a place to focus its energies.

Even as El Chopo struggled to survive against threats of displacement and repression, challenges arose internally as well. Debates were had over how to organize the *tianguis,* or whether to give it any organizational structure at all. Questions arose on how to incorporate new vendors, whether to negotiate with the borough government, whether to allow the sale of pirated discs. The changing times brought more women into the *chopero* fold. The arrival of CDs and DVDs, and the arrival of new subcultures—ravers, skaters, hip-hop heads, goths—also altered the market's landscape. But with each cultural transition happening around it, El Chopo learned to adapt. The market is functionally not retro at all. On the contrary, it has consistently managed to evolve and remain fresh.

Purists will claim El Chopo is not what it used to be. But a few holdouts are still keeping the old Chopo flame alive, through trading. They gather in the back, by the anarco-punks. They barter old Jimi Hendrix LPs for obscure Italian psychedelic rock, or a good anarchist book for a newer album by the Cure. They are men with graying hair or long, ratty ponytails, leather vests, and faded jeans—the kind that must also have been worn at the most mythical concerts in Mexico City's "periphery." One Saturday, as I browse a stack of records lying on the greasy concrete, I ask an old-timer named Jesús what he thinks about the new kids on the block.

"It just feels superficial," Jesús says, in a rolling old-school D.F. twang, where the Spanish takes on a tone that is both tough and soft. "Back then—the hippies, the punks—they stood for something. Now it's just fashion."

A guy over his shoulder named Miguel chimes in. "The principal concept behind all this is bartering. That's how it was born. That's the central concept."

"Pure bartering," Jesús says wistfully.

The hot pre-rain sun burns directly overhead.

"The circle is much smaller," Miguel says. "But the *banda* has adapted to each crisis that has come. They keep buying. I keep buying."

"This," he adds, patting his stack of records, "is an addiction."

Week after week, I wander through the *tianguis,* eyeing pirated concert videos of shows in Mexico City by Metallica and the Strokes, old books, old records. I find myself wondering if I could pull off wearing a fake-zebra-skin belt. I look at rows of cheaply made, mass-manufactured checkered cotton wristbands and wonder about the people who'll buy each one and wear it on their street or in their house with a misplaced bravado. I pick up flyers for concerts and shows featuring names of bands I've never heard of in genres that don't always fit my understanding of rock music's logic. The Cavernarios, Los Calambres, Adicción Fatal, La Julia. Psychobilly, ska punk, Latin metal, indie pop.

I start taking home *chopero* stuff: old punk magazines, a book on the anarchist legend Ricardo Flores Magón, a vintage golf jacket, a first-edition Morrissey CD, that fake-zebra-skin belt, skater sneakers—even though I don't skate. I buy more books about the history of La Onda, charting for myself all the myths and mythmakers of the rock-n-roll underground in Mexico. I pick up flyers, sit against a curb with a cigarette, and try my hardest to integrate myself into one of the *cervecerías* when the market begins to shut down.

At El Chopo, I'm finding, rock and resistance isn't just for sale, it's in the air. It lives with trepidation. In its three decades of existence, it has survived books' worth of relocations and repression in a city well accustomed to both. The PRI regime was dismantled in the elections of 2000. Leftists now govern Mexico City. Instead of state repression El Chopo must now defend itself against the ever-encroaching forces of commercialization and globalization. Less clearly defined as an enemy to the counterculture than the PRI, the Internet makes it presence known at El Chopo despite its guardians' best efforts to keep the market purely "punk." Through

MySpace, YouTube, and an endless stream of blogs, foreign bands and movements that would be obscure in previous decades are now at anyone's fingertips.

It is felt on Aldama Street, especially among those who know their history.

"Look, the kids aren't back here hauling cables, setting up the stage. It's the old-timers," Hernández, the Chopo journalist, tells me ruefully. "This is the generation of the button. Everything is button and finger."

That may be true, I think, but they still come back here every Saturday, keeping El Chopo constantly evolving. There's a working geography to the place, late in this decade. The anarco-punks and the old-time informal vendors clearly dominate the market's rear. Reggae fans, emos, and modern hipsters inhabit the stalls in the middle. Goths, straight-edge skinheads, and hard-core punks keep watch at the front. Here and there they stand around smoking cigarettes, weed, or sometimes the poorer few inhale a harsh and addictive paint solvent known as *mona*. They pass out and receive flyers and revolutionary newspapers. All throughout the market, groups of *choperos* socialize in huddles that remind me of a high school quad. Across the main lateral drag, Mosqueta, the hip-hop heads and graffiti writers keep their own mini *tianguis* called Plaza Peyote, selling national and foreign hip-hop discs, baseball caps, and sneakers.

A few *cervecerías* are around there, too.

One spring day at El Chopo an afternoon rain sweeps across the valley, and the *choperos* seek refuge again in their beer joints. I wander down a side street, following the sound of rock music from a jukebox. A hunched-over old lady claps quesadillas between the palms of her hand, so I knew there is beer for sale inside the archway behind her. I enter a humid, little concrete room with a couple tables and some mismatched chairs, an industrial refrigerator chilling *caguamas,* a jukebox, and older rockers stammering and stumbling about, happy. It's hard to tell, even after many months and visits, how the crowd in an uncharted *cervecería* will respond to a new visitor. Apprehensively, I ask if I can use the toilet. Then I sit down and order a beer and start listening.

There are only free chairs, no tables, so I take a seat and hover near a group of friends. One of them, a baby-faced guy maybe in his mid-thirties, with a black patch over his left eye, smiles and raises his beer at me in salutation. He is wearing a black leather vest and jeans and dusty black biker boots. His hair is jet-black, long, dangling directly down the sides of his head. He introduces himself as Julio. His openness makes him stand out merrily among the rockers around us. We quickly fall into conversation and ritual beer-chugging. I never ask Julio why he wears an eye patch. He welcomes me. We drink, we toast. He is a rocker, all the way, Julio says. He cheerily greets a woman sitting at another table in a corner, then casually mentions to me she is his ex-wife. I don't remember how we start talking about politics, but I do recall that somewhere along the way Julio begins going on about the ways the Mexican government keeps young people down. This is always a fruitful discussion in the orbit of El Chopo.

I ask if I can turn on my recorder.

"Record it! Record it!" Julio hollers. "All right *banda,* all right," he says, leaning in, adding some authoritative heft to his voice. "Here comes a course in sociology, history, and music."

A friend of his laughs and hoots behind him.

"Speaking to you is Julio Ayala," he continues. "Musician with twenty years in rock-n-roll, *güey.* No bullshit. Ask anyone who knows."

Twenty years. I'm impressed. Being *banda* for twenty years

means he is a true survivor. What *hoyos fonquis* did he know? What acts of state violence did he see? What movements did he dabble in? What bands? But Julio at the moment isn't taking questions. He is in the middle of delivering a lesson.

"Well, what is the *pedo* with our country?"

I pause. *Pedo* is the Mexican Spanish word for "fart," but it's more decorative street-level meaning is "crisis," "problem," or "fight." Julio adjusts himself in his seat. "Our country is used to giving its ass to foreign politics. There are treaties, like Bucareli, that say the role of our country is to be the maquiladora"—the sweatshop—"to big capital.

"So, the government gives its ass to remain the dominant class. They give themselves, to be the big dogs, but make no mistake, they still wear leashes."

We are pleasantly drunk, and it is loud inside the bar. Julio's train of thought wanders a bit. "The Chinese. The Chinese have survived Mao, and we Mexicans have survived the PRI, the PAN, and the PRD," Julio continues, listing the acronyms for Mexico's other major political parties.

"The people know how to survive the political parties, and you all know it," he adds, referring to no one in particular. "But the people put on costumes, you know it. Because we know what is happening, we put on costumes."

"One time, I was here at this very spot, and I was talking to a partner about just this. We were talking about how a party like the Green Ecologist party could rise here," Julio went on. "Could it be possible that people need a party to be green ecologists? The party is you, the *patria*"—the homeland—"is you. The *patria* is in your heart. Everyone chooses their own *patria*."

With this, Julio Ayala decides his impromptu course is done. He leans back in his seat, finishes off his beer bottoms-up, then catches himself and leans again toward me, back toward the mic. "My good-bye now to the *banda,* to not bore you. . . . Here at the *tianguis* . . . I'm here, I'll be here, we'll be here next week—despite you." He stands up to go, but he's really just heading to the next table.

"Good-bye," Julio says into the mic. *Click.* Very rock-n-roll.

We say we would keep in touch. I am *"banda,"* he says, patting my shoulder, then making me stand up for a deep hug. Julio ducks out, back onto the streets. I say good-bye to the people in the room, and they all say good-bye in return, nodding, toasting.

I make my way back to the metro in the steady gray drizzle, then decide I'll just walk, see how far I can go. Microbus *peseros* roar down the wide avenues, and people pour out of the main chapel in the neighboring Colonia Guerrero, a spiky Gothic tower. I am pleased. I can be *banda* at El Chopo. And therefore, I have found my *patria.* But there is a catch. Its exact name, official language, and culture will not reveal themselves to me until much later.

Part II | TENSIONS

4 | Fashion & Facsimile

Zemmoa, queen of the night. (Photo by César Arellano.)

The fashion show is held on a Wednesday in early November, at the old Casino Metropolitano downtown. According to lore, the ghostly former game hall first belonged to a socialite romantically linked to President Porfirio Díaz, the former general whose corrupt rule over the country eventually sparked the Mexican Revolution. Today it is again a scene of decadence, but in a way tied not so much to extreme wealth and power but to a more discriminating kind of privilege: fashion.

The casino's downstairs is a long hall with poor lighting and paint peeling off the walls like skin on a banana. The runway consists of metal folding chairs laid out on the faded tile floor, facing each other. Waiters walk around serving shots of tequila in teensy plastic cups. Camera flash punctuates the air. Friends greet each other, posing and floating air kisses. People lustily stare at one another. The show is already two hours late, and a palpable sense of expectation and drama fills the room, a feeling that we are there to witness something spectacular and important—not the fashion show, but one another.

The lights dim and a spotlight catches the rear of the runway. Red lighting from behind an opaque screen illuminates a logo in jagged punk-rock letters, MARÍA PELIGRO, and the show begins. The audience watches the models with determined severity. The line of clothing—subdued large-print flannels in large, angular cuts—is by a young designer named Paola Arriola, who is pretty, has orange hair, and is from Argentina. When she walks down the runway to take her bow, camera flashes sizzle at her from all sides. It isn't Fashion Week, and no major foreign headliner is sweeping into town. Not a single celebrity is in sight, in fact. But no bona fide celebrity is necessary at the María Peligro show because in this world, everyone is a celebrity or behaves like one. It is an independent fashion show in Mexico City, and that means it is—to a certain set, to the fashion-party bloggers—the most important thing happening tonight.

Earlier in the day I stop at Clinica, a small boutique showcasing young, independent fashion designers from Mexico, in the Colonia Condesa. The partners there, Enrique González Rangel and Denise Marchebout, designers from Guadalajara, tell me about the show. I tag along, taking pictures and taking notes. We stop for sushi in the Roma and meet up with more people heading out for the night.

I imagine us as the cast of a droll art-house movie: the gay disco promoter, the strikingly beautiful kabbalist, the German graphic designer, the film-studio executive from Los Angeles and his young Mexican boyfriend. More than enough sexy sceney energy is here to go around already, and the sashimi hasn't even arrived.

We pile into a row of cars waiting outside and head downtown. At the Casino Metropolitana, the clothes by Arriola are interesting, yes. But what really gets the crowd going is the majestic ascent up a glistening marble staircase to the after-party. The dazzling neo-baroque ballroom has lush plants and gilded surfaces and red velvet beckoning from every corner. The city's young and fashionable elite dance into the room, toward the pounding beats of an electro DJ, and to the bars, where men and women in crisp black-and-white uniforms eagerly dispense free cocktails. Every few seconds a new camera is thrust into a random face or group of people. Everywhere you look, instantaneous modeling.

I have never seen posing like this in Los Angeles, and people in Los Angeles carry posing in their DNA. Here, they pose in the gilded sitting rooms, they pose on velvet couches, they pose with their mouths agape and pose grabbing one another inappropriately. The energy keeps rising as the music does, as if there might be no other place in the world worth being at than this fashion party in the Centro Histórico of Mexico City with hundreds of familiar strangers—some Mexican, some British, some American, some a mixture of Mexican, and others of Latin American polyglot heritage. It feels as if a dam has broken, and it is only a Wednesday.

The artist Miguel Calderón, whom I befriended a year earlier, keeps a stash of canned beer near a speaker and scours the room to find me a date. Vicky Fox, a towering transwoman with yellow hair and brown skin, hurls herself dramatically onto the floor and begins contorting about on the weathered tile when I ask to take her picture. For the entire night, a small pixielike character with a bowl haircut and an all-white elfin outfit trails behind me, posing nonchalantly for photographs at any moment and rarely saying a word.

A circle quickly forms and we decide it is time to go. I have lost Enrique and Denise in the drinking and dancing spree. A group of us glide down the stairs to the open street. We gallop over to the plaza in front of the Museo Nacional de Arte, brilliantly lit in the 3:00 a.m. chill. We—it is impossible to say whom with precision— pile into a cab and speed forward, destination uncertain. Crammed in the backseat with Vicky Fox, the pixie in white, Miguel Calde- rón, and a few others, I am so drunk and happy I become inex- plicably furious at the driver. I demand he not drive us around in circles, running up the fare, as cabdrivers in Mexico City often do. In my delirium, I accuse him of cheating us even before we move a few blocks. I curse him and curse all cabdrivers everywhere in the world and on other planets. The driver wisely ignores me.

We arrive at a cramped cantina in the lower Condesa, and I feel transported to, of all places, Paris, circa 2003. Echoes of a visit there. A dance floor, dim lighting, nothing to drink but beer, cigarette smoke, magically liberated young women who appear to inhabit other time zones and cultural genres—1990s rock, 1990s hip-hop, 1990s electro. The pixie trails along with us the entire time, say- ing barely a word. I do not learn his name until the morning after, Quetzalcóatl Rangel Sánchez, a fashion designer and half of the creative force behind the up-and-coming label Marvin y Quetzal. As the sun begins rising, Quetzal and I wind up navigating Ave- nida Revolución in Tacubaya, inviting ourselves into a new friend's apartment at the iconic Ermita building, an art deco landmark. We watch daybreak from the high windows and marvel at the morn- ing traffic roaring below us. The following day, we manage to make it back to our respective houses. I had somehow lost a couple of prized homemade necklaces. Quetzal says we'd find ourselves online and be in touch.

We talk that very night. We come to a solid conclusion: "We should go out again."

For a period in the mid to late 2000s, fashion is *in*, in Mexico City, and I feel compelled to cover every aspect and every minute of it. Mostly, this involves socializing and drinking every night of the week at sponsored parties. The Paola Arriola show is reportedly sponsored by a young party impresario named Rodrigo Peñafiel, a surname seen on millions of bottles and cans of mineral water across Mexico. I quickly learn how the parties work. A good amount of money is always behind the best parties in D.F., the ones where there's no hassle to get in and no hassle for drinks. You just . . . *arrive*. The tricky part is knowing where and when, and with whom. For the next six months or so, as if it is my holy duty, I attend every fashion-scenester-hipster event in Mexico City that I can get into. I network with promoters, DJs, organizers, and producers. I get myself on e-mail lists and then at-the-door lists. I kiss lots of cheeks and shake lots of hands. I watch all the relevant event updates on Facebook feeds. Little by little, doors open, lists expand, access becomes an assumption. If I am not guaranteed access, I learn that with the right attitude and approach, a true Mexico City fashionista can talk his way into virtually anywhere.

I had learned how to network in Los Angeles after living in neighborhoods such as Echo Park and Silver Lake. I was already a dedicated scenester. In Mexico City, I begin gaining access not only to hipster parties and fashion shows, but to the burgeoning stream of film festivals, high-society art openings, mega-concerts, and brand-sponsored cocktail hours. To the movers of the scene in Mexico City, I was "from Los Angeles," and in this moment both cities gave the other equal levels of cool cachet. But I didn't confuse one for the other. The Mexico City scene felt like one sustained climactic moment, night after night, week after week, driven by the sense that in this town more than anywhere else, the party is *it*. In Mexico for as long as anyone can remember, nothing has been more important than to deliver oneself to the rite of the fiesta whenever the opportunity presents itself. And no one in Mexico City at the moment is partying harder and more exuberantly than its fashionable hipsters.

By its very nature the formula is tricky. Devotion to such partying can do wonders for the vitality of someone's professional profile, but without the proper precautions, it can also cause a professional downfall, or worse. This is the world that I fell into right away in Mexico City, a world that is exceedingly welcoming to foreigners. These are the people for whom partying is synonymous with work—and with risk. For me, like them, it becomes an obsession.

"I was supershy at the beginning," the fashion blogger César Arellano tells me over lunch one day in the Condesa. It is January 2008, a year after he launched his blog, Diario de Fiestas. Our conversation takes place in English, characteristic of the first-world leanings within the Mexico City scenester community. César has a lean face, darty eyes—good for quickly scanning a room—and a sneaky grin. He wears neckties and bow ties and shiny wing tips, stuff like that.

The first post on the blog is titled "En el Cultural Roots," referring to an underground downtown club that caters to the Mexico City reggae scene. César had gone to a "weird" art-rock show there. He posted just two images of the night: a shot of the backside of a girl in a pink vintage-looking dress dancing wildly, holding a microphone, and a shot of a person holding a microphone, wearing an absurd sumo-wrestler costume, a silver eye mask, and a silver metallic wig.

"I took these photos in November," Arellano writes on his first post. "They introduce perfectly the tone that I'd like to frequent on this blog. . . . I don't remember the band, but to me they were brilliant."

Photos follow of parties at an underground club called El Patio de Mi Casa, then shots at an opening party for the Kurimanzutto gallery, then one of César's outfits hanging on a door waiting for the night to begin ("Vintage Yale University sports coat, T-shirt by María Peligro, JBrand skinny jeans, and plaid SB Jordan sneakers," he writes). More posts followed, like candids from debauched living-room birthday parties. March came around, and with it, a barrage of posts from Fashion Week. In a short time, Arellano added links, mixing little blogs and big houses: I'll Be Your Mirror, Givenchy, Diary of a Third World Fashionista, Balenciaga, Love Naomi, Mexican Flamboyant, Prada. People started looking.

"I used to go to a party and take ten pictures and that was it," César says at lunch. "But they were my friends, and it was easy to take pictures of them. It was me and it was my close friends and that was it. Then three months later, everyone was looking at it. I don't know, one hundred people were looking at it. The same people who were going out every weekend."

The need to document was apparent. After spending some time apprenticing with a photographer in San Miguel de Allende, and freelancing for an established Mexico City fashion designer, Arellano began meeting young fashionistas who were resettling in the capital and putting on parties. So many had spent time abroad, while many were foreigners themselves: Argentines, Venezuelans, and the Mexican-born but U.S.-raised. In a loose phenomenon, many young Mexicans had soaked up Paris, London, Montreal, New York, Los Angeles, Barcelona, and other world capitals in the early part of the 2000s. They returned to Mexico City around 2005 and 2006 with a refined global sensibility. All were hungry to party—and to prove themselves.

"I felt there was a scene, you know, there was something happening," Arellano explains. "I felt it at Patio. I remember I was at a Zombies party, more than a year ago, and there were at least twenty people dressed amazingly, and the music was great, and the outfits were great." He pauses, as though it sounds so self-evident. "And the night was amazing."

Arellano kept posting. Viewers of Diario de Fiestas rapidly doubled many times over. By late 2007, it seemed every scenester in the city was logging on to the site, looking for shots of themselves from the night before, ogling strangers, critiquing looks, looking for hints for the next spate of parties. From afar, fashion-conscious bloggers in other world capitals started taking notice, adding Diario de Fiestas to their link bars, to peek in and see what the cool kids of Mexico City were wearing on any given night.

Partying, it turned out, is *work*. For his entry documenting the María Peligro runway show and after-party, César expresses some exhaustion with the world he is so faithfully recording. He writes, "At one moment in the night I got tired of the scene and the alcohol and eternally carrying around my camera. After a week, I'm recuperating from it. It must have been the overdose of runway shows and after-parties in October."

"God," he adds in English. "I'm so glad it is over."

It is late spring now, and there is another party at the club called Pasagüero.

"Another party" is how it is described to me and how I describe it to others. Another party, after some other parties, and before a few others to come. I don't know why I am here again. Maybe it is Fashion Week. Maybe it is some other foreign brand in town to penetrate the market: Bacardi, Absolut, Nike, Adidas. Maybe it is someone's magazine-issue release party. I had been to Pasagüero before for one of those. It is in Centro, on a pedestrian street, and the music always bounces loudly up the ditches made by the old buildings facing one another. Back in the early 2000s, which is to say, a million years ago, Pasagüero was *the place* to be in Centro for Mexico City's scenesters. There and at El Patio de Mi Casa, which was more "underground," but anyway that was well before Pasaje America came around, also in Centro, when that club turned into *the place* to be for—oh—about two months.

What are we doing here again? Last time I was at Pasagüero, Mark "the Cobra Snake" Hunter and Steve Aoki were DJing. The leading scenesters in Los Angeles, down in Mexico to throw a party. People were desperate to get in. Now, another party at Pasagüero. My friend Cristal, a dedicated Mexico City scenester, is having a vodka. Cool kids are everywhere around us, talking, drinking, laughing, posing for photos.

"Isn't this, kinda, you know, fake?" I suddenly ask Cristal.

"Nothing that we have is ours," she admits blankly. "We follow the current."

Cristal and I remain concerned with the particulars. Who's taking photos? Where is Diario de Fiestas? Where is Domestic Fine Arts? Who will go home with whom? What's happening later? What am I wearing?

"It's *malinchismo*," Cristal says. I ponder this for a moment. Could the surge in this distinctly new subculture—"hipster," "scenester," "cool kid," whichever you prefer—be yet another expression of the storied Mexican tradition of unduly overvaluing anything foreign and First World? The party is for Nike, we determine. Nike is throwing a party at Pasagüero and we are here even though we aren't sure exactly why. Yet we see no other option but to be here.

"Look," Cristal says, hollering over the noise. "We're here celebrating a transnational brand, not a brand of huaraches."

I nod and take a swig of my beer. It tastes flat and stale, even though the bartender had just popped it open. Cristal is right, I think. Nike would never sponsor a brand of Mexican-made, handcrafted leather footwear, as traditional and old as our precolonial ancestors. That wouldn't be "cool." Transnational, globalization cool, I mean, which is what companies like Nike vigorously sell to young Mexicans.

A camera's flash comes careening into my personal space, ready to capture a moment mindlessly, and I duck. "Us, those of us who are just under thirty, we're growing up without the blanket of our parents," Cristal continues. "But those who are twenty, I feel for them. We got a bit of it, but they completely missed it."

By "blanket of parents" Cristal means the old social order, the way fathers and mothers in Mexico once ruled the household and the entire social structure of a young person's life. Now it is not the same. Hierarchies have flattened. The domestic social structure has disintegrated. Old rites of passage have calcified. Kids come out as gay when they're still in middle school. Everyone has MTV or some form of it on cable at home. Eighteen-year-olds lose their virginity in hotels *de paso* with hourly rates and court one another on hi5 or MySpace. The truly restless and economically desperate become men by surviving the trek to the North. Now every young person in Mexico is an agent of his or her own destiny. The result is that just about every liberated, moderately middle-class young person in Mexico has, it seems, gravitated toward fashion and hipsterdom.

We look around the club. Lights and sounds and flashy faces bombard us on all sides. Yet nothing seems worth a second glance. Another party at Pasagüero. Lines at the bathroom. Lip gloss. Flashy cheap jewelry. Cristal is wearing a bandanna around her neck and glossy sneakers herself. We watch as a friend alleviates her boredom by sitting on a large speaker—she has just discovered she likes the way the sound vibrations feel on her privates. Cristal chugs at her drink and hollers once more: "They're the children of radio and television."

I had first met Cristal on the street one night in Condesa, maybe in December, everyone diving into their last overdose of pre-Christmas partying. Neither of us remembers the details. She must have been getting into a car and I must have been crossing the street. In an instant, we turned around, looked at each other head to toe, and decided with one shared glance, *Oh, we're supposed to be friends.* We exchanged a few words, were heading to different parties, but promised to hang out. In a neighborhood festering with posing, sucking up, and competition, Cristal to me seemed like one person who never hesitated to say exactly what she was thinking, at any moment. That usually involved critiquing someone on their vanity, hypocrisy, or poor fashion choices. The Condesa neighborhood proved to be a fertile territory for this activity.

Although many of the scenester parties happen in Centro, Centro is not where most scenesters hang out or live. The Condesa, a few neighborhoods over to the southwest from downtown, remains ground zero for style consciousness in Mexico City. Correspondingly, it is the neighborhood where most foreigners try to integrate themselves. It is easily the most gentrified *colonia* in all of D.F., if not the entire country. Beset with exorbitant rents, severe parking issues, and, at last count, three Starbucks locations, Condesa is a hub of trendy boutiques, trendy cafés, trendy restaurants, and trendy-looking people. On weekend nights, cocaine dealers in discreet automobiles prowl the neighborhood's leafy streets delivering drugs to thumping apartment parties. No one pretends to be risking anything. This isn't the sort of neighborhood where Mexico City police raid homes looking for narcotics. It is populated by armies of designers, television personalities, artists, politicians, academics, musicians, journalists, marketers, producers, architects, the nouveau riche, and people who work in fashion—the privileged classes, in a few words, and therefore the sort of people who see recreational cocaine use as a matter of social entitlement. Not everyone does it, of course, but it is everywhere. Nearly all the restaurants and bars post signs in restrooms warning customers that if they are caught "consuming drugs," they'll be turned over to the authorities. They never say so, but the messages are clearly directed at cocaine users. *How can one neighborhood's party barometer be so intertwined with a single drug?*

Cristal, who by day trains marathon runners, grew up in the Condesa, as unbelievable as that sounds to many of her recently arrived neighbors. In fact, so did her father and her grandmother, who moved to the *colonia* when she was twelve, Cristal tells me one night. "For starters, there used to be just one *tortería*" in her dad's day, she says. One storefront that sold *torta* sandwiches—in the whole neighborhood. "Café la Gloria used to be, like, a lunch counter. They used to have the only TV in the *colonia* and they charged two pesos to come in and watch it. My dad used to go."

Cristal bemoans the new Condesa, but as a dedicated scenester she also enjoys its spoils. She can walk into four or five clubs within a few blocks of her house, and she hits them all, several nights a week. She enjoys whiskey on the rocks and the olive plate at Barney's, a darkened, New York–style bar with low leather couches. She eats as much savory, if pricey, Mexican seafood at La Ostra as her palate desires and nods her head or throws verbal darts at the DJs who play electronica near the bar, as if the restaurant wishes it were a nightclub. Cristal walks to the 7–Eleven in her pajamas—and gets stared at. *"Me vale madre!"* Cristal swears. (I thought for a while about how this phrase might be translated and came up with the satisfactory option of "I could give a fuck.")

Cristal suffers from the classic syndrome, native-gentrifier paralysis. She is from where she is—the Condesa—and the hipster-fashionista invasion is one she must learn to adopt, willingly or not. "From being a place to live in," Cristal tells me, Condesa has "turned into a place to go to."

The neighborhood's transformation speaks to a wider shift in young people's relationship to popular culture. When the "hipster" happened around 2000, it was the birth of the first global cultural movement predicated on the basic goal of being fashionable. There was no other value as dominant. It was about knowing what to listen to, knowing what to eat, knowing what to read, and knowing what to wear. Genre boundaries were obliterated. You could dress like a sixties hippie while listening to Run-D.M.C. and reading Ayn Rand. That was sort of the ideal, being as eclectic and obscure with your tastes as possible, and being an expert in everything deemed "good," and in everything deemed not good as well, just to be safe. Punks or goths use fashion to identify themselves as part of a group, but hipsters in the abstract sense use fashion for the sake of using it. To stand out, not blend in.

A decade into the phenomenon, hipsterdom expanded into the mainstream at an alarming pace. The "hip" dominates pop media, from movies to marketing. It penetrates the consciousness yet remains a cipher. Hipsterdom's cultural borders are constantly shifting, or potentially nonexistent. For ten years it has largely maintained a heavy load of internal baggage. There is a strong element of self-loathing: Nothing is worse than being called a hipster, even if you are one—and at the same time, hipsters tell themselves, everyone *wants* to be one. It is the price of successful penetration: Hipsterdom cannibalizes itself, an internally built mechanism. Its death is announced every day. Hip is so mainstream it's not even hip anymore. But don't ever forget the important corollary: Some people still manage to be really, really hip.

To that end, at some point in the last couple of years, it didn't matter what city you lived in. What mattered was that you were plugged in, turned on, and had all the right tastes. When it all comes down to being fashionable, fashion becomes important. In Mexico City, that remained a relatively renegade obsession. An element of risk is central to life here, with the specter of holdups and kidnappings, with epic traffic jams, pollution, and arbitrary pauses in the water and electricity supplies. In Mexico City, living with risks translates beautifully to street fashion. The trend-conscious urban adventurers think nothing of risking a look that might register as too bold or outrageous in other places. The city's young fashion designers take this conceit to its maximum reaches, then detonate it. New currents in clothes by young designers are bold, aggressive, and distinctly androgynous. Clothes meant for partying.

But there are stark differences between hipster iterations north and south of the border. In Mexico, young people may follow through close and constant Internet analysis the street-fashion trends in Los Angeles, London, Paris, and New York. But unlike many of their American counterparts, the hipsters of Mexico City make no pretense of being "poor" or "D.I.Y." Most Mexican hipsters do not dream of living in run-down lofts in far-off, frightening reaches of the city, but prefer orderly upper-middle-class districts such as Del Valle and Coyoacán, or the established chic hoods. There is no Mexico City version of a "trailblazing" Bushwick or South Central. In Mexico City, hipsterdom is essentially an expression of middle-class comfort.

I begin thinking hard about this, after some months of hitting up scenester parties, night after night of free access and free drinks. I am burning out. I am seeing the same people over and over, and having the same sort of night with them, each time. In Mexico City, the coolest of the cool were still congregating and partying for the most part in one neighborhood, Condesa. Many remained proud of it. And those who weren't had made themselves a miniculture of saying so—without ever leaving, of course. "Condesa was at its best four years ago," Arellano tells me the day we sit down for lunch. "I'm about to leave this neighborhood. It's too commercial, way too commercial. All these people from Coapa, Satélite, coming over to Condesa. It's over. It's time to look for a new place."

It is easy to say so, but far less easy to put the thought into practice, as he and others of us know. There is still a party around the corner that night, and another one around the next corner, and another one after that. Night after night, like it or not. We keep going.

"The *onda* right now," a scenester bellows into my ear one night at Malva, a club, at another party, "is that there is no *onda,* and there is all the *ondas.*"

5 | The Warriors

Welcoming the emos to El Chopo, kinda. (Photo by the author.)

Erik is sixteen and lives in Ecatepec.

—*Why emos?*

—Well, I don't know, it's the style of dress that we like, the
way of thinking, too.

—*How is that?*

—Well, I don't know, sometimes we have to take our emotions higher and make them more dramatic.

—*And what is that for?*

—Well, I don't know, that's each person's thing, it's like one
day you want to be happier, and be sadder another.
—*How do you make things more dramatic?*
—It's when you feel anxious, without knowing what to do,
and you start going to other things.
—*Like what?*
—Well, cutting your skin, I don't know, it's about looking dif-
ferent than the rest.
—*Where on your body do you cut yourself?*
—On my wrists, my chest, my legs.
—*What do you cut yourself with?*
—Razor blades.
—*Why do you cut yourself in these ways? (In zigzags, crosses,
words, and hearts.)*
—Because I started getting bored with the normal cuts and
so I gave them forms and figures.
—*And this is what you do when you feel depressed?*
—Yes, or mad.
—*What makes you mad?*
—Well, I don't know, sometimes when they don't listen to
me, or they don't try to understand me.
—*When are you depressed?*
—Well, most of the time, well, I don't know, there might not
be that much motivation.

(From Sergay.com, "Special Coverage on the Attacks Against
Emos and Gays at the Glorieta de Insurgentes," filed March 16,
2008, under "News.")

At the risk of sounding clichéd, the building in Tacubaya where I
live is like something out of a magical-realism novel. Right on Ave-

nida Revolución, a frenetic southbound artery on the city's west side, it looks a little dilapidated on the outside but offers clues of a previous golden era, ribbons of delicate tiling, spurts of florid interior detailing, a lingering sense of harmonious geometry and interior grace. Through a large, rounded metal door and down a cool tunnel, a series of row houses face a garden with trees. Everything about my building—the ancient plants, the sagging wooden floors, the rounded doors and interior corners, the chipping paint—makes me feel transported to a different time, an imagined place. My bedroom in our house is on the second floor, with a window facing a square interior patio that opens onto the kitchen and always smells like wet garden dirt.

My roommates share the building's history with me. Officially called Edificio Isabel, it was built in 1920. Juan Segura, one of the era's most revered architects, designed it back when Tacubaya was a western "vacation town" for people from the capital. In the 1970s and 1980s, Tacubaya was made famous as the territory of one of the city's most feared street gangs, Los Panchos. Long since engulfed by the marching blob of urbanism, the neighborhood today is just . . . here, hanging on, nothing more than a metro station to most people.

One bright Saturday morning in the spring, my roommate Diego pokes his head out of the kitchen window below me and calls up to get my attention. "You have to look at this," he says. I peer down. It is a story Diego has just clipped from *La Jornada,* the daily newspaper that caters primarily to students and bookish liberals. We open the paper flat on the kitchen table to a far-inside page with regional news. The headline reads like a joke: "Members of Urban Tribes Attack Young Emos in Querétaro." The article describes the scene:

March 8, 2008. Querétaro, Qro.—Some 800 youth belonging to "urban tribes," like punk, *metaleros,* darks and *skateros,* attacked young people from the emo movement—identified by their philosophy of acting according to their emotions and feelings—with the objective of preventing them from gathering at a plaza in the historic center of Querétaro's capital.

A mass emo hunt? The story says mobs chased emos through the streets, beat up the few they could catch, and overwhelmed the police and authorities. The story continues, "Cherry, an adolescent belonging to the emo movement, said that the aforementioned groups are opposed to their musical style, which is a mixture of trends from other groupings. 'This whole generation of darks and punks are angry at the emos because they say we're a copy,' she said."

We chuckle and then head separately to our rooms to work. I can't shake the thought that this story is screaming for a follow-up. I peek around the Internet. The primary social-networking sites used by young people in Mexico—hi5 and MySpace—are teeming with chatter about the "emo riot in Querétaro" from the night before. It is already all over YouTube, too. Querétaro is the capital city of the state of the same name. A friend is from there. Three hours north of the D.F. in the lush highlands of the Bajío region, Querétaro is a quintessential "provincial capital." Clean and conservative, very normal. I remember the cult film *The Warriors,* where gangs in almost cartoonish costumes battle for control of the streets of a dying seventies-era New York. Querétaro is not the sort of place I imagine a real-life version of this story could play out. In Mexico, in real life, the *banda* are supposed to be fighting a common enemy—authority—not one another.

Who *are* the emos anyway? The following Monday I call my friends in Querétaro and pack a bag. I ride the metro in the rush-hour slog to the North bus terminal, where Volvo-made passenger buses heave in and out every few minutes to the great northward expanse of the republic, back and forth, around the clock.

Glorieta de Insurgentes, I write in a notebook wedged between my window and a blaring bus-cabin television set. The rolling green countryside races past me. The sky is bright gray and cloudy, moisture hanging low and lazy on the horizon. I am happy to get out of town. One of the great things about living in Mexico City is when chances present themselves for you to leave it. Though I am leaving the city, I keep returning in my brain to the *glorieta,* or roundabout, back in the heart of the D.F. It binds together a major intersection—Insurgentes and Chapultepec Avenues—with a metro station, a dedicated-lane bus line, and a circular pedestrian plaza sunken below street level. I should have made the connection earlier. Circular, bulging a bit at ground level, as though the station below were pressing upward against the concrete, the Glorieta de Insurgentes plaza conjures the linear, muscular, and functional design so idealized during the height of the PRI era. Walls are painted orange and pink. High-rises and massive blinking advertisements loom above, and traffic swoops continuously in the out-of-view lanes overhead. A sustained buzz in the air at the Glorieta de Insurgentes is generated by two kinds of people: those passing through, on business, transferring from this line to that; and those sitting around doing nothing but watching them, and each other.

In cities and towns large and small in Mexico no social tradition is stronger than watching the world go by at the local plaza. Plazas are where brass bands play on Sundays and where people gather to chant and give speeches when they are discontented. Plazas are still the places where things start. At the plaza of the Glorieta de Insurgentes, a remarkable shift happened in late 2007. The emos began showing up. Sitting against the walls of the metro station, huddling in packs, they claimed the *glorieta* as their unofficial meeting place. Little by little, the emo crowds grew, until by springtime the plaza was overrun by emo youth on Friday and Saturday nights and sometimes on random afternoons, the after-school jam.

Hurrying through one day, I thought, *I gotta come back and talk to these kids.*

Average harried city dwellers find it difficult to tell the emos apart from any other teenagers wearing disaffection on their sleeves. Before 2007, the term *emo* had never achieved common usage in Mexico. In the United States, *emo* had been more or less forgotten with the era that saw it popularized, the 1990s. Here, however, they look different. These are not the suburban teens in heavy-rimmed eyeglasses who listen to Weezer and Dashboard Confessional in Middle America. The Mexican emo supersedes any global stereotype—the lackluster outward demeanor, the profound full-bodied melancholy, the habit of cutting oneself to enhance sensations of fury, emotional pain, or hopelessness. These characteristics might have been found among a minority of the emos who emerged in Mexico, but most of them, in passing, seem pretty happy. For self-identification purposes, emo in Mexico really comes down to one essential characteristic: a chosen look.

The emos at the *glorieta* wear elaborate, meticulously crafted hairdos. Bangs slicing dramatically down over an eye, fake bedhead stylized to look like a peacock fan sprouting up from the back of an emo's head. Hairdos are cut with streaks or stripes of radiant purple, red, pink, or blue, sometimes punctuated with pristine baseball caps or sparkly plastic tiaras. Makeup is indispensable. Boys and girls alike wear theatrical levels of dark eye shadow and eyeliner, often purposefully smudged down their cheeks, suggesting an exhausting sobbing session that never actually took place. (Sometimes the smudges are hot pink.) Clothes, too, are crucial: Skinny, too tight jeans tapering rigidly down the ankles are sometimes fixed with crudely sewn patches or rows of safety pins or chains. Falling-apart Converse or skater sneakers are the footwear of choice. The bolder ones have stud or ring piercings on their lips. There are lots of plaids, skulls, stars, and, inexplicably, the cartoon character SpongeBob SquarePants hanging from key chains. For emos in Mexico, black is the dominant color of choice for any garment or accessory. Black goes really well with spurts and streaks of purple, red, pink, or blue.

This new subculture practices an unfamiliar mix of goth and punk, with a sprinkling of metal, skate, indie, and even anime and candied pop. In abstract terms, it descended from somewhere between the pristine shopping centers of Southern California and the landscapes of suburban tracts in the hillsides of the Valley of Mexico. My first impression: This is like satire, only when it isn't self-aware.

The emos get together at the *glorieta* and smoke cigarettes, joke, play, touch up their makeup or hair or that of their friends, and flirt with new arrivals. It turns out that this is happening not just at the Glorieta de Insurgentes but in plazas large and small, new and old, all over Mexico, including in Querétaro. At some point, their arrival transforms into a nuisance for some young people who do not identify as emo. And by the twisted logic of collective identity, some members of Mexico's established urban tribes decide that the nuisance has to be eliminated.

———————

Querétaro is the sort of place where cloaked nuns still live in seventeenth-century cloisters and sell *pan dulce* from a window in a wall to the street, like medieval drive-throughs. A church is on practically every other corner in the historic center. Unlike Mexico City, where downtown churches feel more like museums nowadays than houses of worship, Catholic chapels here maintain actual congregations. On my first day in Querétaro, around lunchtime, I go for a coffee at the Plaza de las Armas, a slanting square directly before the central state-government building, the site of the emo riot the previous Friday. Everything appears normal. The benches are packed and lunching couples sit at tables at cafés tucked behind the surrounding buildings' arching columns. Live easygoing marimba is playing from somewhere.

I see some young people who look vaguely emo, and I approach them to strike up a conversation. Four of them are sitting together on a bench and on the floor in front of the bench, under a dense tree. Yes, they say, they had been here on Friday night. They seem relieved someone is asking them about it. I kneel down.

"They've been saying it was the punks and *skateros*," I say.

"No, no, they were anti-emos, *chakas*," kids from poor suburbs, says a girl, Vanessa. She looks only slightly emo, but close enough. One girl and three boys, two of them puffing on cigarettes. They must be fifteen or sixteen.

"It started with a Metroflog," says Arturo, cutting in.

"What's Metroflog?"

"It's an Internet page," three of them answer in unison. "Where you can put pictures up," Ángel finishes. "So they made a Metro' that said, 'We're going to get you, be careful.'"

The riot had been premeditated and publicized online. "They

were saying that we were supposedly taking over the plaza," Ángel says.

"Because the emos hang out here?" I ask helpfully. Heads shake no.

"This is just like a meeting point," Ángel explains, a little annoyed. The others nod: *"Aha."* Arturo and Ángel and Vanessa speak, the other boy stays quiet.

"To get together, before a show, a party," Vanessa says.

"Like a social space," I offer.

"Ahaaaaa," all of them say in unison.

"Like the Glorieta de Insurgentes—"

"—in *México*," the kids finish, brightening up with recognition. Being emos in Mexico, they know it is their new epicenter, in *México*, the capital. I ask the kids if it got ugly. Ángel admits that he had been chased. The mood briefly becomes grim.

"What were they saying?" I ask.

"'Death to the emos,'" Ángel says.

"'Fucking emos,'" Vanessa says.

"'If you don't jump, you're emo!'" Arturo adds, to all-around laughter.

"What *idiots*," the boy who has remained quiet suddenly says to himself, to my surprise. It's a classic slang phrase in Mexico usually used in football hooligan sections—*If you don't jump up and down, you're from the other team!* So everyone starts jumping like crazy. I am momentarily struck by how these four kids manage to see humor in the phrase being used against them. A profile of the attackers is coming into focus: a mixture of young sports fans, and anti-emo *chakas*, as Vanessa describes them. *Chaka* is a more polite way of saying *naco*, the most obscene slur there is in Mexico. *Naco* is so bad people refer to its use as "racist," even though its connotations have nothing to do with someone's race and everything to do with someone's class, social status, and tastes. Think of what a well-off urbanite in the United States might consider "hick" or "white trash"—that's *naco*. Vanessa in fact uses *naco* at one point to describe the emo-bashers.

"They had been bothering us for weeks, sending their little messages," she sneers. "We didn't give it much thought, 'Well, nothing will happen,' because of all the security, you know? There's always police here."

"But they paid the police," Arturo says.

"*Ahhhhaaaaa*," they all reply. An unverifiable but—to the teenage mind—completely plausible rumor: The police allowed the emo-bashing to happen. They stood back on purpose.

"Yes, the police didn't do anything," Vanessa says.

I gradually put together the pieces of what happened that night, from talking to these kids, from the clips on YouTube, and from press reports. The emo kids of Querétaro had been gathering at the Plaza de las Armas for several months. Like the Glorieta de Insurgentes, the plaza became a meeting point organically, a space where emos could get together, look at each other, then take off to a party or to see a band play. But these gatherings became bothersome to other teens in Querétaro who did not identify themselves as emo. The annoyance transformed into rage.

A bulletin circulated on Metroflog, then on MySpace, and on hi5, calling for a "rescue" of the Plaza de las Armas from the loitering emos. On the night of Friday, March 7, about eight hundred anti-emo youth poured into the square, hunting for emo blood. A mob developed. The crowds began taunting the emo kids, who had gathered for their usual Friday night out. The taunting turned into pushing, the pushing turned into blows. One emo boy was videotaped being pummeled repeatedly as he sought refuge against a stone wall. Later identified by his nickname Ácido, the boy was seen helplessly holding on to two girls, his lower lip quivering in humiliation.

"He wants to cry! He wants to cry! He wants to cry!" the mob chanted.

The police, reportedly caught off guard, arrived in force long after the incident had started. By then at least a dozen emos had been left roughed up, and the rest of them scattered away from Querétaro's Centro Histórico, chased through the streets by the mobs. The media arrived, allowing the anti-emo youth to explain their grievances. "The emos don't bother me, what bothers me is that they take a place as if it were theirs," one young man told a local television newscast from the plaza that night. He talked as though he was pleased with himself about what had just occurred. He was clean-cut and otherwise plain. Just a kid. "It also bothers me a bit," he added, rolling his eyes, "that they look more like girls than boys."

This became a common point of spite against emo boys, repeated over and over in the digital dialogue that exploded across Mexico after March 7, 2008, that emo boys look "gay." From day one, the wave of anti-emo violence had an antigay undercurrent.

It must have been a weird night, adrenaline pumping through mobs of teenagers, confusion and excitement fueling the violence. The kids I meet on the Plaza de las Armas say they heard that injured emos were left lying on the sidewalks. Ángel's father caught up with him that night in the Centro. Like a scene out of an action flick, Dad pushed his son into the safety of a doorway and told him to hide. On the Monday after the country's first emo riot, the kids on the plaza revealed that they were dressing "less emo" because they were afraid a rogue basher might still be prowling Querétaro's streets. They were dressing down, essentially in disguise, for their own safety.

"What's the emo culture about anyway?" I ask.

"Thing is, well, I say, it doesn't have words to define it," Ángel says. "I think you just decide you're emo. It's a way of life, it's not a style."

"The problem is people think they cut themselves," Arturo says.

"That they're bad," Vanessa adds.

"I have some scratches, but . . . it's something else," Arturo says, trailing off.

"People made a mistake with the definition of emo, because they say they're loners, and they like being depressed, but that's not true," says Vanessa.

What do you listen to? I ask. They list subgenres of music I hadn't heard referenced before: "Hard core, screamo." I jot down more notes. "The Devil Wears Prada . . . Alessana . . . The Horrors . . ."

"It's not new," Ángel insists. "It's just, now, it's more visible."

The kids are getting ready to get up and do whatever teenagers end up doing on a Monday afternoon downtown. "You should talk to Ácido," Vanessa suggests.

I'd look for him, I say, and we give our good-byes.

More clues about the emos' general profile emerge over two days in Querétaro. I talk to several kids, to a sociologist, and to the local human rights commissioner, a bland middle-aged man who speaks about the incident in impenetrable officialese. I find Ácido on MySpace and contact him, asking to meet. His profile online is drowning in emo imagery. In one of his photos, Ácido is dramatically smooching his own reflection in a mirror. His hair drapes over the entire top half of his face, and a studded bull-ring is embedded in the bridge of his nose. We speak briefly on the phone. Ácido sounds scared. Overnight he had become the poster boy of emo victimization. He doesn't want to draw any more attention to himself. But I press him, and he says we could meet at a mall the next day. *Aha,* I think. The emos, I'd come to find out, also constitute in their core a recognizable type in the era of globalization: middle-class mall kids.

Ácido doesn't show up. He stops responding to calls and text messages. The mood in provincial Querétaro seems calm and peaceful early in the week, and so I return to Mexico City that Wednesday. In the strict geography of the city's *tribus urbanas,* it has already become a different place.

Gay and human rights groups in Querétaro call a march for peace and tolerance for the following Saturday, March 15, but elsewhere in Mexico the clashes are just heating up. Something in the universe of young people has caught a spark. The anti-emo wave spreads virally across the country. In the hot Pacific coast state of Colima, five schools cancel classes after a message circulated on the Internet urging local teenagers to "join forces" with their "compatriots" in Querétaro to "clean up Mexico, clean up Colima, and make a better place for everyone." It is signed, "Association: Death to the emos." That same night in Durango, in Mexico's north, police detain eighty anti-emo activists who gather in the state capital city with the intent of hunting down emos. The next afternoon, while people march for peace in Querétaro, emos in Mexico City gather at the Glorieta de Insurgentes to face off against their enemies in an all-out rumble.

Miscalculating my day, I spend the afternoon at El Chopo, expecting the *glorieta* to ignite in the evening. News footage of the afternoon confrontation shows squads of young people arriving at the plaza in waves, eager for trouble. The aggressors include punks, goths, rockabillies, and skinheads, kids beating each other up simply for how they are dressed. The emos hunker together and fight back, chanting, *"Emos! Emos! Emos!"* The youth strike one another with studded belts. Girls behave particularly ferociously against one another, yanking, pushing, and cursing.

"We're against the emos! They're copying our style!" one long-haired youth in dark attire says to the cameras.

Riot police from the nearby police headquarters are called to disperse the crowds, but confrontations reportedly spill into the neighboring streets. Only a band of peace-loving Hare Krishnas, who paraded and chanted through the plaza, are able to quell the tensions, "as if it were a joke or scene from a surrealist film," a newscaster remarks.

No serious injuries are reported in any of the confrontations, yet the violence seems to bring on a kind of collective ecstatic release. The Internet swells with messages about the brawls in Querétaro and Mexico City. Older adults are bewildered. Younger adults—people who see themselves as truer rockers from preceding generations—look upon the anti-emo phenomenon with embarrassment and disdain. These "kids," rockers of older generations are saying, have no idea what they're doing. Since their arrival, emos have widely been seen among other subcultures as being superficial copycats. And—their worst crime of all—as being new on the scene, with no history, no apparent values.

The anti-emo wave spreads further. Emos start appearing on daytime talk shows, decrying the violence. Newspaper editorials weigh in. Members of the international press send dispatches back home. Some Mexicans begin to view the whole affair as one long and embarrassing punch line. "They're beating up the emos," I report in a text to Cristal one of those nights. "Good," she responded curtly. "They want to cry anyway." The emo riots and the emos in general are seen as indicative of a larger fault in modern Mexican youth. It raises an anxiety about the free-market free-for-all culture invading from the North: that limitless appetite of consumerism, that middle-class malaise personified by a fifteen-year-old, bone-skinny boy in purple stripes and sneakers. On one offensively crass (and therefore hugely popular) blog called Hazme el Chingado Favor—roughly, Give Me a Fucking Break—one contributor summed up the emo disdain in an exasperated comment: "I don't know if I should shit myself with laughter or start crying to see that my country is going down the drain."

Sunday, March 16, the day after the riot at the Glorieta de Insurgentes. It's a cool, calm night. I'm standing here, lounging against the walls of the metro station, looking for more emos to interview. Clusters of kids are mingling in the plaza's shadows. In a corner, I spot a group standing around, laughing, hollering at one another, and playing music on their cell phones. A quick attire scan—jeans narrow as tubes and hairstyles of the slash-and-spike variety—confirms I should approach. They are boys, but most of them are chattering like young girls, their voices pitched and nasal, their mannerisms effeminate. I can hear them refer playfully to one another as *chica* and *hermana*—"girl" and "sister." They are gay teenage emos.

I strike up a chat. The boys are well versed in the mainstream talking points of what is happening. It is "discrimination," they say, because lots of emo boys are "bi, gay, whatever you want."

"You know the movie *The Warriors*?" asks one of the boys, José Luis. "That's the best way to describe this."

5 | The Warriors

They all nod and laugh and chatter away. Capital police cruise around the plaza, elevated on Segways like motorized puppets. With the gay district Zona Rosa nearby, I am not too surprised to observe a muscular older American with blond hair and blue eyes hovering around the boys, making his best effort to just "hang out." The boys tell me they were at the confrontation between the emos and their adversaries on Saturday. They are back at the plaza now in defiance. And because there really isn't anything better to do on a Sunday than hang out and shoplift from the *glorieta*'s tiny pharmacy.

"Yesterday you saw who was really an *emo* emo, who showed up," says Aldo, a wispy-haired sixteen-year-old. "Because a lot of them are *poseurs*."

"And how long have you been an emo?" I ask innocently.

"Since November," Aldo says.

It doesn't dawn on Aldo that his answer provides exactly the kind of fodder that makes the emos of Mexico so many passionate enemies. The idea that poseurs could infect a scene has always been considered a threat to the most serious adherents of the established *tribus urbanas* in Mexico. But now an entirely new current is emerging seemingly built on the very idea of posing. So could a young man like Aldo and his friends in this sense be considered authentically emo? *Of course he could,* I think, and the realization leaves me a bit stupefied. You cannot authenticate "emo" because emos are by definition authentically inauthentic.

"So how do you define emo?" I ask Aldo.

"How do we define ourselves?" Aldo looks puzzled. "What do you mean?"

I try to rephrase the question. One of Aldo's friends insults him from across the group, and Aldo snaps, "I do know, *idiota*," and turns to me, admitting, "Well, more than anything, I like the style."

Aldo and his friends tell me that they heard a demonstration is planned at the municipal justice department, where gay rights groups would be urging better protection for emo youth. I tell them I'll be there. The next Wednesday, only a few dozen teens show up at the protest, and barely any of them dress in identifiable emo style. They hold up signs calling for tolerance and more security, along with an enormous rainbow flag. A few photographers show up. I am the only person I see holding a notebook. Aldo and José Luis and other kids from the plaza on Sunday are there, but we don't have much time to talk. The protesters decide to march to nearby metro Balderas and return to their territory, the Glorieta de Insurgentes. They descend into the metro station as a moving clump, chanting, *"Emos! Emos! Emos!"* the entire way, kissing and holding hands. Police escort them.

Theatrical and disorganized, the gay-emo march may be politically ineffectual, but it does prove that some young people are exploring emerging sexualities behind their emo fashions, taking refuge in the look's androgynous codes. Still, some of the young protesters did not want to be publicly acknowledged as emos, much less as gay. That week Sergay.com, a popular gay Internet portal, collects explanations as to why some marchers refuse to be interviewed on record at the demonstration: "My mom thinks I'm at Mundo E," responds one, referring to a major suburban mall.

"I live here nearby in the Colonia Juárez," says another.

"My friends don't know that I am emo."

These kids are already conscious of the risks involved in joining the emo wave. At the gay-emo demonstration, one young protester stands out. His head is entirely shaved. Andrés wears thin-framed glasses and says he is twenty years old. He tells me that after the big brawl on Saturday at the Glorieta de Insurgentes, he was walking home along the streets of nearby Roma when a group of young men jumped him, held him down, and chopped off chunks of his long emo haircut. He went home and finished the job himself.

"I felt impotent," Andrés says, looking directly into my eyes. Asking more, I make a reference to his being emo. "I am not an emo," he interrupts. "I am me."

Andrés's declaration stops me. I wonder if the media has been grouping emos together too hastily, negating each young person's individuality. I wonder if am I profiling the emo look irresponsibly.

The following afternoon I return to the *glorieta*. Reporters and cameramen are prowling around for quickie interviews. They've become as much a part of the landscape now as the emos themselves. I sit down among a group of emos and wait. Next to me sits Pablo, a seventeen-year-old guy with long bangs, stretch-tight jeans, and purple eye shadow. He wears skater sneakers and a skater cap, but I don't see a skateboard on him.

"Just yesterday my mom told me to leave the house," Pablo says, whistling through his teeth. "Well, she told me to come back at nine p.m., because some friends of hers were coming over."

He is listening to My Chemical Romance on his iPod, smoking, and waiting for a friend. "She asked you to leave because you embarrass her?" I ask.

"Yeah," Pablo says a little sadly. "Sucks, huh?"

Nearby, I notice one of the flamboyant gay emos I had met the previous Sunday, with Aldo. The emo is sitting against the station wall. He had been at the gay-emo march, too, but I hadn't asked for his name. I crane my neck to see if he'll notice me, to see if he'll say hello. Instead he avoids making eye contact. Still dressed emo, the kid looks genuinely depressed. From afar I could see an enormous black scab dominating the crown of his nose, as if he was hit across his face with something heavy and blunt.

Poor guy, I think. *The wound looks painful.*

News of the emo riots in Mexico ricochets across the globe. Kids are talking about Mexican emos in the United States, Germany, Vietnam, Australia, on every continent, in dozens of languages. Comparisons are drawn to similar youth movements that are also just emerging, the *fotologers* in Argentina and *pokemones* in Chile. MTV and *Rolling Stone* cover the story in the United States. In Mexico, analysts of every stripe and sector are attempting to apply some level of reliable logic on the outbreak of youth tribal warfare. *La Jornada* quotes a battery of specialists to help readers figure out the wave of emo-bashings. The paper surmises its roots are in "violent conservatism," and that young people are reacting to "a lack of opportunities for work and education."

"What I see is a deeply conservative connotation, the object being to divide [young people], because they cannot offer them expectations for the future," Ignacio Pineda, coordinator of the Multiforo Alicia, an alternative-oriented music venue in Roma, tells the paper. In a separate report, *La Jornada* quotes a specialist who argues emos do not constitute a "classic" urban subculture because they do not have a political or social platform as the punks, goths, or skinheads do. Emo is "pure fashion," says "youth expert" Héctor Castillo Berthier, a response to the forces of the market.

Among the emo buzz online, one amateur commentator catches my eye. Harry24, a user on the music site Last.fm who identifies himself as a resident of Mexico City, offers readers a meticulous sociocultural explanation of the anti-emo violence, in a learner's

English, blaming the phenomenon on five basic points. First, Family: "A lot of Mexican families are disfunctional." Second, Music: "90 percent of the bands from that wave are totally crap." Then Harry24 sets blame on Media: "The main TV companies here in Mexico are full of crap artist[s], fake bands and stupid shows, and anti-cultural shows." He also lists Culture: "Fact: Mexico is full of ignorant people." Finally, he places some blame on Government: "Emo boys are the perfect target to turn them into stupid and ignorant adults, to be manipulated."

It is true, in general terms and as Cristal had explained at the hipster party at Pasagüero, that the family structure in Mexico is under duress, resulting in part in armies of isolated teens. It is true that many mainstream bands labeled emo are amateurish. And, yes, the media that promote such bands are partly to blame for their staying power. So crappy bands and crappy shows produce a crappy movement. But Harry24 loses me with "Culture" and "Government."

I am just not sure. The anti-emo wave generates its own self-referential satire—emos as the subject of intense discussion on the Internet, emos appearing on the covers of tabloid newspapers and glossy magazines, emos and punks in "debates" on the radio. One fact becomes lost in the chatter. Emos are *new,* and anything new is a potential threat to the existing order, the equilibrium of the subcultural landscape in Mexico. Freshly arrived, emos bewildered everyone. No one knew where to place them, so the question of whether they should be incorporated into the geography of the city's subcultural symbolic bodies is answered with the hurried fist of violence. In that sense, the anti-emo movement had to have emerged organically. If there is a media-authoritarian conspiracy behind the anti-emo attacks, as Harry24 suggests, no one apparently told Kristoff.

Kristoff—he goes by one name—is a popular host on afternoon cable TV, on *Telehit,* one of those programs with loud music and graphics and crude jokes arbitrarily thrown into each segment, like a quota. Kristoff talks about stars, sex, and music and movies that he likes and dislikes. As the anti-emo movement began rumbling on the Internet, before the first altercation in Querétaro, one video clip was posted and reposted on the social-networking platforms most frequented by young people in Mexico. It is of Kristoff, in a live broadcast in January, leaning into the camera, his dusty blond hair styled dramatically upward, his fair-toned face rippled and colored red in fury. Kristoff, a Mexican of eastern European descent, wears leather cuffs on his formidably thick wrists. He is unloading about a new trend, the emos.

"Emo is bullshit," he starts. "What is *emo*? It's something for girls who are fifteen, because they've just gotten hair you know where. They've just become *emo-tion-al,* because they like the singer in the band, not because they like the music. . . . Is it necessary to create a new genre that says, 'Dude, all the rest are emotionally incorrect, they don't satisfy us'?"

And then in English: *"Fucking bullshit, kids!"*

And back to Spanish: "There is no movement, there is no way of thinking, there are no musicians. You guys confuse punk, hard core, you confuse screamo, you combine all the currents, just to give meaning to your stupid and idiotic movement."

He is practically spitting his words. *"There. Is. No. Movement."*

Watching the clip for the first time made me squirm. Whether his points were valid or not, Kristoff's on-screen persona is cocky and self-important. Which is to say, I need to meet him. I want to look plainly into the eyes of emo hatred and extract if possible what makes that hate burn. I contact Kristoff and he agrees to an interview at the Televisa studios where he works, near downtown. Television studios are never as glamorous as a television fan might expect, and Televisa Chapultepec is no exception. I walk in through a long metal gate and over a field of asphalt where various trucks and crates and unused light booms lie about. Inside the plain office building on the lot where Kristoff shoots *Telehit,* we sit down on a red velvet couch abandoned in the middle of a hallway. A thin and busty blond woman named Daniela, Kristoff's girlfriend, sits with us as we talk. Daniela remains cheery, with a flat smile plastered upon her face. It is early afternoon, and Kristoff is preparing for that day's show, giving instructions to editors and assistants who are rushing past.

Sitting next to me, chatting casually, Kristoff is significantly less, well, douchey offscreen. It turns out Kristoff is less a tool in a conspiracy against the emos than an unwitting spark that the emo hatred needed to ignite itself. "I *always* express myself that way on television. It's nothing personal," he explains. The anti-emo rant had been taken out of context—the context of performance anger that he peddles on *Telehit.* "I express myself that way about everything."

As soon as the anti-emo violence struck, many emos and commentators openly blamed Kristoff's rant for the confrontations. The clip of Kristoff berating the emo culture was most reproduced on blogs and MySpace profiles that called openly for violence. Emos mention his name in interviews and call him out with signs at marches. Before me, Kristoff does his best to appear at ease, as though he is bemused by his unexpected brush with worldwide infamy, but I could sense a good week's worth of stress and fatigue flaking off him.

"It's that minute on YouTube . . . ," Kristoff complains ruefully.

On cable programs such as *Telehit,* shock is what grabs viewers' attention: "This is cable. This is not open television."

Kristoff was born in Russia to Polish parents. His family emigrated to Mexico City when he was eight years old. Raised in the capital most of his life, Kristoff considers himself fully Mexican. He worked in radio for a while, he says, then found his place on television. The target audience for *Telehit* is the wide bracket of thirteen to thirty-four. Kristoff tells me his most popular weekday slot is Mondays, when he takes callers' questions about sexuality and dating. Despite the uproar over his comments on the emos, Kristoff is not publicly reprimanded by his show's parent company, the media juggernaut Televisa. Kristoff himself responds to the first anti-emo riot in Querétaro with a characteristically fiery challenge to the initiators of the violence.

"Leave them alone, assholes!" Kristoff screams in the clip about the Querétaro rumble. "What's the fucking problem? What kind of balls do you have? If you're such badasses, why don't you go after the *reggaetoneros*? Because the *reggaetoneros* will rip your faces apart!"

But it doesn't help. In the days and weeks following Querétaro, Kristoff is still labeled the king of emo hate. I ask him if he still believes what he said about the emos in general. He basically says yes. "I repeat, when you hear them, when they say, 'Nirvana is emo,' I have to say, 'No, you're confused. You just like certain kinds of melancholic music, and you like dressing a certain way because it's the clothes that they sell, right?'"

"Or putting on eyeliner," I offer sneakily.

"Eyeliner," Kristoff repeats. "And black with pink," he went on, switching to English, "because it's cute, you know. Because pink is the new black. But it's okay. I don't care about that."

Surely, I think to myself. Yes, the emos are products of the rising consumer class in Mexico. But Kristoff—working for Televisa, the country's de facto state media company, in his designer jeans and leather jacket and gelled hair—would be just as much a product of Mexico's new media-saturated consumer culture as the average mopey emo kid. Or maybe even more so.

"Do you really think this is a passing trend?" I ask.

"No, I think it's going to stay, especially now after what has happened. Little by little, they're defining themselves, looking for their bands, looking for their ideology, but they haven't achieved it." He pauses, baffled by his own train of thought. "Maybe they're not even looking to do that."

I watch Kristoff record a show inside his studio the day I visit. It doesn't seem necessary to take many notes. Daniela sits next to me, still smiling. The routine is mostly crass, forgettable stuff. But something that Kristoff tells me in passing near the end of our interview stays with me.

"They said somewhere on television—I don't know if it's true," he begins, sort of smirking, "but, that there are gay groups putting themselves in there, because you know, they accept boys kissing boys, girls kissing girls, without being gay." Kristoff is speaking conspiratorially, as if sharing a deep and disturbing secret, although it is well-known to anyone who has been following the emo-violence story that gay rights groups have called for tolerance. "So there are a lot of gay groups getting involved. I mean . . . I don't know. It's what I heard the other day."

He seems bemused by the thought, and I am partly awaiting a Kristoff-like punch line, mocking the emos once more, mocking their tangential gayness.

The emos of Mexico are here to stay, and that is the problem. They are not just a new "urban tribe," they are an entirely new breed of it, genetically different from punks or goths because they are not formed in reaction to a repressive state but born in reaction to MySpace and the mall. This threatens tribal equilibrium and inflames the sensibilities of self-respecting alternative-leaning young people. Acknowledging the transformation of the subcultural landscape has, for some, meant turning to violence—pure, raw brawling—against the new kids on the block. It is the emos' welcoming ceremony, their swearing in. In the battle over the public and social spaces shared by the subcultures, the emos' rapidly advancing numbers would eventually guarantee them a place at the table. But not without a fight. Throughout popular-subcultural history, young people have demonstrated a gleeful willingness to indulge in a primal human lust for blood and bruising when tribal allegiances call for it.

I see this firsthand one Saturday, three weeks after the Plaza de las Armas popped in Querétaro. A surge of sympathy and goodwill for Mexico's emos has poured in from blogs and Web sites all over the world. Day after day, I am doing my best to explain or at least help illuminate the phenomenon over the telephone with journalists in Germany, New Zealand, and the United States. By now, I can no longer ignore my emo-fatigue.

It is a hot and overcast Saturday. Emos—by then enjoying the aid and support of the leftist establishment in the D.F. government, who considered them the victims of reactionary forces from the right—announce they will march from the Glorieta de Insurgentes to El Chopo, to demand inclusion and tolerance at the place where inclusion and tolerance among *tribus urbanas* is supposedly sacred. This time I don't want to miss any of the action. I know the emos will be heavily guarded and heavily watched by reporters and photographers. So I come in on the event through the rear. I go directly to the market, earlier than the emos' expected arrival, to wait with the *choperos*.

5 | The Warriors

The scene is a typical Buenavista station Saturday, crews of punks, skinheads, rockabillies, indies, *skateros,* rastas, cholos, *darketos,* and even a few straggling emos, everyone just hanging out. Large cloth signs slung between poles near the market's entrance welcome the emos and remind everyone that El Chopo is dedicated to tolerance for all. The signs feel a little out of place, as if hung there begrudgingly. I sit down on the ledge of a sidewalk, next to a pair of friends, and wait for a few minutes to pass before I turn and ask if they are waiting for the emo march.

Paulina, an eighteen-year-old who says she lives in the northern Aragón region of the city, says she is. "I wanna see what happens. Is it gonna get rough or what the fuck?" She has dyed-black hair, wears black eyeliner smudged down to her cheeks, and has a mean-looking stud in her nose. Paulina looks tough and mischievous. I like her immediately.

"Are you *darky* or something?" I ask.

"I'm punk rock." Paulina makes a fist. Her friend is somewhat overweight and doesn't say a word. He looks a little emo, I think.

"So are you going to Christian Death tonight?" I ask.

"Yes. Are you? No way!"

Old-school punk friends of mine had mentioned that the legendary dark metal band from L.A. is in town. We have tickets to see them. This coincidence makes Paulina open up a bit. Glancing at her timid emo-like friend beside her, I ask her if she is anti-emo. "Whatever . . . ," she responds, without much conviction.

"What's gonna happen? What's it gonna be?" Paulina says, rubbing her hands together. She adds, unable to hide her delight, that at the *glorieta* "everyone was pounding on everyone, even the girls, they looked like *perras.*" Bitches.

At about 4:00 p.m., as rain clouds grow darker overhead, a large contingent of police cruisers rolls on to the scene. "The pigs just got here," Paulina sneers. The air is tense. A Chopo organizer speaks into a microphone plugged into a large set of speakers, reminding everyone, conspicuously, that "all types of people" are welcome at El Chopo. But no one I see looks pleased with the idea of a police-led march by little emos heading their way. When the emos arrive, rows of them, arm in arm, holding up signs, marching and cheering, they are outnumbered by a ring of police and reporters. Punks and goths and skinheads and rockabillies gather up, as if the Chopo has suddenly become a tub of gasoline, ready to be lit. No friendly handshakes, no warm hellos, are offered. As soon as the march comes up Mosqueta to the entrance of the market at Calle Aldama, the Chopo crowds form a line along the edge of the sidewalk. The street erupts in human noise. Punks and goths and others throw their middle fingers into the air and chant, *"Death to the emos! Death to the emos!"*

The emos throw their middle fingers back in reply. Only the presence of police with shields and batons prevents a riot. Behind me, behind the punk line, I see a spiky-haired kid grab a slab of loose sidewalk, slam it onto the ground to make small rocks, grab two of the biggest chunks, and prepare to hurl them into the opposite crowd. In a moment when the police seem poised to lose control of the situation, they allow traffic through on Mosqueta, and a sudden gush of vehicles separate the tribes. Rejected, the emos retreat, pull back, and leave, not once coming into direct contact with the market or with those waiting for them. The emos march onward, to rally for peace at the monument to Benito Juárez—Mexico's Abraham Lincoln. The confrontation lasts only a few minutes.

The anti-emo forces rejoice. They are incensed that the emos dared to come as a group to El Chopo—with police, no less. *"Fucking emo pigs! Fucking emo pigs!"* they chant. A spontaneous mosh

pit gets started. Bodies pounding against one another, elbows flying, knees hopping.

In the crowds I lose Paulina. But in a few moments I see her
squeezing out of the moshing punks. "Where's your friend?" I ask.

"He got scared!" Paulina laughs. The friend has run off.

"It was a shitload of police," Paulina says, panting, her voice
shaking with adrenaline. "Let them come alone, fine, but with
police? Come on!" We walk together into the market. Paulina's eyes
are ablaze. She wants more. As she speaks, Paulina is pounding one
fist into her other palm.

6 | The Lake of Fire

(Illustration by Rodrigo Betancourt.)

You can't really appreciate the enormity of Mexico City until you leave it on the ground. Merely landing at or departing from Benito Juárez International Airport belies the city's physical contours, the ranges of mountains that ring its basin. Flying in or out conceals what you're really dealing with. You must experience Mexico City's hugeness as a journey of distance, inch by inch, mile by mile, traffic allowing. On a late afternoon, nearing sunset, during the smoggiest season of the year, winter, your bus or car is climbing the mountains to the east. The road curves and pitches. You can feel the air outside get colder and colder. The mountains in every direction are suddenly covered in brilliant green trees. To the west the sun disappears behind a dark cloud hanging over the enormous valley. It is not a rain cloud. It is a blanket of pollution permanently fixed over the city. A nasty thick black cloud, so dark in the shrinking light of dusk that you cannot see anything underneath it. The only way you can tell the city exists below is because from miles away you can still feel its hum. It's almost impossible to believe, like a vision of some futuristic hell.

People live there?

I survive my first smoggy winter in Mexico City by applying a gee-whiz sort of awe to it. I hack up alien-looking green phlegm in the mornings for weeks at a time, but I can't really comprehend just how toxic the city gets around Christmas and the New Year. In my second winter, I have moved to the Centro, to a second-floor apartment facing a street choked constantly in the daytime with traffic. It is a Saturday in late January when I wake up with a violent cough. Throughout the day the air feels as if it is sagging on my back. By Sunday I have a nagging headache. It is cold at night, but it still feels hot out somehow. Something on the skin, a stickiness, a barely perceptible unnatural film.

The news bears out my suspicions. It is a thermal inversion, an unkind weather phenomenon that afflicts places dense with people and pollutants. In the mountain bowl of Mexico City, a thermal inversion can be acute and dangerous when it strikes during the dry season. Warm air that gathers in daylight is trapped on the valley floor by cold air that moves in at night. The warm air mixes with what's already there, all the pollutants of everyday urban activity. It has been an especially polluted weekend in the capital. Toxicity levels spike to a point that prompts the D.F. government to activate its environmental contingency plan, calling for limited outdoor activity, temporary restrictions on the manufacturing sector, and circulation restrictions on certain vehicles such as older models and cars from neighboring states. I scribble in a journal, *My throat feels like a cat pissed in it and my head feels like it's spent four hours listening to the same Daddy Yankee song on full volume, on loop.*

A few merciful breezes visit the city. By that afternoon, the government lifts the contingency alert. All activity returns to normal, but the following day the air still feels outrageously toxic. This makes me a little nervous. Mexico City's current official slogan is Capital in Movement, so by necessity we can have it no other way. A Mexico City with fewer cars and trucks on the streets, with less commercial and manufacturing activity, less *movimiento,* is a Mexico City that loses money by the hour. Can't have that. So eyes are puffy and dry, coughs are chronic, and just a few flights of stairs leave you winded. That pinched sensation of nastiness lingers on the skin. In the schools, recess is held indoors. TV Azteca reports that scores of city children show up at doctors' offices complaining of bronchitis. They say the chief pollutant that weekend is ozone. But . . . whatever. No one really knows what to call the cocktail we breathe in Mexico City. It is a mixture of ozone with nitrogen oxide, sulfur dioxide, carbon monoxide, and hydrocarbons—inhaled and exhaled in a continuous cycle by some 20 million people, day in and day out. What can you call that, really?

In the dryness of winter, the form and effects of the pollution are strongest. But winter or not, it is always there, hanging invisibly over your head, even when the summer rains come and clear away the sitting atmosphere for a few hours a day. At seventy-three hundred feet, the valley's altitude, the air pressure is dramatically lower than on coastlines, which heightens the pollution's least favorable effects on the human body. People get sick chronically. The Mexico

City smog affects your entire person, body and mind. Knowing you are inhaling an atmosphere once famously described as being equivalent to a habit of daily chain-smoking (which plenty of *capitalinos* do anyway) is enough to make you question your and your neighbor's sanity.

On the worst days, the cocky cigarette-sucking of so many proud Mexico City natives grows exponentially. What else can you do but gather friends and hunker inside, to booze up, suck in the nicotine—"Might as well"—and to think fondly of the days before the birth of the world's first Smog City, a capital internationally known for being caked in pollution. It was just the way the story went, when Mexico shifted from a largely rural society of communal farmland and the slow lifestyle of the hacienda to a rapidly urbanizing one of crowded highways and factories coughing purple fumes. Starting in the late 1950s, people came to the big city in the valley from the provinces, near and far. They kept coming, and kept coming. Urban immigrants came looking for work because in Mexico City, they were told, it did not matter how poor or marginalized you were, you could find a hustle and provide for yourself. The city was irresistible. Slums sprang up around the outskirts, unplanned and all but ignored. The same phenomenon would eventually change cities in East Asia, in other parts of North and South America, and in Africa and Europe, but for much of the twentieth century it did not happen at the scale and velocity anywhere else that it happened in high central Mexico. A lack of proper infrastructure in an accelerating grid of humans and industry soon bred the first poisonous clouds over Mexico City, never to leave. Environmental misery followed.

Planners and regulators would dub it uncontainable, a city whose apparent destiny of failure was rooted in its ability to attract endless streams of new residents. The city grew, by the thousands a day, by some accounts, and its situation worsened. During a memorably bad period of thermal inversion in 1991, when the city's smog was at what is now considered its historical peak, the *New York Times* quoted a local expert: "If the meteorological conditions remain the same, then we could have a thermal inversion that could equal the killing smog of London in the winter of 1950–51."

There is no such panic today, even on bad days. The city has grown accustomed to itself. In the bowl, no one seems to notice the poison. The sky above you is some shade of blue, right? Why complain? The locals say it is normal. They don't seem to mind. They look at you with pity. During this extra-smoggy weekend in January, residents in my building make an effort to go outside as little as possible. We open beers and talk. In the darkened interior of an apartment upstairs, my neighbor Ponce, a cartoonist and illustrator born and raised in the capital, calmly explains the air of normalcy while smoking a few singles. "We're mutants," Ponce says.

I down my can of beer, ask for an extra smoke, and retreat back to my apartment. What Ponce says makes my eyes pop in recognition. To be raised in Mexico City, or to willingly assimilate yourself to it, is to relinquish control over your natural state. The environment *physically alters you*. Because we've physically altered it. Ponce has uttered a cosmic truth. The Mexico City mutation is real.

Smog levels have steadily been dropping in Mexico City in recent years, but it remains above us, operating more than anything else as a totem. It symbolizes our species' irrevocable dominance over the planet. In places like the Valley of Mexico, where industry, urbanization, density, and the centuries have made the earth our violated dominion, the consequences of this reality haunt us. It is, as Ponce says, unnatural. It leads us into conflict with the elements, with fellow men, and with the gods.

The planet seeks payback in Mexico City. Earthquakes remain a spectral threat. The massive 8.1-magnitude temblor that swept the city on September 19, 1985, is a wailing ghost that still rings far in the back of people's minds. An estimated ten thousand people died, but no one knows for sure. The city was brought to its knees. Off in the distance, usually invisible behind the smog, the Popocaté-petl and Iztaccíhuatl volcanoes pose a subdued terrestrial menace. They're dormant, but—*could they wake up one morning?* There are the freakish rains and thunderstorms, bringing pounding blasts of wind. Neighborhoods flood, drowning kids and old ladies. Hills or asphalt streets give way. Trees snap and crush small cars. The land and sky remind us every day that they remain older and more powerful than anything we can bring to them.

Among people, the threatening qualities of the environment sometime ignite a primal urge—the urge to kill. Mexico City is by no means the most dangerous metropolis on earth. Cities such as Washington, D.C., for example, have higher homicide rates. But in the Aztec megacity death and murder acquire a disquieting inti-macy with everyday life. In page after page, the red-note papers are filled with practically gleeful reports on the cruelest deaths, often accompanied by graphic photographs. A French scientist who is held up on a busy road and shot in the face after being followed from the airport, dying days later. An Italian man who is shot dead after refusing to cooperate with thieves on a bus. The transgendered sex worker in Ecatepec whose head is rammed to mush by a huge cinder block at the hands of a client. Bodies are found beheaded, burned in tanks of gasoline, mutilated, or beaten to death, blow by blow. There are robberies gone bad, executions carried out in shad-owy alleys, and crimes of violent passion. In the age of narco warfare and the growing cult of the Santa Muerte—the unofficial saint of "holy death"—the killings numb us. News of a death to start off the day and news of a death before going to bed at night. Killings presented as common and as in-your-face as the traffic and smog.

Every day the papers tell us how the urban claims its victims. There are drownings, freak car accidents, vehicles turning over, indoor carbon monoxide poisonings, and horrible falls. The claiming of victims is indiscriminate. A wealthy person dies just as terribly as a poor one, and only the opulence or humility of their gravestones will mark their differences during life. Living in Mexico City becomes a long risky slog through an infinitely treacherous landscape. Some people are keenly aware of it, and it can drive them mad.

William S. Burroughs once described Mexico City as "sinister and gloomy and chaotic, with the special chaos of a dream." That was in the late 1940s, when D.F. had a small fraction of the population it does now and the mountains and volcanoes that ring the basin were crisply visible on the horizon. "No Mexican really knew any other Mexican," Burroughs wrote, some fifty years after the experience, "and when a Mexican killed someone (which happened often), it was usually his best friend. . . . Mexico was basically an Oriental culture that reflected two thousand years of disease and poverty and degradation and stupidity and slavery and brutality and psychic and physical terrorism."

Reading this, I instinctively respond with disgust of my own, tallying up all the offensive phrases. Then I think about it again. I think about all the writers whose attempts I've seen to sum up the soul of Mexico in a single argumentative statement, from the romantic or the nationalistic, to the postmodern or celebratory. Few are as raw, and as honest. Burroughs looked in the city's heart and it looked alien, violent, and sinister to him, like a pathogen. His experience illustrates the city's ability to swallow and permanently transform an individual. This was where Burroughs perfected his dark bohemian lifestyle—drug use, alcohol abuse, chasing young American guys for sex, fixing up his heroin on Dolores Street in Centro, just around the corner from where I sit. In Mexico City, Burroughs forged his twisted relationship with death. It is said Burroughs never lived or wrote the same again.

The problem that Burroughs and so many others have identified, and which is not going away anytime soon, is a sustained struggle over equilibrium, a lost balance with the elements and with history. The Aztecs who witnessed the original encounter with the Europeans must have felt the coming chaos. Their entire system of things, they believed, was at the mercy of their gods, the custodians of the elements. The earth they knew demanded sustenance. To them, the citadel of temples at the center of their city—Tenochtitlan—was the "belly button of the moon." As it was the center of the universe, according to their spiritual logic, all their gods were present. The god of war, god of fire, the god of earth, the sun god, the moon goddess. They had to be thanked somehow. So the Aztecs built their empire on sacrificial credit, submitted untold amounts of human souls in ritual sacrifice to ensure the rising of the sun, the rains, and their way of life.

They fed the land with blood. Children and infants were sacrificed to Tlaloc, who required the tears of the young to wash over the earth with rain. Slaves, virgins, and prisoners of war were slaughtered to dedicate new temples and to ring in the new year. Their severed heads were placed on *tzompantli* racks on the city's central plaza for all to see.

When they arrived, the Spanish regarded these practices as barbaric. But in conquering Mexico, they replaced the system of ritual sacrifice with something arguably bloodier and more brutal. The Conquest was a spectacularly violent encounter, a "foundational holocaust." Once subdued, the surviving Indians watched their cities and temples be dismantled. Their gods were replaced by images of Jesus Christ, his saints, and the new mother, sweet Guadalupe. In the early years of the consolidation of New Spain, indigenous survivors succumbed to disease in overwhelming numbers, killing off entire lineages and turning thriving urban settlements into ghost towns. Their world had been upended. Cities disappeared, their ruins willowing into the brush, forgotten. The force of the Conquest was so fierce, many Indians, one troubled priest wrote in the late sixteenth century, became "apathetic." Many refused medicine when they became sick, the priest wrote, choosing instead to "die like brutes."

I can't imagine the agony, unable to render to their gods—Tonantzín or Tlaloc or Huitzilopochtli—as they had done since the dawn of their world. But history marched on. In the ensuing generations, Mexicans of all castes intermixed beyond order and recognition, spawning the new, idealized mestizo civilization. With the boost from the Virgen de Guadalupe, everyone became a Roman Catholic. Mexicans eventually let go of the Aztec gods, but that didn't mean the deities just disappeared into the cosmos. In Mexico City it is regarded as a sad spiritual irony that the Metropolitan Cathedral—built on pre-Hispanic holy land—is sinking into the earth.

The spiritual imbalance heightens the sense that Mexico City is a geography of real, physical risk and hostility. But to blame the awesome power of a hostile environment on human religious practices alone would be impertinent. Historians often categorize Mexico into three major periods: its pre-Hispanic, its colonial, and its modern. During all three, the society's center is Mexico City, and in all of them, the city is driven by a culture of violence. Violence against humans, violence among humans, and violence between the human race and its surroundings. At each defining step in the history of Mexico, blood and death were on the watch. Something deeper is at play here.

In another one of those awful smoggy winter days spent huddling indoors in the Centro, smoke choking the room, Ponce and I meet again for an afternoon tequila. His hair is wild and his skin is earthen bronze. He is always dressed as if he's ready to run out his door and never come back, in trainers and sweatpants. Ponce is so inspired and terrified by the air outside that he paces around, tensely holding an invisible ball of energy between his two open hands. I am sprawled on the floor, illogically looking for cool air from the wooden planks.

"Mexico City," Ponce whistles, "is a lake of fire."

He sits down to keep drawing a psychedelic comic strip taking shape before him. My mind races back to that winter bus ride to the east, at dusk, turning back to the image of a futuristic hell. Mexico City shrouded in poisonous smog, proof of man's dominance over the elements. In the shrinking light, I imagine brontosaurs lumbering up the hillsides and an orange pterodactyl soaring above me. Is this how it looked since the beginning of time?

Around the first or second century A.D., on the south end of the valley, the geological record tells us, the Xitle volcano erupted near the Cuicuilco settlement, washing over the land in scorching lava. This primordial violence wiped out the earliest known civilization that existed on the basin's ring. The settlement was virtually liquidated, leaving hardly an archaeological trace. The lava cooled, slowly transforming into the stone with which later Mexicans built their pyramids and, later, used to build the Spaniards' churches.

A dramatic painting depicting the Xitle eruption is sometimes on view at the Museo de la Ciudad de México. On one side, a few of the earliest human inhabitants of Mexico—nearly naked, holding spears—stand bravely above the hot hell below them. Their expressions are grim but determined, as though they are thinking, *This is where we were made to live. This is who we are.* The valley at their feet is a belching sea of red and orange.

7 | Kidnapped

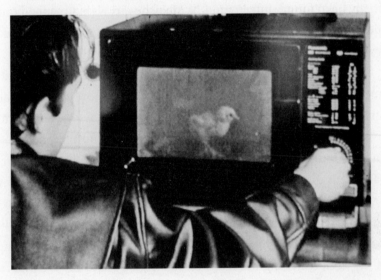

Violence in art, like violence in society. (A still from *Rinoplastia*, by Yoshua Okon.)

The news report I am reading online says authorities discovered the remains of a young woman late in the evening of Friday, December 5, 2008. The body was found buried in a shallow dirt ditch beneath a metal staircase in the garden of an abandoned home in a comfortable neighborhood in a southern borough of Mexico City. Hours later, according to the report, Nelson Vargas, a prominent businessman and the former head of Mexico's national sports commission, entered the headquarters of the top organized-crime investigators in Mexico, stone-faced. He offered no words to reporters. By the following Friday, December 12, on the Virgen de

Guadalupe feast day, DNA studies confirmed the widespread spec-
ulation: the body of Vargas's eighteen-year-old daughter, Silvia, has
finally been found, fifteen months after the girl was kidnapped one
morning on her way to her exclusive private high school, snatched
from her car by armed men.

In Mexico City, this grisly discovery would have been the end-
ing to just another kidnapping case, coordinated, professional,
terrifying. Kidnappings are common, occurring by one conservative estimate as often as twice a day across the country. That ratio
ensures individual cases rarely make the news. But the Silvia Vargas case is different. Every single development, no matter how tiny
or inconsequential, has been broadcast nightly on the TV news
and updated by the minute on news sites. When the confirmation
finally comes, that Silvia Vargas's body has been found, I am sitting
at my desk watching the feeds online. I go over to my neighbors'
to share the news, but my announcement meets with little interest. It's a warm Friday night. Ponce and the crew just want to play
cards. I go back to my screen, scanning the news, checking for an
announcement from the Vargas family. The girl's story has been
haunting me. I am hooked. And I can't figure out why exactly.

An hour or so after the first news report, I check the Silvia Vargas vigil Web site. For months it has displayed photos of the girl and
the family's contact information. It is now updated with an open
letter to the public informing supporters that a memorial mass will
be held the following day for Silvia at the Panteón Francés in Colonia San Joaquín, the French cemetery. The family's note appears in
elegant script and requests that mourners wear white. The Vargas
family thanks the media—"Without them, we would have never
found Silvia"—and the media get the message. It is past midnight,
and right now even at the left-leaning *La Jornada* the top story is

about the transfer of Silvia's remains from the morgue to a private crematorium. Not a particularly earth-shattering update.

"She Is with God," banner headlines in the daily papers announce the next day, quoting the Vargas family. Once again, the familiar image of Silvia appears on newsstands on practically every other street corner in the capital. Her soft, round face, sandy brown hair, deep brown eyes, a bright smile suspended forever in death at eighteen years of age. Standing before a newsstand, in the thick of the downtown traffic and noise, I am motionless looking at Silvia's face on the newsprint. Sadness yanks at me, but I am not comfortable with this emotional response. I never met Silvia Vargas. She was practically a whole generation younger than I. I doubt that— had she lived—our paths would have crossed. Yet seeing her image so many times in the papers and on television confuses me into believing that I *may have* known her, and by extension that I can sympathize with the grief felt by her loved ones.

As soon as the mass for Silvia is announced, I know that I want to be there. Why be present at the grieving ritual for a person I never knew? In my head, I can't formulate a reply. The only thing I'm sure about is that I am not sharing my Saturday plans with my neighbors.

Kidnappings in Mexico fall into three basic categories: express, virtual, and ransom. The *express* variety refers to quick pickups, with the victim hauled off to a few cash machines, taken on a joyride, then dumped on an unfamiliar street. The *virtual* kidnappings are characterized by trickery. Families are called and told a loved one is in the hands of criminals, so they hastily fork over money, even if no kidnapping has actually taken place. *Ransom* kidnappings bring more risks for the organized kidnapping rings, but also the potential of much more profit. Professional kidnapping negotiators are called in, and the kidnappers settle into a position of power, terrorizing relatives of the victim with harassing phone calls or, in some cases, by sending over a minor body part to the waiting loved ones—an ear, a finger—proof that the stakes are severe. Victims are held for cash ransoms as large as millions of dollars or as small as a few thousand pesos. Often they are permanently "disappeared," killed and never returned home, even after families pay up.

As many as two-thirds of the kidnappings in Mexico go unreported, up and down the ransom scale. The phenomenon took off during a soaring national crime wave that followed the economic crises of the 1980s and '90s. People in Mexico City will tell you that everyone was broke and desperate back then. Kidnapping circuits have since become a frightening and lucrative branch of business for drug-trafficking cartels, which have diversified their revenue sources as the government has tried to crack down on narco smugglers. Recent official tallies suggest that more than sixty kidnappings occur in Mexico monthly, but civil organizations says the true number is closer to five hundred. Law enforcement authorities remain widely distrusted by a public accustomed to hearing of cases in which police are found to collude or even lead kidnapping crews. Privacy, without any contact with the police, is the preferred approach in such circumstances. As a result, the fear grips all of society—most kidnapping victims belong to the lower- and middle-income brackets—but in Mexico only the wealthy and well-known are capable of thrusting their problems into the public eye. Only in rare cases do they do it in so dramatic a fashion as Silvia Vargas's parents, in the full glare of the media machine, and with a total appreciation of their privilege even in grief.

The Vargas family broke its silence in late August 2008, hanging an enormous five-story banner over Paseo de la Reforma, featuring a photo of Silvia and a toll-free number. PLEASE GIVE ME BACK MY DAUGHTER SILVIA the banner read. YOU SHALL BE REWARDED. They were determined to make the case of their missing daughter a public matter.

Days later, Vargas called his first press conference. He wept uncontrollably before a wall of news cameras. He pleaded with investigators and the news media to do everything possible to locate Silvia. It had been months of agonizing silence for his family, he said. They followed all the instructions given to them by Silvia's kidnappers, and then one day, the family just stopped hearing from them. While Miss Escalera, long separated from Nelson Vargas, was reserved in her press appearances, Mr. Vargas allowed his grief to be a painfully open affair. Here was a grown, gray-haired, distinguished bureaucrat weeping and cursing his way through the intolerable nightmare of having a daughter snatched away from him. The press was riveted.

Vargas—who has bushy, gray eyebrows and wears thin spectacles, and almost always appears in public in a suit and tie—was then featured on the cover of the high-society glossy *Quién*, or *Who*, alongside the quoted words "I am dead in life." This was unusual for a magazine that normally publishes puffy profiles on prominent politicians or celebrities. The piece on Vargas included photos of Silvia as a small girl, taking swimming lessons, along with revelations by Vargas that he had three meetings with President Calderón himself over the case, as well as numerous face-to-face interviews with the public security secretary and the attorney general. "I have access to that," he told the magazine. "But imagine those who don't, they are truly screwed."

Vargas added, "Society has no idea how much evil can exist in this country. We are inhuman."

As summer and fall wore on, little progress was made in locating Silvia, but her name remained in the news. By October, Nelson Vargas, apparently frustrated with the pace of the official investigation, called yet another press conference. This time he presented the findings of his investigation into his daughter's case, which implicated his family's former driver, Oscar Ortiz González, in the kidnapping. González's brother was a member of a kidnapping gang known as Los Rojos, or the Reds. Vargas told reporters he had alerted the authorities about the connection but was essentially told to butt out. At the press conference, the grieving father vented his rage. "The authorities have told us that we have nothing that may lead us to Silvia. If this is nothing, a man who worked for almost two years for our family, who we know is related to a gang that has already made abductions, that's not having anything? *That's not having a mother!*"

You could almost feel a ripple of scandal sweep over the city after Vargas's outburst. In essence, he called the investigators motherless bastards—an especially emphatic slur in mother-obsessed Mexico. To the public, a grim truth emerged. For all his connections to friends in high places, for all his public pleas, Nelson Vargas was powerless to save his daughter. Her rescue was completely out of his control. And in the hands of Mexican law enforcement, the case was more or less a lost cause. We had all known this since the beginning. That is the sad part. Where it gets weird, I realize, is in the collective response, the way the psychosis of the Mexican elite can play out in the public sphere, trickling down into our brains.

The trend—if it can be called that—started a few weeks before the Silvia Vargas case went public. Another well-connected member of Mexican society, Alejandro Martí, owner of the Martí chain of sporting-goods stores, went to the press with his family's kid-napping nightmare. His fourteen-year-old son, Fernando, had been picked up in early June, along with his driver, at what was described as a false checkpoint set up by men posing as mem-bers of a high-level Mexican investigative agency, the AFI. Weeks later, the boy's decomposing body was found in the trunk of a car parked on a street in a tough southern D.F. neighborhood. His family had already paid the kidnappers as much as $6 million for the young Martí's return, according to one report. Adding to the outrage, subsequent arrests in the case indicated the chief suspects behind the Martí kidnapping were federal police officers. The rev-elations proved so shocking that President Felipe Calderón himself attended an evening mass in honor of the young Fernando Martí. The president sat in the front pews beside the stricken Martí par-ents, accompanied by First Lady Margarita Zavala.

This made me a little sick to my stomach. The president's appear-ance at the Martí funeral was meant to signal to the Mexican pub-lic that the executive and his *primera dama* are concerned about the awful kidnappings and killings of children in Mexico and are committed to doing something about it. But this was apparently more urgent now that the elite were becoming so public about their plight. Which begs the question, as Nelson Vargas himself imag-ines in his glossy magazine interview, *What about those who are not rich and famous, those who do not have a platform on which to transmit their case?* The missing are ever present in Mexico. Missing-person signs adorn the public-announcement panels in metro stations and government buildings like flapping black-and-white sheets of wallpaper. But where are the public and political displays of empathy for thousands of nonwealthy families who are suffering the same nightmare? Where are the cameras and heads of state at those funerals?

In the days after Silvia Vargas's body was found, this discrepancy was overlooked by just about everyone. The Martí and Vargas names, and Silvia Vargas's innocent face, saturated our visual landscape. The media continued to stoke the flames of selective outrage. Anger swelled. New groups on Facebook channeled it: "ENOUGH! No More Violence in Mexico," "For a Secure Mexico," "Let's Make an Anti-Kidnapping Squad," "Yes to the Death Penalty for Kidnappers and Killers," and the darkly humorous "I Don't Put My Photo on Facebook for Fear of the Kidnappings."

As he mourned the loss of his son, Alejandro Martí took his considerable assets and connections and transformed himself into a high-profile antikidnapping activist, speaking before lawmakers and government panels. He founded SOS, a civil group meant to lobby for solutions to the kidnapping wave. But he was not alone. Members of the general public began joining him in taking a stand. Some began calling for capital punishment for convicted kidnappers. Joining the chorus was the Mexican Green Party, a move that critics in the left called cynical and politically motivated.

In this atmosphere Martí and his supporters called for a massive march in Mexico City against *"inseguridad,"* in August 2008. On a cool night, under a purple sky, tens of thousands of people clad in white clothing marched from the Angel of Independence monument to the Zócalo. They held candles in memory of the victims of Mexico's crime wave. I wandered around the plaza, listening, looking at posters, signs, and photographs of the missing. A middle-aged architect named Juan Manuel in a plain shirt and jeans told me he has been held up twice recently. "The authorities need to see how many people are upset by this," he said, holding on to his ten-year-old daughter. Before, he added, "You could walk at any hour of night, houses didn't have bars on their windows. Even the muggers were more decent, in some form."

"What can be done?" I asked.

Juan Manuel paused. He searched the plaza with his eyes. "What can you expect if the police themselves are involved?"

I ran into a friend named Jorge, a D.F. native who has an office job in a foreign embassy. I was surprised to see him at the *inseguridad* march. Ordinarily Jorge is a fun-loving, joke-telling person I see at bars or parties. Tonight he looked furious, and a little nasty. I approached him and said hello. "Enough, enough, enough," Jorge was saying to the person standing next to him. "We've had enough."

We chatted. "What can be done?" I asked.

"Death penalty," Jorge said flatly, his eyes locked upon me.

Mumbling a good-bye, I backed away. I felt as if I were entering a twilight zone. Around us, people holding small Mexican flags were chanting in unison, *"Pena de muerte! Pena de muerte! Pena de muerte!"* as if "Death penalty!" were a college sporting cheer. I began feeling claustrophobic—more so than usual when the Zócalo is choked with protesters. It was not the crush of people that was making me panic at the moment, it was the *type* of people on the plaza. I looked around. I noticed a certain class stature to the demonstrators. People were in white, as planned, but it is mostly what I'd call designer white. Chanel, Gap, Dockers. Shopping-mall white. A goodly amount of these marchers were taller and paler than the average Mexican, a characteristic that is difficult not to notice in a Centro so identified with its poorer, more racially mixed residents. Several homemade signs openly blamed leftist mayor Marcelo Ebrard for the spike in crime. Demanding answers, they chanted the exact message that teary-eyed, white-haired Alejandro Martí transmitted to authorities as he buried his fourteen-year-old son: *"If you can't do it, resign! If you can't do it, resign! If you can't do it, resign!"* Do what, exactly, was never made clear. I wonder who would take the place of resigning politicians unable to magically obliterate the criminal threats. More politicians?

As I struggled to make it out of the plaza, it hit me: Most of these marchers must be conservatives, National Action voters, PAN people. These had to be *panistas,* people who in a lasting stereotype live in walled mansions and rarely travel away from their guarded neighborhoods, people who read *Reforma*. With their slogans and signs, the marchers did not aspire to anything beyond seeking revenge or justice for their particular cases. These are Mexicans who insist on wearing class blinders.

There was virtually no discussion in the *inseguridad* protest movement of the need to address or tackle the root causes behind the kidnapping wave. No talk of the crippled public education system, which almost guarantees a dead-end path for millions of young people. No talk of the corrupt and stagnant justice system and its army of police officers who are so severely underpaid and undertrained they see taking petty bribes as a necessary slice of their monthly income. And certainly, no talk of an economic and tax structure that overwhelmingly benefits large companies and the extremely wealthy, leaving millions of working-age men and women on the margins of Mexico's development and with no other option but to flee for work in the United States—or to stay in Mexico and join a gang of pirating, extorting, drug-smuggling, kidnapping criminals.

In Mexico's cycle of corruption, marginalization, and crime, its actors were oblivious to the social inequalities that breed criminals and criminality and to the instincts of greed and self-preservation that perpetually feed the cycle with new victims. Standing in the Zócalo that day, watching the protest, I wondered if it will ever be broken. I wondered if we will ever stop feeding ourselves sad tales of the Silvia Vargas variety. And I wondered what purpose those tales truly fulfill.

114

The Panteón Francés San Joaquín is known for services with prices that guarantee a certain uniform pedigree among the interred. The decaying, old mausoleums inside are laid out in orderly concourses, offering a parade of names that have had their hand in shaping contemporary Mexico. Familia Haddad Asha, Familia Nader Carrillo, Familia Julian Slim, Familia Dessafiaux Sánchez. It is a week since Silvia Vargas's body was found. I arrive in time for the mass of the ashes in her memory, following in a couple holding hands and dressed in white to a large stone chapel in the middle of the cemetery, Capilla Lorraine. Mourners have been gathering since morning. President Calderón stopped by before noon.

The mass inside is officiated by Father Mario Contreras Martínez and is broadcast from speakers directed at the outdoors, as though overflow crowds were expected. But the only people outside are members of the press and a few curious passersby. Every so often someone strolls out of the chapel in sunglasses to get some air or to walk a restless child. I merge with the reporters behind a grape-colored velvet rope that marks an indistinct boundary between the press and the mourners. I sit on a curb, shielding my eyes from the sun with a notebook. Photographers angle for a useful shot. Radio reporters toy with their equipment. More than anything else, the reporters around me seem bored.

A *Milenio* scribe is sitting beside me. "Here we are again," he says gruffly under his breath. "And we will be here again, and again, and again. In six months," he adds, standing up to stretch, "I'll see you here again for the same kind of story." He whistles. "The truth is, it's embarrassing, man."

The high valley sun shines hard and bright, maximizing the

visual effect of the mourners' attire. Except for a woman dressed in purple and gold and a few men who wear jeans or track suits, all the mourners are dressed in white, just as the Vargas family requested. Many wear it from head to toe. White loafers, white sundresses, white dress pants on the men and women. The reporters and onlookers outside watch in silence. I am struck by a sensation that the mourners are fundamentally alien to us, with their unshowy yet self-conscious markers of wealth: jewelry, heavy makeup, oversize $1,000 sunglasses. The fully assured gait of privilege of Mexico's rich, even in mourning, unattainable behind the purple velvet rope.

It sounds like a beautiful mass. There is music, prayer, reading of Scripture, and a poem read by Silvia's mother. When the priest bids the mourners to "go in peace," many more people emerge from the chapel than I imagined were inside. Some immediately light cigarettes. Fashionable women gather in clumps, talking on cell phones. Young men stand in groups talking. One teen with intensely curly yellow hair and rosy red cheeks catches my eye as he walks briskly out. He is clearly rattled by the service and disappears into the passenger seat of an SUV, a stone-faced driver behind the wheel. I am thinking about Silvia Vargas, wondering if in her life she ever went to the funerals of kidnapping victims.

A few media celebrities catch the attention of the waiting reporters, who rush to capture their reactions. One is the track athlete Ana Guevara, a silver medalist in the 400 meters at the 2004 Olympic Games in Athens, and recently an officer in the national sports commission along with Nelson Vargas. The Olympian, with her pronounced features and baritone voice, is a favorite of reporters in Mexico looking for a juicy quote. Guevara wears a tight-fitting white suit and a white turtleneck underneath. Video cameras, microphones, and tape recorders crowd around her face. I duck into the huddle and crouch near Guevara's left leg, balancing a small recorder upward.

"Ana," a male voice calls. "You're a public official. In whose hands is the city, in the hands of the delinquents or the authorities?"

"In the hands of the authorities," Guevara says firmly. "But I repeat, many of these things shouldn't be happening, and they wouldn't happen if there was more citizen participation."

"Who is failing?" asks a female journalist.

"There are failures on both sides," Guevara answers. "So many theories are out there, that it's coming from inside the prisons if it is gangs, that it's coming from inside the very government or the authorities. What has happened here should really open our eyes. We've seen two stories in these past months of well-known families, distinguished figures from the business community, that have made a lot of noise. But what about the families also that don't count with the economic means, what about the families who remain with a permanent complaint, still waiting for an answer, for the bodies of their loved ones?"

I move away. Everyone here is playing his or her role: media, mourner, politician. Since the case broke, I had believed that I could separate myself from the frenzy of coverage on the Silvia Vargas kidnapping and not be engulfed by it, but here I am, both covering the story and wearing white myself. I had told myself while getting dressed this morning that a white shirt might better my chances of getting inside the Panteón Francés San Joaquín in the event that access was restricted. The rationalization is now unconvincing. I am unwittingly a party to the mourning and to the media storm. The kidnapping story has kidnapped me.

Reporters are now preparing for the golden shot at the front of the Capilla Lorraine. We move back to our proper place behind the purple velvet rope. The family spokeswoman has informed us that the Vargas family will come out and release a flock of white pigeons. There is to be no formal statement to the press. The stage is set. Videographers jostle into position. Given Nelson Vargas's tendency for outbursts, every cameraman wants a choice shot. Momentary chaos. "If you're not here working, then you should just go home," one photographer proclaims out loud to no one in particular.

When the family and its closest friends finally emerge through the glazed-glass doors of the chapel, Nelson Vargas is among them. The old man seems calm and at peace as a cage full of white pigeons is placed before a gaggle of screeching toddlers, all dressed in white. Vargas makes an effort to acknowledge those who have closely followed his story, taken his photograph, called out questions.

"Thank you for your solidarity!" he calls to the reporters, raising an arm. "Thank you! Thank you! Thank you!"

The crowd of mourners behind him breaks into applause. When the cage is opened, most of the birds are too bewildered or undernourished to do much besides flap their wings. A few fly off only to land a couple meters away, near the media photographers. We dutifully keep documenting.

8 | The Delinquent Is Us

"I am a delinquent." (Photo by the author.)

It's back in the summer of 2005. I am visiting Mexico City from Los Angeles for a short vacation. I want to see friends that I miss. I take a day to visit the Uruzquieta family in Iztacalco, and that's when I witness my first Mexico City street fight. It begins with a couple of guys after somebody who owes them money. It happens in the middle of the street, by the graffiti-scrawled gymnasium and soccer field in the middle of Colonia Zapata Vela. The fight is sloppy and rowdy, happening right in front of us as we visit the home of Don Alfredo's brother around the corner. A few more young guys run toward the commotion and try to step in. Another one comes to defend the one in the middle of it. Whistling cascades down from the narrow concrete streets, and more men rush out of doorways and driveways and into the fray. In seconds the fight is a hollering brawl. We watch as a single police patrol cruiser rolls into the scene, turning on a lazy siren warning. The fight continues. We stand inside the house watching from the living-room window. The children are outside watching blankly from the covered driveway, as if this were television. The police officers finally catch on, leave their patrol car, and rush over.

They are outmatched. They cannot get inside the brawl to neutralize it. A female officer tries to yell orders but is drowned out. People gather to watch from the gymnasium and from inside the shabby fenced-off soccer field. More police cars arrive. More police officers. Still no order. The officers appear threatened. It is as though their arrival and their attempt to interrupt the neighborhood's social-ordering-in-progress amplifies the local men's impulse to solve everything by blows and the rules of the streets.

Where is Don Alfredo? I wonder.

Sebastián—Don Alfredo's nephew—and I go outside to get a better view. The kids are now hopping and laughing at the perimeter of the brawl. Something exciting is happening outside, a fight with police that looks out of hand. Inside the house the adults are chattering and pointing and making jokes among themselves. Their tone suggests less enjoyment than nervousness. As the fight gets out of control—pushing, punching, falling, screaming—the cops must respond now purely in defense. More people gather to watch.

Where is Don Alfredo?

Just then he barrels into view, trodding over, chewing on a plastic drinking straw, the dome of the bald top of his head gleaming in the sun. Don Alfredo reaches into the melee with one hand, with the determination of a lightning bolt, and pulls one of the fighters out by a shoulder. More police cars are pulling up.

"Maybe it's time you should go," Sebastián suggests, smiling, "I'll walk you." He leads me around the center of the brawl and across the gym and recreational complex, to a main drag with *pesero* routes that will take me to metro Iztacalco.

"*Cheeeeeeeeen,* that got intense," I tell Sebastián.

"Yeah," he says.

He doesn't seem too perturbed. His uncle stepped in, and that meant, here in the *colonia* where his family are the unofficial community leaders, some level of order will eventually be restored. Eventually.

I head back that afternoon to areas of Mexico City more orderly in the imagination of the transient visitor—Condesa, Roma. Places where the police keep the peace, I tell myself, where their presence as an institution is generally respected. So it seems anyway. In the poor, rough barrios, the police may fear the people. In its more genteel enclaves, the reverse is true. The people have plenty of reasons to fear the police.

In November 2004, two undercover federal police officers were lynched in the small pueblo of San Juan Ixtayopan on the outskirts of Mexico City. A mob had gathered, accusing the officers of raping a neighborhood girl. The incident horrified the public. How could something like this happen? Marcelo Ebrard, then the city's police chief, told the papers the day after, "The problem is that between the moment that the lynching started and in the time that it takes you to move authorities there, they had already accelerated the lynching and we could not arrive in time."

In August 2008, five "delinquents" dressed as federal investigators who had attempted to kidnap a man in the town of Tlapanalá, Puebla, were captured and nearly lynched by an angry mob. The bleeding and wounded men were turned over to actual uniformed authorities only after a lengthy negotiation. "Delinquents," whether their uniforms are fake or original, are nuisances that the *pueblo*— the people—will deal with on its own, justly or not.

I'm never quite sure when the laws apply to their full social strength in Mexico. The laws are there, in books, on paper, mentioned in the press, cited by the politicians and angry victims of this injustice or that, updated daily in the dry, dense text of the Federation's Official Diary. But laws in Mexico are really more like starting-off points for negotiations between parties. Between victim and perpetrator, between lawmaker and political leader, person to person, a million times over every hour in every day in the megalopolis. Everyone is hustling everyone, in the micro sense or in the cosmic sense. At the checkout counter, over business deals, in real estate transactions, over drugs, a set of keys, in bed.

They say the screw-or-be-screwed dynamic is most ardently practiced in Mexico City. For people from *provincia*—the provinces—all *capitalinos* are automatically *rateros*—petty thieves. I don't want to believe such a nasty stereotype, but, to put it simply, I also take taxis here. Cabs provide daily examples of how artfully people screw each other in Mexico City. One summer night after a mellow cab ride of relaxing conversation with the driver, the friendly old man gives me a fraudulent ten-peso coin for change. I don't realize it until I get home and I feel the coin is lighter than it should be. *20 CENTAVOS* it reads, *1944*. The coin is essentially worthless. Most impressive of all, in hustler terms, it appears to have been painted to look like a modern ten-peso coin, with a ring of "gold" around the inner silver. I smile. *City of swindlers,* I think.

I take the coin out with me for two days, thinking that maybe I'll be able to return that sneaky cabbie's favor to all of Mexico City. I step onto the action of the sidewalks with the fake ten-peso coin in my pocket. A potential victim: the hunched-over, old newsstand man on the corner of Bolivar and Uruguay Streets. In my head I'm rubbing my palms together. I'm also thinking, if I get caught, the situation could get extremely embarrassing, fast. No one likes being swindled. Making that sentiment known as loudly as possible when you realize it is happening is a customary response here.

I can't do it. I give the old guy a real ten-peso piece for my paper, then show him my bogus ten, casually. The old man explains amiably that it is a worthless coin, and to watch out. I tell him what happened. He laughs and suggests I take the coin to an antique-currency shop down the block, which I go ahead and do, with no luck. When I leave the old man at his newsstand, I could tell that although he is being friendly as we chat, he must be relieved—and also probably a little perplexed—that I didn't try tricking him out of ten pesos.

Millions in Mexico City scrape by on just a few dollars a day. Living amid the city's culture of hustling, I see clearly why so many *capitalinos* cut their losses, take their chances, and embark on the treacherous journey to the United States, smuggling themselves across the border to reach the mythical pastures of dollars. *At least,* they must also think to themselves, *people follow the rules there.*

In Mexico City, it is wit versus wit. No other rules, when it comes down to it, really apply. Money is tight, work is scarce. Rent, water, what will I eat for dinner tonight? I begin to see why people would want to do whatever it takes to feed and clothe themselves, even if it means breaking the law. One night, walking on a street in the

Colonia Portales, I become startled by my own train of thought. I am desperately poor right now, surviving on coffee, orange juice, beer ("grain juice"), and tacos. Gigs for writers don't come easy. I am angry and depressed and feverish. I had moved to Mexico City on a whim and I knew it would be hard. What I fail to expect is that the delinquency mind-set would take over my brain. Who would stop me, I think, who would catch me, if I hop into that cab coming my way and start barking directions? Who would know or care if I held a knife to the driver's throat, demanded all his money, and threatened to kill him if he made any funny moves? How would I feel when I got home at night, finally able to eat properly?

How would I sleep?

At the height of the Silvia Vargas kidnapping saga, *delinquency* was on everyone's lips. "We need a strong fight against delinquency," they'd call. "Just say no to delinquency." The extremists proclaimed, "Death penalty to delinquents and kidnappers." The trouble is the "delinquents" are rarely identified in specific terms. Who are these maddened, heartless criminals who are terrorizing the city? Your neighbors? Aren't many of the major crimes that grab the headlines—the Silvia Vargas and Fernando Martí kidnappings, for instance—committed by police or "delinquents" with ties to police? Politically conscious youth responded with their own answer. "To the administrators of this city," read a poster that appeared overnight around the city. "I AM A DELINQUENT / I am 20 years old / I am young / I have no right to / An education, to work / To housing, to health care / And to many other things." It is wheat-pasted in repetition along tagged-up walls, hung or taped upon the blue-tarp layers of stalls at El Chopo. Stamped with the logo of the Multiforo Alicia, the independent-rock venue in Roma, the poster glows with defiance.

I find young people know better. I hear it mostly in casual conversation. At a cantina in Centro, young university students are sitting around having a few cheap beers, discussing the ins and outs of the government's connections to the major cartels. Which cartel runs which route. Which cartel runs which city. Which cartel is cutting deals with which major political party. The deals struck between capos, and between capos and politicians. They chat as though it goes without saying that the political system is wedded top to bottom to the narco industry. It sounds like baseball stats. When twenty-seven government officials in the state of Michoacán—including ten mayors—are arrested in May 2009 for alleged ties to La Familia Michoacana, the cartel that controls much of the state, no one bats an eye. Pedestrians stop and browse the headlines at the newsstands, maybe someone shakes his head, and we carry on. Occasionally investigative reports in the newsweekly *Proceso* detail one such relationship between this kingpin and that state governor, but otherwise, the generally assumed truth operates entirely outside the political and media discourse. (In Michoacán, a year later, most of those allegedly narco-related mayors and officials were free. The top-notch federal prosecutors just couldn't come up with many charges.)

In March 2007, pharmaceutical industrialist Zhenli Ye Gon, a naturalized Mexican of Chinese origin, was accused of hiding hundreds of millions of narco-dollars in his Mexico City mansion. Facing arrest and trial, Zhenli responded to the allegations in a public letter, which the newspapers reprinted. He detailed a long episode of torment at the hands of PAN operatives and police who threatened him and his family, frequently kidnapped him for short periods, and left cryptic letters with instructions coded in star symbols. "Those funds are and were secret funds belonging to the political party, used for the presidential campaign, and to buy arms and finance terrorist activities," Zhenli wrote. "I am an innocent victim and I was tricked into these participations in the corrupt politics of Mexico."

Calderón dismissed Zhenli's allegations, calling them a *"cuento chino"*—or a Chinese tall tale. It is a cynical and blithely racist remark, and the press just laughs along.

Everyone is touched by the narco trade in one way or another, and countless numbers are direct players. The commodities at stake are not just drugs. Narco cartels are believed to have their fingers in *every aspect* of Mexico's vast underground economy. The smuggling of desperate undocumented immigrants across the border in the northern deserts. The smuggling of weapons south into Mexico from the United States. Prostitution rings. Kidnap-for-ransom and extortion rings, the kind that so terrorize Mexico's high elites. All the way down to the organization and policing of innocent-looking street vendors. You never know who is the criminal, whether overtly or covertly. The white-collar-looking guy might be taking narco money, or making narco money, or washing it clean. The grandfatherly cabdriver might be in on an express kidnapping ring, which is likely a branch of a cartel anyway.

The combination of demand for drugs in the United States and the overarching reach and penetration of the cartels into Mexican society mean that on current terms the government cannot possibly win its war against them. Before, the governments merely made pacts with the cartels, turning a blind eye to the flow of drugs leaving Mexico for the United States in exchange for order and tranquillity, and maybe a kickback or two. This president's approach—attack, attack, attack—underestimated the traffickers' willingness and thirst to draw blood in the effort to protect their enterprises. Their desire to succeed easily dwarfs the feeble civic motivation of the average cop or soldier who is supposed to be fighting them. Resistance to their way of doing business, the cartels seem to say, will not be tolerated—from anyone. So they kill and kill and kill. And the citizens are stuck in the middle, absorbing daily servings of funerals, images of human grief and agony, stories about unclaimed bodies dumped into communal graves, videos of torture and beheadings. The strategy is failing. Headlines roll around in my brain: the scandalous Martí and Vargas kidnappings, the narco-terror grenade attack in the provincial capital of Morelia on Independence Day 2008, and the violent death of Juan Camilo Mouriño, Calderón's right-hand man and heir-in-waiting, on November 4, 2008, a night when almost every country in the world except Mexico is united in momentary jubilation with news of Barack Obama's election as president of the United States. A Learjet carrying Mouriño slammed into rush-hour traffic on the swanky west side of town as it approached Mexico City from the state of San Luis Potosí. Mouriño, the interior secretary, along with Mexico's former antidrug czar, a widely respected man named José Luis Santiago Vasconcelos, and seven others were killed in the plane. Eight more died on the ground.

The government rushed to declare the incident an "accident," but suspicion remained that one of the cartels—or even more sinister internal forces in the shadowy corners of conservative power—might have brought the plane down. Attempts had been made on Vasconcelos's life already, and eliminating the president's top cabinet member struck a direct blow to the government. Days later the book *Accomplices of the President* hit stores. In it, journalist Anabel Hernández lays out her evidence of endemic corruption up and down Calderón's cabinet, including allegations against the now deceased Mouriño and Genaro García Luna, the public-safety secretary. I don't know anyone who went out and bought it; the details were almost beside the point. For most Mexicans, insinuations that their top political leaders are tied to criminals—the national enemy—were nothing new. Same story, new faces.

Sandra Ávila Beltrán, a powerful female figure in a narco underworld dominated by men, fell to the authorities in September 2007. She is known as the Queen of the Pacific, a strong and elegant woman who built a mini-empire of power and money. Now she sits in prison. At one point in early 2009, as panic crested in the United States over the perception that Mexican narco violence was "spilling over" the country's southern border, the CNN anchor Anderson Cooper walked into visiting hours at the prison that houses the Queen of the Pacific and somehow got a sit-down interview with the notorious prisoner. Ávila Beltrán repeatedly pressed upon Cooper the idea that the Mexican government is not part of the solution but part of the problem behind the current wave of bloodshed.

"Can they win?" Cooper asked her.

"I don't think so," the Queen responded. "You'd have to wipe out the government to wipe out drug trafficking."

The soft social chaos in Mexico makes me edgy. People are nice to each other, of course, in far more elaborate rituals than anything I've ever seen in the States. The *Thank you* and *You're welcome* and *Until next time* and the *Until next time* in reply happen everywhere all at once, until I think that maybe the formalities will never end. But underneath all the florid etiquette, a cosmic violence is always ready to erupt.

"It reflects a violence that is inherent to our society and the form in which we relate to each other," the artist Yoshua Okon tells me one day, as we are walking in Condesa. "There is conflict and resentment and . . . there it is, no?"

I want to pick Okon's brain on this topic because he once made one of the most graphically violent art piece on Mexico that I've seen, a narrative video titled *Rinoplastia*. In it, a wealthy *junior* from the city's rolling hillside mansions takes a joyride around town with a friend, just as the sons of the power elites do when they are, as Yoshua says, "existentially bored." That is often. Along the way, the *juniors* terrorize day laborers and maids walking on sidewalks, hurling racial and sexual slurs at them. By the end of the night, they are denied entry to a swanky nightclub, and the main character finds violent release from his social anxieties by attempting to rape his maid. The video, Okon tells me, was inspired by a series of scandalous accounts in Mexico in the 1980s and '90s of spoiled *fresa* kids abusing their inherited power and their help around the house, including reported instances of rape.

One police chief from the period was notorious for ordering the Periférico highway closed so that his son could have his motorcycle races in peace. "Mexico is a society where a lot is denied in the official discourse," Yoshua tells me. "It's a country where a great majority of the population is either colonizer or colonized." The *Rinoplastia* piece, produced in 2000, became a moderate hit during screenings at galleries and museums.

In Mexico the severe social stratification, the severely lacking pace of economic development, and the widely held impression that elected and law enforcement officials are as fundamentally corrupt as the average street hoodlum combine to create an atmosphere where there is no actual order, only a mimicking of order. No one is in control, not the military, not law enforcement, not the infrastructure of government, not the unions, not even the cartels. "For me the true crisis in Mexico, the real crisis, fundamentally, is the lack of a rule of law," Okon says. "The entire judicial system in Mexico is incredibly rotten.

"Now, no modern society is not violent. All modern societies are based on exploitation. But the fundamental difference between Mexico and other nation-states is that the legal system is incredibly corrupt." Marches against "insecurity," he adds, "are ridiculously foolish, incredibly superficial, and reactionary."

The result is moderate anarchy. There are masks and rituals to suggest there is order, but these are inadequate in convincing the average person that he or she should trust the officials, trust the police, or trust the cartels. Intrinsically aware of this, the cartels, brotherhoods of businessmen, want only to sell a marketable product—narcotics. They wish to satisfy the insatiable demand in the United States for marijuana, cocaine, heroin, and methamphetamine, and maybe drop a bit off along the way for Mexicans with disposable incomes. The capos wish to live "the American dream," or the Mexican Dream of What the American Dream Looks Like: big families, big houses, big cars, and other essential luxuries such as private zoos with exotic animals.

No wonder the people of Colonia Zapata Vela in Iztacalco prefer to take matters into their own hands. If the cops represent a rotten state, who would ever allow them to meddle in the dispensing of justice? It is a saddening admission. We are all responsible. We look in the mirror, and the delinquent is staring back.

Part III | TAKING CHANCES

9 | A Feathered Serpent in Burberry Shades

Illustration by Ector Garcia.

From the night of the María Peligro fashion party, one memory that sticks out clearly among the haze is my first encounter with Quetzalcóatl Rangel Sánchez, the semi-androgynous party boy who never seemed to say a word but appeared to be everywhere at once. He shows up in many of my photographs from that night. He is impossible to miss, in that way that people who treat what they wear as an act of creative expression and not merely a tool for social acceptance are always impossible to miss. In my photos, Quetzal wears a gold headband over a shaggy pageboy haircut and an outfit consisting of lots of white and ruffly fabric, accentuated by trim white leggings and white platform shoes. The overall look is of a frail, little cyber-elf plucked directly from some kind of futuristic Middle Ages.

Friendships in big cities are so often built on the premise of proximity. In late 2007 and early 2008, Quetzal lives with roommates in San Miguel Chapultepec, the next *colonia* over from where I live in Tacubaya, making it easy for us to hang out on a whim. Quetzal is a rising fashion designer hungry to make a name for himself in the Mexico City creative circuit. He has no steady employment, and therefore no steady income. Yet like a lot of people our age here, he and his partner, Marvin Duran, make it work with the support of sponsors, parents, and small jobs here and there. Sometimes I see them together in Condesa or in San Miguel Chapultepec, walking to an appointment or finishing a meal. Quetzal, in his mellow declarative voice, stops me and says, almost sadly, *"Oye, te quiero."*

Hey, I love you. And he and Marvin both blow a friendly air kiss.

Whose social spectrum doesn't thrive on a steady dosage of mischief? We get together on Saturdays at the market nearest to our houses, have hangover quesadillas, talk about our careers and our projects, and gossip. His public persona is undeniably that of a party monster always digging down into the spiral. But in conversation Quetzal is astute and intuitive. It becomes one of those friendships where the two parties have very different aspirations and histories, yet can quickly reach some form of synchronicity.

134

We get together one Saturday in December 2007, shortly after that wild Wednesday-night fashion show. Quetzal wants a pet Chihuahua, so we decide to head to the Mercado Sonora, to look for one. Halfway between my place and metro Tacubaya, he announces nonchalantly, "I fainted in the metro once." I laugh. Quetzal speaks seriously, flatly, making everything he utters sound unintentionally humorous.

"It was so crowded and all the windows were closed, so I fainted. Like, in a woman's lap, then to the floor," Quetzal says.

We laugh.

"This line," he adds as we descend into the system at Tacubaya, where three lines meet, "the orange line, this is where all the gay cruising happens."

"Really?" We descend on two long escalators, down orange-painted, dome-shaped transfer tunnels, to reach the platform on the pink line.

"I once saw a guy get a blow job, like at Constituyentes."

I ask for more details. We are riding under the city, in the hot, crowded subway, moving east. Mercado Sonora, known informally as the witches' market, is ten stops in this direction. Mexico City has dozens of *mercados,* one for each major neighborhood, or sometimes even two. Several are specialized: the fish market, the gourmet market, the flower market, and so on. Vendors at the Mercado Sonora sell anything you might need for the kind of spiritualities that require your direct and concentrated control: Santería, black magic, indigenous healing, the cult of the Santa Muerte. They also have animals for sale.

At metro Merced, we emerge to street level into a crush of people pushing their way down to the platforms by the hundreds. Women pull along small children and balance enormous bags on their shoulders; Christmas shoppers. The station opens directly onto the

Merced market, a confusing maze of covered stalls. Fruit, meat, cleaning supplies, party decorations. Everyone pushing against one another. My sense of direction is immediately scrambled. In a small clearing a snake charmer attracts a crowd.

"La brujería, la magia," he chants into a microphone, dancing with his snakes. "Do not be alarmed if I call out the names of people in the audience." Quetzal says he is frightened and urges that we move along. The day is hot and bright, so bright the light is loud. Mexico City's altitude brings me closer to the sun and to the sky than I'm used to. The air is thinner. Sunlight feels as if it can penetrate clothes and ceilings. Quetzal and I cross a crowded, shaky pedestrian bridge over a noisy boulevard to reach Mercado Sonora. The air smells like rotting chicken parts.

"How did you get a name like Quetzal?" I ask.

"My dad was a hippie," Quetzal explains. "He's a biologist. They didn't know if I was going to be a boy or a girl. He had a dream one night, that I was a boy, and that my name would be Quetzalcóatl."

It's an elegant and timely choice. Quetzalcóatl is the most potent god in Mesoamerican cosmology, the Feathered Serpent, the one who returns. Among some educated parents of recent generations, it is seen as wise to give newborns at least one pre-Hispanic name. Crossing that bridge to Mercado Sonora, Quetzal walks gamely forward, a pixieish figure, with his womanly legs, bushy black locks, his delicate air. He is a striking presence. I stop for a moment. Here is Quetzalcóatl present before me in modern Mexico City, the divine made manifest in the figure of a spritely young fashion designer wearing fitted gray jeans, boots, and Burberry sunglasses, indoors and out.

Although born and raised in Tabasco, a swampy state on the southern coast of the Gulf of Mexico, Quetzal has become a product of this delirious place and of the moment, I think. He expresses an asymmetrical worldliness in the way he dresses and moves, in his interactions with the urban white noise around him. He is a mutant walking among mutants.

We move into the Sonora market, into a long hallway lined with stalls. It is a witch's row, the Disneyland of witchcraft. Old women with deep, fiery eyes and pursed mouths and too much makeup calling out after you, *"What do you need? . . . Go ahead and ask. . . . What are you looking for?"* The space is jammed with the sort of items you are warned as a child to avoid—while praying. Pentagrams, voodoo dolls, magical stones and beads, candles, ointments, ritualistic instruments made of hollowed wood and seashells. The smells of esoteric teas and incense hover before the nostrils, new smells around every corner. Some stalls are supply shops for Santería, their merchant dressed head to toe in white, images of Changó and Yemaya for sale as if they were portraits of beloved movie stars.

"Excuse me," Quetzal asks an old man. "Where are the animals?"

"Uuuuuhhh." The old man grins. "There's a shitload thataway."

We can already smell them. A heavy, airless stench alerts the approaching visitor of endless litters of whimpering little puppies; walls of cooped-up chickens, roosters, and baby chicks; squawking parrots, caged goats, and snakes; frogs and fish. The cages are filthy. Bins of drinking water are empty or filled with a gray-brown slush. The place smells of droppings, stale dog food, and misery. Dogs howl for freedom. Even the amphibians are unable to hide their hopelessness. I watch as a frog in a fish tank leaps desperately up the clear glass walls of his prison in pathetic repetition. Quetzal and I cover our mouths and noses. He is visibly disgusted, but marches on, searching for a Chihuahua to his liking.

"The problem with the animals here," he says while browsing,

"is that you take them home and a few days later they die on you."
Mexico has a quite underdeveloped notion of animal care. I wonder if the conditions in the market are intended as a backhanded
sales pitch. *Have a heart, save a puppy.*

"This little one, this precious thing, would cost you ten thousand pesos at a mall or in Santa Fe," a young vendor tells us, indicating a homely little Chihuahua in her hands. We squint at the
puppy but it is impossible to tell how pure a breed he is, or if he is a
Chihuahua at all. The poor animal's skin is crumpled and colorless,
his eyes unable to focus. He looks near death.

"Three thousand," the girl says. "What a precious thing."

Quetzal hesitates.

"Well, what are you looking for?" the seller asks accusatorily.
"What can I offer you?"

We move along. "They're so pushy," Quetzal whispers.

Although the conversation flows naturally, it doesn't escape me
that Quetzal and I are speaking in English. When the opportunity
arises, young Mexicans who have spent some time living abroad
look for places in their speech to insert playful Americanisms and
exclamations. Quetzal has never been to the States, but he spent
time in Montreal studying fashion design and living as a "hippie"
in what he describes as an ambisexual, drug-addled three-way relationship (*"No es el sexo, es la persona"*). His English is as good as
or better than any immigrants' with a few years' experience in the
United States.

We continue along, to the section of the market dedicated to
items for *despedidas,* bridal showers. This area features decorations
in white lace and many toy versions of the male penis. A few transwomen browse the offerings. Many transwomen are at the market

today. Busty female figures, some with obscene nose jobs and others made to be electric blondes, shop among the stalls of magic and witchcraft, examining their products with the severity of well-informed regulars. Transgendered witches, I think. A potent combination.

Quetzal pulls me by the arm, close to his body. "Come," he says. "I want to show you the hookers."

Our Chihuahua mission abandoned, we leave Mercado Sonora and cross the bridge back toward the Merced area, the city's reddest red-light district. We make our way up a congested avenue, down sidewalks packed with unlicensed vending stalls and, after a short while, prostitutes. They stand out, as intended. Merced streetwalkers wear heavy eye makeup, miniskirts, and high heels that are outrageously high. Many are small, very young, and deeply brown, with prominent Indian features. These women are often human-trafficking victims, brought into the city from the provinces to be sex workers. Entranced, we walk on, the prospect of getting back on the train at Merced forgotten. The afternoon grows dark and dense, and with Christmas just a couple weeks away, the Centro is more packed than I have ever seen it. People with large shopping bags stand in long lines for buses headed to the far-off fingers of the urbanized valley and beyond. As we head toward the Pino Suárez intersection, the hookers become more commonplace.

"They're everywhere," I say.

"Yes," Quetzal answers. "You should see it at night."

We stop briefly at an opulent sidewalk altar for Santa Muerte, the popular death saint. The altar is lit by a black fluorescent tube and guarded by a few ratty dogs that lie about, resigned to the monotony of a life lived in no one's service or care. Quetzal gazes and studies, sparking some introspection in me as well.

What is this figure about? I wonder. Death, in a state of reverence, a saint for the lake of fire. *Why does she flourish here? Why Mexico City?*

Our conversation moves to the world of independent fashion design in Mexico, always a ripe and complex topic for those of us who love it. Unlike the flesh market of the Merced, Mexico's emerging fashion industry suffers from a lack of buyers and collectors. He and Marvin have had some success in their insular world, but widespread sales of their collections have so far evaded them. In Mexico, the proximity to the United States often draws the distracted eyes of design consumers northward instead of around the corner. "With Marvin, we've been out there for like three years. People know us, people come to us, and we do a lot of party dresses and stuff like that. But collections, no."

Yet little by little the global eye is turning to new Mexican fashion, and it is exciting to watch. Young designers are stepping around the traditional platforms of brand-name magazines and department stores and selling their designs online and in boutique showrooms both in Mexico and abroad. "There's something going on. There's a movement," Quetzal agrees. "We're making something that has references to our backgrounds. Everything I make I have Mexican references."

He says the Marvin y Quetzal line has been inspired by the Tarahumara and Mazahua Indians, the Mexican military, and piñatas. I feel the city evoked in their clothes as well. Colors are neon and chemical, almost confrontational.

"I always make references, but take them to a more global level, and not so obvious," Quetzal adds. "Otherwise it's just kitsch." You can see it in other young designers here as well. They are merging the global with the local, applying the austere lines and geometries

140

of international couture with the playfulness and surreal qualities of everyday life in Mexico. They are also disciples of the power of androgyny. Among independent young labels, garments are offered as unisex, expressing in a simple article of clothing a belief in the idea that the male and the female exist equally within the self. The self speaks in what it decides to put on when it rolls out of the bed in the morning. Or when the self is preparing to go out at night, to a party in Mexico City. The fangs of the party monster, of this generation's newfound sexual liberation, is the garment, the look.

"Why did you decide to do fashion?" I ask Quetzal as we walk the crowded sidewalks. His reply is assured. "Love."

The sky is now purple, the air is barely there. In this valley high in the mountains, I think, just too many people are breathing at once.

"I was living in Montreal," Quetzal continues, "and I went through this huge depression, because I was drinking too much and doing a lot of drugs, and it was during the winter, so I got, you know . . ."

Soon after moving to Mexico City, Quetzal tells me, he met Marvin at a party during Fashion Week. Quetzal, raised in Tabasco, and Marvin, raised in Venezuela, formed an instant bond. They became partners. Quickly the pair became a fixture of the growing D.F. fashion scene. They began appearing together in magazines. They showed up on the Diario de Fiestas blog. They became a *thing*.

Quetzal and I decide we need to celebrate our surviving Mercado Sonora. We head toward the Zócalo. In the center, the plaza is bathed in Christmas cheer. Massive arrays of twinkling lights hang from the buildings surrounding the square and over the streets feeding into the Zócalo's traffic ring. There are people everywhere, cotton candy, clowns, women dressed as angels in blue wigs and plastic wings. We take photos and wander around while Quetzal gabs on his cell phone endlessly and with absolute seriousness.

The night comes upon us and adventure beckons, so Quetzal decides we should check out the gay cantinas that furtively ring the Alameda Central.

We enter a place that calls itself Cineclub, near the Diego Rivera Mural Museum. The indistinct entrance has a rainbow flag hanging over its door, and that's about it. Quetzal leads me into the *cuarto oscuro,* the dark room where men watch porn and feel each other up or have sex. "Be careful in here," he warns. "People steal."

We have two beers each, and then, a little creeped out by the place, but still looking for trouble, Quetzal and I go around the corner to El Internet, a *cervecería* hidden behind a bodega. Passing cramped rows of synthetic snacks and coolers of sugary Coca-Cola products in the shop, we walk through a passageway and up a narrow flight of circular metal stairs to a room John Waters could have conjured—only slightly more threatening. Small, dank, drenched in glowing blue light, the room is painted like the skin of a zebra. A few tiny circular tables and knocked-over chairs are scattered about the sticky black linoleum floor. Scratchy music is playing from somewhere. The ceiling is hardly higher than the top of my head. Quetzal and I sit down, order a *caguama,* and start making friends.

It is loud. There are vaqueros, construction workers, transsexuals and transvestites, their male suitors, round Mexican black women, guys who are probably packing guns somewhere under their leather jackets. In the blur, we strike up a conversation with a tall transwoman seated at a table next to ours. She has pale brown skin and poorly treated yellow hair. Everyone is friendly and jolly.

142

At this point Quetzal loses his cell phone somehow. His Black-Berry has disappeared from under his eyes. Somehow. Because right then the transwoman gets up and goes downstairs without saying a word, clearly expecting us not to notice in the hollering and laughter.

Quetzal becomes frantic. "Wait," I tell him. "Look carefully." He searches through his bag and all the pockets of his jacket and jeans. Nothing. Near tears, Quetzal wails in English again. "That cell phone costs nine hundred dollars!" he cries, maybe embellishing a little.

"Come on," I urge. "It has to be somewhere."

Tension. The people around us lift their legs and look below their seats. Hadn't he been holding on to the phone, on the table? "The trannie!" Quetzal screams.

"Where did she go?" I ask.

Upset, Quetzal gets up and begins marching to the stairs. "I want to leave this fucking place." I follow him down as I keep calling Quetzal's number on my own phone, searching with my ears for its ring. "*¿Dónde está?*" I ask the plainclothes guard at the bodega downstairs. "Where is she?"

The guard asks us what happened and I explain that someone, possibly the girl with the bad yellow hair, has stolen my friend's phone.

"Well, if you saw the *acción,* why didn't you say anything?" he challenges.

"I did!" I say. *I mean, I am.* "She stole my friend's phone! Where is she?"

"Let me go get her," the guard says, and he goes back up to the bar.

Quetzal is nearby, pounding his feet in frustration, cursing her. I am still calling the cell phone, ears up, scanning the bodega's rear storage room, below the joint upstairs. A huge bald man sits with a beer at a table pretending to be sending a text message on his phone, but I can see a curious bulge in his front pocket, and it is not his anatomy. *Did the evil trans girl pass the phone over to this guy? Was he the getaway crook? Was that the system? Was I making up the scenario in the loose logic of intense anger?*

I am a split second away from approaching the man, thinking about what I might say, when the girl with the bad yellow hair appears, pulled by the arm by the guard. And I am preparing for a confrontation because he places her right in front of me and says in between us, "He says you stole his friend's phone."

The girl is absolutely shocked, absolutely scandalized by the accusation. She speaks in rapid-fire, defensive *chilango* Spanish. "I don't know what you're talking about. . . . I came here to drink with my friends. . . . I don't know who you are . . . I don't need to steal!"

Her aggressively defensive attitude feeds my suspicions. "You took it," I say slowly. "I saw you." This was potentially going to get ugly. It is the start of the dance of violence, our faces only inches apart. Am I really about to get into a physical altercation with a trans girl at an illegal gay cantina in the Centro of D.F. over a friend's lost "$900" BlackBerry? "You took it! You grabbed it, then brought it downstairs and gave it to someone!"

The guard steps in. "Then you should have said something."

"I did," I protest a bit unrealistically.

It is useless. The bald fat man in the back has disappeared. Quetzal's cell phone is gone. The guard shrugs and looks at me as though we both know it would be pointless to make much more fuss. The girl keeps gabbing away, defending herself to no one in particular as we turn our backs and walk off.

Quetzal is drunk not with alcohol but with rage. I'm pretty much beside myself, too. Tired? Drunk? Mad as hell? Not sure what, exactly. In the span of a day Quetzal has gone from an intrepid guide and urban adventurer to a hapless victim in the risky games of the Mexico City streets. We play with the night, and this time, the night wins.

At El Internet, people inside and outside the bodega are watching us. Quetzal and I tumble out onto the street, walking down the middle of Doctor Mora. A couple of D.F. transit cops observe us with halfhearted attention. Quetzal is screaming, *"Fucking trannie! Motherfucking trannie bitch! My phone!"*

We begin walking away.

"She needs the money more than I do," Quetzal bellows. *"Whatever! IT'S MEXICO!"*

10 | Negotiating Saints

Absorbing the beat at a *sonidero* in Tepito. (Photo by Livia Radwanski.)

It is an overcast Sunday afternoon in the bleak D.F. suburb of Tultitlán, where a few dozen people are gathered for the one-month
anniversary rosary for Jonathan Legaria Vargas, the man they called
El Padrino and El Pantera—or the Panther—now deceased. In the
yard of Legaria's unofficial outdoor church on a desolate industrial avenue next to a used-car lot, families with grandmothers and
infants stand alongside tables offering tamales, fresh juices, and
beef stew. With flowers, a mariachi band, and the recitation of the
rosary, the ceremony has all the trappings of a traditional Mexican
Catholic mourning ritual. Two elements, however, stand out: the

altar before them, enclosed with a miniature skeleton dressed in a gleaming white robe and a tiara, bony jaw agape, eyes hollow; and an enormous seventy-two-foot-tall statue made of plywood and fiberglass that Legaria had erected to his chosen spiritual mother, the Santa Muerte. Death is in a black robe, her face shrouded by a hood, her skeletal arms outstretched, like something out of a theme-park ride, crazed and nightmarish. Glancing up at it every few seconds, I half expect the structure's robe to mechanically split open and reveal the entrance to a hall of mirrors.

"O Most Divine and Most Precious Holy Death," the mourners chant in unison, kneeling before the Santa Muerte altar. "Cure the jealous . . . guard the moribund . . . bless El Padrino . . ."

The prayer is led by Legaria's widow, Constantine, a young woman with pale, freckled skin and furiously curly, lemon-colored hair. She wears jeans and a small, stylish jacket and holds a microphone. "O Most Holy Death . . . ," she chants, curving the tone of her words from down to up, as if conducting a hypnosis. And the people repeat each line.

"In silence I remain here . . ." *"In silence I remain here . . ."*

"Waiting for the moment . . ." *"Waiting for the moment . . ."*

"That will take me to you . . ." *"That will take me to you . . ."*

After a while, I am mouthing the chants myself, letting them roll through my brain. I am treated cordially and warmly by the attending women, Constantine's assistants. I have tamales, and when the prayers are over, after the mariachi sing "Amor Eterno," the traditional ballad of farewell, each person places a white carnation before another large Santa Muerte figure dressed in a crimson gown, crossing himself or herself. Constantine then leads a procession of her dead husband's followers along the avenue out front. They carry flowers and candles and banners and march behind a limousine that El Pantera had custom-painted with images of the

Santa Muerte and the call letters of his Santa Muerte radio show. Throughout the afternoon, the mariachis play, the food and drink flow, and the children run happily around the huge Death statue and a small field of humanlike skulls spread out on patches of grass, in grids.

A month earlier, on the night of July 31, 2008, Jonathan Legaria had been shot more than a hundred times by high-powered assault weapons after a car-to-car chase on a busy boulevard in the neighboring suburb of Ecatepec. Police say the killing, spectacular and saturated in press coverage, had all the markings of a coordinated assassination, far from the peaceful passage befitting a revered spiritual leader. Legaria, just twenty-seven years old, was not an unknown figure in the red-note tabloids. He had verbally clashed in the press with the proprietor of another Santa Muerte sanctuary, in the central Colonia Morelos, and with the archbishop of Ecatepec, who labeled him a "charlatan." He fought with the municipal authorities of Tultitlán when they attempted to prevent him from building his massive Santa Muerte statue. In life, the tabloids note, El Pantera had plenty of enemies.

With his piercing eyes, his eloquent and hypnotic manner of speaking, his neck and wrists covered in Santa Muerte scapulars and Santería-like beads, the self-anointed priest had developed an enthusiastic following in the northern suburbs of the city. Hundreds of people, including a fearsome biker gang, attend Legaria's funeral.

After the Panther's murder, his mother, Enriqueta Vargas Ortiz, determined to defend her son's honor, announced a quarter-million-peso reward for any information leading to his killers. The local authorities declared themselves "incompetent" to lead the investigation and handed the case over to federal authorities. This was read as an automatic defeat. Given the "spiritual" ramifications of the case and the nature of Mexican law enforcement, Legaria's murder will be forgotten and piled away with mountains of other unsolved killings, both high profile and not. From one day to the next, the press stopped visiting.

It occurs to me that the Panther's towering Santa Muerte statue is perhaps the largest personification of Death any mortal has ever built. At Legaria's "afterlife" party, we stand below it in a ritual of mourning, not minding the irony. I wander around the yard listening to people who swear that the Holy Death image and El Padrino have saved them and given their lives new meaning.

"I think it's unjust that whoever did this is eating and breathing, while they took away our Padrino, someone so valued, who did so much good in my life, in my family," an old woman named Margarita tells me. "Look at what it's done for me," Margarita insists, smiling broadly.

I look. She has dark, rough skin, eyes set close together, and fairly crooked teeth that protrude outward from her grin. Margarita tells me how she came to the Santa Muerte sanctuary in Tultitlán. She says she had been in the darkest point of her life when she saw the large Santa Muerte statue in passing. "One day it was raining, and I came in, and I saw a . . . beautiful man, white, who saw me, because I was crying and crying, and I said to him, '*Buenas noches,* is the prayer over?'"

Margarita's eyes grow wide with wonder at the thought of her memory.

"'*Señor,* can I come and see her?' He said yes. 'Are you in a rush?' He said, 'A little.'"

"Who was it?" I ask.

"Blessed be God and my Holy Mother, it was my Padrino," Margarita says. "He opened his doors. He let me pray. And once inside the door, he listened to me. I told him everything that I had been through. How I had arrived here, destroyed, without family, without friends, without a house. I had been on the street for four days."

Margarita is tearing up now.

"People think you're crazy, that you're not functioning right," she goes on. "Yes, I consider myself crazy. Yes. I am crazy, but for love for my fellow citizens. When my Padrino listened, as you are listening to me now, he stretched his hand out to me." Margarita reaches out for my own hand and holds it. "And he said to me, 'You . . . are good.'"

Margarita's eyes are aglow with the rapture of belief. She is literally channeling her faith through my recorder, and in her mind speaking to the universe. "Now, I am a fortified beauty, a beauty who believes in the love and mercy of our Mother."

Her "Mother" is the Santa Muerte, Death itself. And then, at the height of the party, the clouds above part. It is sudden, as if on cue. The sun bears through the gray moisture in radiant light, catching new colors and textures before our eyes. El Pantera's followers are joined in wild applause and ecstatic cries. Margarita dances, shakes her hips, raises her arms to the sky, and weeps.

"You've witnessed it," Constantine says into her microphone, fierce with devotion, her own mourning aside. "El Pantera is here with us. . . . He cannot be here in body, but he is here in soul."

To understand the phenomenal growth of the cult of Santa Muerte in the last decade in Mexico City and across the Mexican diaspora in the United States, it's worth reminding yourself, first of all, that everyone dies. No matter your class, country, sex, or net worth, we all eventually face death. It is life's built-in defect, its greatest source of sadness. Looking to mitigate the banality of death, societies and religions turn it into an existential mystery. Great significance is attached to what sort of circumstances in life affect what happens to the soul in the afterlife. Churches teach us that death carries a clean spiritual logic, one that virtually anyone can follow: Be godly in life as we dictate, ascend to heaven in death.

The Santa Muerte challenges that entire structure, which is why the Roman Catholic hierarchy in Mexico so violently despises the cult, calling it "satanic." The Santa Muerte—the Little Skinny One, as she is sometimes called—violates the Church's order by bringing the omnipresence of death into direct contact with everyday life. Worshipping a Death figure amounts to worshipping the one sure thing that life offers, its end.

In criticizing the Santa Muerte church, authorities only feed fuel to its followers, who number between 2 and 5 million, according to some estimates. Pushing back is pointless. How could the Church compete against a readily accessible icon that offers the average mortal more agency and spiritual independence than any religion's doctrines? With prayers and offerings, people are learning to charm Death into doing their bidding in life. They ask her to find them jobs or spouses, to take away enemies, or to protect their own selves from her eternal embrace, for a time. Such options understandably draw the morally marginalized to her cult: drug traffickers, prostitutes, petty criminals, politicians.

The origin of the Santa Muerte is disputed. Some believe the image is a descendant from pre-Hispanic times, on the lineage of the Aztec god Mictlantecuhtli. Anthropologists maintain the Santa Muerte is a refashioning of San Pascual Rey, a Catholic saint with a long cult history in the Mayan lands of Chiapas and Guatemala, and whose traditional image is a frightening skeleton. Historian Claudio Lomnitz casts Santa Muerte's following in an economic light, arguing that it exploded after the onset of the North American Free Trade Agreement, when the modern northern exodus of Mexican migrants across the border really took off. The argument is that the economic uncertainty defining Mexican society created an opening for a spiritual icon that could respond to deep social rifts and the widening distance between the government and the average citizen.

"The spread of this cult can be understood as a symptom of Mexico's second secular revolution—the nation's increasingly tenuous relationship to the state," Lomnitz writes in his book *Death and the Idea of Mexico*. "She is, from the viewpoint of her devotees, for all intents and purposes, an independent agent."

This hypothesis seems the most apt to me. As I witness in Tultitlán, worshippers of the Santa Muerte retain their national Catholicism without necessarily involving themselves in criminal or corrupting acts. But if nothing about the Santa Muerte cult is specifically criminal, I ask myself, why does so much passionate unease exist over its growth? In Tijuana, in the north, the government has gone out of its way to destroy Santa Muerte sanctuaries in a rampage that believers everywhere consider a direct assault on their religious freedom. Santa Muerte followers feel compelled to come out of the shadows. One day in April 2009, they march for their religious rights in the Zócalo, carrying their Santa Muerte right up to the gates of the Metropolitan Cathedral. It is a veritable confrontation of gods.

My work is ostensibly that of a dispassionate journalist, but I have to admit the truth. I am looking to see if I can assimilate the Santa Muerte into my spiritual diet. Her altars beckon to me from inside shops and on street corners. Her gaping cackle and hollow eyes, her scythe and globe, her colored gowns, her knobby fingers, calling out in witness behind a veil of cigar smoke or incense. She is in tattoo form on a man's arm or chest, in sticker form on the back of a cab, in scapular form around a young person's neck. In Mexico City, where history is an epic parade of death and bloodshed, no religious icon is more rooted in the place's essential identity. A saint of death for the land of death.

For weeks I wander the major altars found in the center of Mexico City, meeting people who are otherwise "normal" in their lives but are somehow drawn to a cult considered "pagan" by Mexico's ecclesiastical leaders. I find myself returning to a basic idea. *There is nothing more certain in life than death. . . . There is nothing as certain in life as its finish.* The cult of the Santa Muerte is simply an elaborate acknowledgment of fact.

So why, I wonder, must I keep repeating this to myself?

The most famous Santa Muerte altar in Mexico City lies deep in the mythically "rough" barrio of Tepito, the most notorious neighborhood in all of Mexico. I have long tried to remain aware that a neighborhood's notoriety doesn't always correspond with its actual profile, but Tepito is a special case. It is the capital of pirates, the capital of gangsters, of those making do on their own. It is more or less off the grid, and it's been this way for centuries. The sidewalks are choked with vendors selling cheap pirated and stolen goods, tons upon tons, below long stretches of colored tarps that block out the sun, disorienting the senses. Street vending dominates the landscape in Tepito; there is street commerce, then everything else. So many stalls sell bootleg movies that they are sometimes divided up by genre, with pornography dominating over westerns, horror films, art-house and classic-Mexican cinema, and so on. If you know whom to ask, and how, you can get anything. *Anything.* Drugs, guns, animals. Anything for the right price. "In Tepito everything is for sale but dignity," the maxim goes.

The neighborhood is Mexico's incubator of great boxers, great football players, legendary *pachucos* and *sonideros*. It also tends to operate as a slate upon which all kinds of theories are hung, on globalization, developing economies, criminality, the underworld, on Mexico. In films and books, Tepito is a muse. Carlos Monsiváis called it a "cemetery of ambitions, a congregation of thieves." In Tepito, he wrote, "everything happens, everything fits."

I dig regularly into the market. What draws me is that Tepito's primary purpose is shopping. The endless options, the prevalence of the idea that anything can be had, commerce above morals, laws, or codes. Today, some businesses in Tepito are kept by Korean immigrants, recent arrivals to the Tepito landscape. Most of the merchandise is said to be smuggled in from China—always a reliable bogeyman for Mexico's economic warts. But authorities also believe much of what is sold within Tepito is manufactured inside the walled-off *vecindades,* self-contained neighborhoods occupying whole city blocks where unofficial factories pump out CDs and DVDs, and caches of weapons and drugs are stored. Police officers are present but rarely enforce any laws. Whenever the government's "special forces" attempt to eradicate pirate manufacturing and drug distribution in Tepito with predawn raids, the incensed residents, women and children included, beat back the armed agents. The metro Tepito station symbol is a boxer's glove, a nod to the many fabled boxing champs who got their earliest training in Tepito's streets and gyms. But the symbol for the station could just as well be a silhouette of the Santa Muerte. This is where the cult first came out of the shadows.

Deep in the neighborhood on a street called Alfarería, the most popular public altar to Santa Muerte is watched over by a well-regarded woman known as Doña Queta. She passes the time cleaning and decorating the glass case in which the life-size Santa Muerte figure stands, just outside her *vecindad*. She dresses her Death in extravagant gowns and tiaras, as if preparing her for a wedding or *quinceañera*. The display is always color-coordinated. If the Santa is dressed in green, candles and fabrics will be in green. Every Halloween at midnight Doña Queta's altar is the site of a Santa Muerte rosary ritual that draws so many adherents that, on the night I go, I am unable to get closer than two blocks away. Thousands of people as far as one can see face Doña Queta's door, reciting the Santa Muerte prayers, honoring their "Santita." When I depart, the cabdriver tells me the local narco capos bring their automatic assault weapons to Doña Queta's on Halloween, so that the tools of their trade can be blessed by Death.

Jonathan Legaria's Santa Muerte sanctuary up in Tultitlán is a distant and unknown place for Doña Queta and the people who worship the Death figure on her doorstep. Weeks after Legaria's funeral, I visit Doña Queta in the daytime, hoping to clear up some questions. She is sitting on a stool before the altar. People approach to deliver flowers and fruit to the skeletal figure in the glass case. "We all respect one another here, each person to his own," Doña Queta explains. "No one would attack you here."

Doña Queta regards the image with an almost childlike affection, talking about the manner in which she dresses her, keeps her "pretty." I ask her why the cult has grown so much. "It is the faith of the people, my child."

I ask again, "But why now?"

"I already told you. Before, there were no altars on the street. I put this altar, and people came."

So, *if you build it, they will come,* I think to myself.

A shock of white races through the old woman's black hair from the top of her forehead, like a crown. Doña Queta's eyes are fierce, intense, yet she exudes tranquillity. Doña Queta is at peace with her life, her office. The Santa Muerte's caretaker. "Does the Santa Muerte protect you from death?" I ask.

Doña Queta is momentarily annoyed. *What a foolish question,* her expression says.

"You are born with a destiny, from the day you are born. This is separate. This is for asking that she protect you, that she accompany you." Doña Queta shrugs, coming up with suitable examples. "That she might get a son out of jail, that she might find you a job, that she might stop you from losing your house. But your destiny is marked, my child."

I have more questions. I bring up the allegation that cartel men pray to the Santa Muerte for help in the wars against their enemies. The papers always say that the Santita watches over assassins, I tell Doña Queta.

"And do you know a narco who has told you that?" she shoots back. "Well? That is just talk. I don't go there."

People continue to stream past the altar. Some hold small children by the hand or carry babies in their arms. Some touch the front panel of the glass case so that the Santa Muerte's blessings might channel through at the touch. Doña Queta insists to me that nothing is too otherworldly about the Santa Muerte.

"She is inside of you just as she is inside of me," Doña Queta says, lifting a pinch of skin on her forearm, her eyes ablaze. "Once you peel this . . . *you* are the Muerte. You already have her . . . in you."

My pen stops. I feel myself pitch slightly backward. I feel Doña Queta's words sear right through my skin and envelop my skeleton. The idea is so powerful. The Santa Muerte, living inside of us all. The veracity of the image, my journalist's brain thinks, is now "provably true." There isn't much more to discuss.

156

Doña Queta offers to walk me to the nearest big street to hail a cab. Tepito is thick with noise, smells, human energy. "You have to be careful around here," she warns me, holding the back of my arm.

I make small talk. "Do you have children?"

"Oh, yes, but they're *cabrones*"—little shits—"just like you."

I admire Doña Queta's arts of perception. "Do they go out around here at night?" I ask.

Yes, Doña Queta replies, but she says that her motherly advice is always the same: "'Only whores, thieves, and cops go out at night. Which one are you, asshole?'"

Every twenty-eighth day of the month is another day of chaotic pilgrimage in Mexico City. Beginning early in the morning, the pilgrims crowd into the metro, huddles of young people carrying their statues of San Judas Tadeo, or St. Jude, the one they called Thaddeus, an apostle to Christ. The pilgrims travel from the city's far outskirts to the church of San Hipólito, above metro Hidalgo in the city's center, taking part in a specific act of ritual passion. The streets around the church—including a section of Reforma—must be shut down to traffic to accommodate the masses. The young pilgrims are partying even before they arrive. They are laughing and holding on to one another, and some are preparing their doses of *mona* to inhale.

They press in toward the church's doors and crowd to the point of human gridlock, much like at the basilica every December 12. Thousands, tens of thousands, are crowding the surrounding streets, selling San Judas beads, garments, key chains, and lots of food and drinks. For those to whom San Judas has delivered a miracle, handing out prayer sheets or flowers to strangers becomes a spiritual duty. The church is their beacon. They want blessings, they want guidance, they want love. Couples caress, children are carried upon shoulders, *mona* is consumed. Religiously, I guess.

San Hipólito, baroque in style, built partially with volcanic stone, was erected in the early 1700s. It was designated a chapel in honor of the saint whose feast day falls on August 13, the day Tenochtitlan fell to Cortés—but most of the kids here could probably not care less. They gather at San Hipólito because a shimmering San Judas statue is on the main altar inside, and San Judas is the patron of lost and desperate causes. By the size of the crowds, it appears Mexico City has plenty of those at the moment.

Like the Santa Muerte, the cult of San Judas Tadeo is experiencing a surge of new adherents in D.F. in the first decade of the new millennium. The saint's annual feast day, October 28, is the biggest religious party in Centro by a wide margin. The believers adorn their San Judas statues with beads and threaded necklaces, colored lace, scapulars, and roses. The saint is traditionally depicted wearing a green robe, but his adherents generally prefer white. On October 28, 2008, I head to San Hipólito with Uriel, my partner in many ventures into the cultural soul of Mexico City. We are in attendance partly out of curiosity and partly out of a quiet suspicion. *What's this about, really?*

We arrive late at night to the San Judas carnival, walking a handful of blocks from my apartment and diagonally across the Alameda Central. Uriel and I find the streets around San Hipólito, first and foremost, to be drowning in trash. Sidewalks and curbs are almost entirely submerged. The San Judas image—bearded, a flame of holy glory alight atop his head—is still bobbing above the people by the dozens. Most of those holding him are just teenagers. Kids are crowding around old men and women who are giving away long-stemmed roses as a San Judas–inspired charity. Clamoring, actually, while whistling, laughing nervously, and chatting and calling for "one more."

Up against a metal riot barrier placed by police to control the masses, we meet an older gentleman who is about to be overwhelmed by kids desperate for a rose. Jesús Enrique Hernández wears eyeglasses and has that timeless air of a devout Roman Catholic, upright and serene. He says October 28 is the most important day for his faith.

"He is our miraculous patron, San Juditas Tadeo, so on this day we venerate him," Hernández manages to say to me. He is about to be knocked over as kids push their way past us, clamoring for more free roses.

"He is not pagan, not pagan," the old man hastily adds, making what I figure is a veiled reference to the cult of the Santa Muerte.

I try interviewing some kids about their faith in "San Juditas," but none that I approach have anything coherent to say. They stammer and shrug. "It's just faith." We watch as police officers snatch up teens smoking marijuana too brazenly on the stoops at metro Hidalgo. We watch small children and teens line up to take photos with a fully costumed clown who is roaming the grounds. Even clowns must seek spiritual protection in their most desperate hour, I think. Standing on a curb, resting, Uriel and I are approached by a young San Juditas adherent who starts chatting us up. He wears sunglasses in the dark, talks excitedly, then tells us he has ecstasy and acid for sale. At a good price for other *"cuates"*—homies—in the faith, he says. We consider this. An "incredible" rave is coming up, the guy tells us, out in the forests in the state of Hidalgo. He gives us a flyer and his cell phone number.

As we walk away, Uriel sums up our suspicion: "This is trendy."

In Mexico City, San Judas Tadeo demands not only pilgrimage to San Hipólito every twenty-eighth day of the month from his faithful, but apparently also the donning of specific garments. It is a deeply urban costume worn religiously by youth in the Centro, and always shifting. Right now it consists of white San Judas T-shirts or white tank tops, white sneakers, and white baseball caps. Jeans are rolled up and cuffed at the ankle. The boys wear their hair cropped short and tight, sometimes with gelled tips, or with intricate patterns cut in by skilled barbers. The girls put blond streaks in their hair, and both boys and girls are fond of necklaces, bracelets, and piercings. The look makes reference to the cultures of hiphop, reggae, *cumbia,* drum-n-bass, California cholo, and Cuban Santería. They get together at *sonideros,* deep-barrio street parties that include a unique transnational element. Shout-outs and messages on signs are transmitted to the MC, who reads them back. The entire *sonidero* is recorded and then turns up on the streets as a bootleg disc. The discs make it across the border, and the shout-outs reach their destination. Through *sonideros*—at least those I've attended—Tepito and all its subcultural styles become an export product of sound.

It all feels familiar, like a piece of home. Who cares if this is "trendy"? Is trendiness not in its own way authentic, as the emos prove? Over time, almost without noticing it, I begin wearing San Judas Tadeo myself. I begin burning candles in his honor inside my house, if only out of a sense of solidarity with my neighbors. I live in downtown now, and in D.F. his cult is strongest here. It is the most pragmatic and elastic of those available to the young people of the Centro, I realize, a happy refuge halfway between the Virgen de Guadalupe and the Santa Muerte. The Holy Death feels true, in that sense that there could be no doubting the reach of her power. In a sense she is in competition with her inverse, the Virgen de Guadalupe. Santa Muerte as the custodian of death, the black and skeletal reflection of Guadalupe, source of mercy and light. One requires a resignation to the totality of death, while the other requires a resignation to the totality of the Church and the Conquest.

Neither, however, is as useful to tending to the challenges of everyday life as is San Judas Tadeo, or as adept at making it look so big-city cool. These streets are San Judas's streets. These obstacles—making money, commuting from here to there, evading police—are his to mediate. There's no use questioning it. "Why do the kids of Centro like San Judas so much?" I sometimes ask my *tepiteño* friends. The answer is usually the same: "We just do."

I decide to leave it at that. Every twenty-eighth—every *veintiocho*—I am there at San Hipólito, working my way through the crowds, among the statues and woven and airbrushed images of the patron saint of lost causes. I am one myself. Life in Mexico City is tough. Every day is a series of trials. Survival is always in doubt. I'm hungry. I'm broke. When the tests take me to the breaking point, I look to St. Jude and beseech him. *Just one more day,* I pray. *Just one more chance.*

11 | Originals of Punk

On the outskirts. (Photo by William Dunleavy.)

Reymundo, known by his punk name, El Reyes, is in his mid-thirties, a large and burly guy. His belly is formidably composed, not by fat or muscle exactly, but by the stuff of strength. His head is shaved. That makes him a *punk pelón*, he explains to me on the day I meet him. Being a shaved-head punk means he is often mistook for a skinhead, or worse, a fascist skinhead. That sometimes leads to trouble with strangers.

I meet Reyes in late summer 2009 at a music space known as El

Clandestino, out in Ecatepec, the suburb to the north reachable on Line B of the metro, the one colored green and gray. It is another Sunday-afternoon *toquín*. Bands of spiky-haired, patch-covered punks, guys and girls, gather outside on a busy avenue under the blazing sun, the smell of car exhaust and stagnant channel waters bouncing against the traffic and the raw rock sounds from inside. Some kids are inhaling *mona*. Reyes is working the door. His job is to make sure the punks lingering outside won't rush in without paying the steep hundred-peso cover, payable at a makeshift box office: the passenger-side window of a small white car parked near the door. A shirtless guy sits inside, drinking, smoking, and collecting cash.

Several bands are scheduled to play on a bill described as the Festival Katártiko Punk de Aniversario, with a tagline of "Because Catharsis Is Still Valid, Liberating It Is Our Way of Life." I tell Reyes I am a journalist from Los Angeles here to cover the event. He asks me to wait about an hour, then introduces me to El Clandestino's manager, who welcomes me in along with a friend visiting from California. The space—nothing more than a large box with a dirt floor—is filled with guys covered in tattoos and girls with studded dog collars around their necks and their hair in tall, pink spikes. Murals on the black walls depict skulls, silhouettes with their fists raised, the Addicts. Although we are obviously outsiders and not full-fledged punks, no one regards us with suspicion or hostility. I settle in, buying from the concessions stand a large cold *caguama* and a plain *torta* of ham, cheese, mayonnaise, and chili.

Síndrome plays, one of the oldest and most well known punk bands in Mexico. Everyone moshes wildly. A little guy who looks about sixteen or seventeen but is deeply afflicted by dwarfism is hoisted upon someone's shoulders in the slam pit. Rising above everyone's heads, the little guy makes it to the stage, where the Síndrome singer Amaya—who at forty-seven years old is still going strong—lifts him up, and they both go into a rage, raising their fists to punk glory. I move closer to the stage. I lift my boots up and down to pound upon the dirt beneath me. I holler in nonsense. I push and shove my way about. People are bouncing around, elbowing strangers. The whole action feels very communal.

When I leave El Clandestino, I thank Reyes at the gate. He shakes my hand energetically. "I'll show you the real roots of punk in Mexico. The *chavos*," he adds, the young people, "need to know." Something about Reyes's demeanor makes me trust him immediately. Six days later, I call him.

Reyes tells me to meet him on the platform at metro Salto del Agua, at 1:00 p.m. It is the following Sunday. I arrive in time, and after a half hour of watching trains go by, people heading in and out, I finally spot him walking toward me from down the platform. Reyes's stance is wide and his strides long. He wears camouflage trousers and laced-up boots and a worn black T-shirt with the sleeves cut off, the phrase REBEL: PUNK AND SKIN PRIDE, ANTI-FASCISTS on front. After we greet each other, Reyes makes a lightning movement without warning. He sticks his hands against the closing doors of a metro car before us and yanks them back open, prompting an automatic siren. Riders dutifully open up space as we enter. Reyes wants us to get on right there, so that's where we get on. He smiles widely. He is excited by the start of our journey. We are going to a suburb called Chicoloapan, he tells me, to meet his family.

"A lot of reporters come," Reyes says as we ride the train, "and they want to write about us, about the punk movement. But they only care about what's happening in the moment. They don't get into the roots. Some of us have been twenty years with the movement, some even up to thirty. Me, I think I've been punk for maybe twenty-six years."

I listen as we race eastward under the capital, deciding it best not to ask Reyes about his age. People move in and out of our car at each stop, the everyday movement of the subterranean city. "We're older now," Reyes says. "The *chavas* are now *señoras*. Their husbands died or were killed. They have their own kids now."

He shows me the tattoos that decorate his thick arms. One of them is marked with the letters *P.N.D.*, the name, he says, of his punk group in Santa Fe, where he grew up. He tells me others often mistake the acronym to mean Punk Never Dies, but Reyes explains, "It's Plan Nacional de Desarrollo." The name—National Development Plan—expresses the idea that liberation from government repression, that a radical state of total autonomy, the core tenet of punk, is a project not just for his neighborhood in Santa Fe but for the entire nation. "And that's what it still is, Plan Nacional de Desarrollo," Reyes says seriously, looking straight at me. "We still believe it."

Reyes grew up in the slums that rose unchecked around the vast garbage dump in Santa Fe, a long canyon-dotted region on the west side of the Federal District. For decades, the Santa Fe dump epitomized the disarray of a megacity growing beyond its capacity. The city in that period was widely recognized as the world's largest, and at the Sante Fe dump, extreme poverty mirrored an extreme environmental crisis. The Associated Press reported on the area in 1988:

> The foul-smelling dump, spread over about 150
> acres on the western edge of Mexico City, was one
> of the largest in Latin America. . . . The garbage

was estimated to be 230 feet deep in some places, forming enormous cliffs from the refuse deposited there for more than four decades. . . . Spontaneous fires broke out, sending noxious fumes into the air. There was also concern the wastes were seeping into aquifers and contaminating the city's already scarce water supply.

Today much of Santa Fe is an overdeveloped business district of high-rises and exclusive business complexes, a place of impersonal living. Some call it Mexico's mini-Dubai. Despite its veneer of hyperdevelopment, Santa Fe is to this day still surrounded by many of its original slums. In this radical transformation, Reyes explains, Santa Fe's history of massive displacement has completely been erased.

In the early 1980s, the federal government decided that Santa Fe would eventually be developed into a first-world-styled "central business district"—as far from the city center as possible. For that to happen, the garbage dump and the people who lived off it had to be relocated. Little by little, the trash pickers and residents of the Santa Fe slums were pushed out, making room for hotels, a massive shopping center, and the campus of the Universidad Iberoamericana. The small barrio in the slums where Reyes grew up was Tlayapaca, one of the last holdouts. The government wanted it to be the new home of the Mexico City campus of the Tecnológica de Monterrey, one of the country's most prestigious universities. The neighborhood had to be razed. Residents were offered money but many families did not want to leave. The people of Tlayapaca resisted as much as they could, but on December 28, 1998, a date Reyes invokes gravely, police swept through the barrio and forcibly removed its residents. The December 30 edition of *La*

Jornada reported that six hundred people were removed that night by authorities who operated with "the luxury of arrogance and violence." Reyes's family was among them.

For years the most ardent families of Tlayapaca battled the government—"at war," as the victims still say—over their land. For much of that time they lived sit-in style in front of government buildings or wandered the urban geography as refugees, homeless. The university eventually settled with the people of Tlayapaca by offering to relocate them to new houses, some in Chicoloapan, far off in the eastern reaches of the city, far from Santa Fe.

Reyes sees the dislocation as central to his punk identity, the basis for his stance of resistance and self-determination. Santa Fe was teeming with punks in that period, he says. The whole city was, from north to south, east to west. In testimonies and video footage that survive from the era, punks explain themselves in a manner that is conscious and politically aware. To most of the city, however, the marginalized youth of Santa Fe were known as *chavos banda*, the media-coined term that essentially criminalized young people, casting them as thugs and thieves. After the government sweeps, the people of Santa Fe spread out. They emigrated to Ciudad Nezahualcóyotl and to the borough of Iztapalapa, or even farther away. Reyes's sister La Flexi—a leader in the Tlayapaca resistance movement—was among those offered new homes in Chicoloapan. Exhausted with the struggle, the families moved.

Time passes, and the dislocation corresponds with a physical transformation. Reyes tells me that the last true remaining punks of Mexico City, the ones who didn't die an early or violent death, might no longer wear cascades of chains and buckles or mold their hair in spikes. A lot of them have children now, jobs—or at least a source of income. Nonetheless, punk in Mexico City remains one of the most enduring and complex subcultures to emerge after

1968. Mexican punks in many cases maintain close ties with their counterparts in Spain, Germany, and the United States. Years later, original D.F. punks still see resistance not merely as a stance or a costume but as a way of life.

Reyes and I get off at metro Boulevard Puerto Aéreo, near the airport. In the underground tunnel leaving the Puerto Aéreo station, he explains that he makes some of his living by selling mesh shirts knitted in colored cotton, stitched by hand by his sister Flexi. The shirts are popular with punks wherever punks live. He stops in the flow of people in the passageway and pulls a red garment out of his backpack. It looks like cotton chain-mail soaked in blood.

"Put it on," Reyes says. "Wear it." I hesitate, stumbling to make up an excuse. "No! Put it on."

No point in arguing. If an original punk in Mexico City tells you you should do something, you just have to do it. I don the cotton chain-mail and immediately feel goofy. The thing hangs unflatteringly over my bony shoulders. "Looks good!" Reyes laughs in approval.

We pile into a *combi,* one of the low-roofed minivans converted into stop-and-go public transit units that are as common to the long-range commuter experience in Mexico City as the metro. Most people who live in the city's faraway reaches use both, *combis* and the metro, to go about their everyday lives. The insides of the vans are hollowed out and fitted with small, carpeted seats. Reyes and I squish into the van's back corner. We are going to ride shoulder to shoulder, knee to knee, in an airless minivan packed with strangers, for at least an hour in traffic.

"I want to show you something," Reyes says, pulling a new item out of his backpack, a worn manila folder. Reyes holds it with both hands as though it were a holy book. He passes the folder to me and I open it delicately on my lap. Inside, page after page of old-school punk testimony. Drawings, crudely typed or scrawled personal histories, photocopied flyers and photographs. "I want to make a book," Reyes says, pressing his fingers against the papers inside. "The true history."

He begins telling me stories, about the fascist punks he's had contact with, the confrontations, the brawls, about fellow punks who hide their identity while working in the police or the army, and—more astounding—about Nazi-sympathizing punks. The fascination among some Mexicans with violent national socialism from a different place and a different era lies beyond the realm of comprehension for me. Reyes says he once found himself inside a Mexican cop's domestic space, where he saw Nazi flags on the walls.

"I've tried to talk to them," Reyes tells me as we ride along. He sighs. "You have to let everyone believe what they want to believe."

Through the window, the landscape is a blur of broken structures, lonesome figures, wide treacherous expanses of traffic. Right next to me, skin to skin, sits a stout brown woman whose body mass is so packed with maize and earthen living I feel as if I am a pesky bag of twigs disturbing her personal space with my sharp edges. We are nearing Chicoloapan. The road has turned ruddy and brown, and traffic moves inch by inch. Light *ranchera* music plays from the radio up front. Cars and trucks and the smell of exhaust push in from all sides. Reyes turns and asks me, "And you, what drew you to punk?"

The various simultaneous strains of thought racing in my head come to a screeching halt. *What drew me to punk?* Reyes has small eyes and a steady gaze. He is waiting for an answer. "Well . . . ,"

I start. "I don't know. I think . . . I think punk is something that . . . you just carry."

Reyes nods.

"I like a lot of movements," I go on. "I feel like . . . like you can draw some things from this and some things from that . . . but deep down . . ."

I trail off. Reyes seems satisfied with my response. I look down at myself. I am now wearing one of his mesh cotton punk tops, over a T-shirt with an image of a skeleton playing a guitar and the logo of the L.A. punk band the Screamers. I had been at a *toquín* out at El Clandestino and had moshed to Síndrome. I understand what Reyes means when he explains Plan Nacional de Desarrollo, and I understand what he means when he talks about resisting the government, and the need for histories to be told. To Reyes I am *banda*. To Reyes I am punk.

In Chicoloapan, this flat, eastward-spreading section of the metropolitan region, greater Mexico City looks more like a forgotten war zone than a collection of interconnected suburbs. Cinderblock buildings sit unfinished out in the fields, and dogs and the most destitute people carve out their living spaces along the black muddy roadside. By the time Reyes calls up to the driver to ask to get off, I am relieved to unglue myself from the lady next to me. This could be any other desolate street in the reaches of the valley where the urban rubs uncomfortably up against the rural. Nothing to speak of, nothing to note, just buildings and fences and dogs and the big cloudy sky above us. We walk down an empty side street, past closet-size paper stores, Internet shops, and cleaners. No one is around. The street is quiet enough to hear my own breathing.

Reyes does not live here; he stayed in the orbit of Santa Fe after Tlayacapa was swept off the map. But he moves around Chicoloapan with the assuredness of a local. We are headed to his sister Flexi's house, to see who is home.

"Tell me what happened when they kicked you out of Santa Fe," I say to Reyes. "How did your family end up here?"

It happened in the middle of the night, Reyes says. There were mounted police, police from all the boroughs, police right outside his door. Old people, women, children, all woken up and forced from their homes. It sounds violent and traumatic. After the initial dislocation battle, Reyes and his community formed a resistance movement. They camped out in their territory. They camped out before government buildings. "Every night, at two or four in the morning, the riot police would come and push us out of where we were, like at the Zócalo," Reyes says. "Even with our kids, with our old people, who got sick. Those who resisted were beaten, beaten bad. We lived for four years in struggle and resistance."

We pass a dirt soccer field that is still wet from rain the day before. After four years of fighting, the Tec, as the school is known, offered new homes to the displaced families of Tlayapaca. "We were tired of living on the streets like nomads," Reyes says. "We were one of the original seven hundred families. By the end of it, there were thirty families."

Flexi's house is near the back of a dead-end street, along a row of brightly painted block homes, the kind that tend to spring up on the outskirts of developing megacities. Driveways in each home are made of the same concrete as the street, white and cracked. Reyes rattles a rusty white gate. "Open up!" We wait. Flexi and one of her daughters emerge. Flexi seems happy to see a new person in one of her chain-mail punk tops. We have handshakes and hugs and kisses as we enter the darkened living room. The floor is smooth gray cement.

Inside, I meet Reyes's nephews and his father, an old man hunched over a carpenter's workbench. Flexi, in short, curly hair and a camo fleece, immediately begins referring to me as *manito,* shorthand for little brother. She is preparing an early supper of *consomé,* a chicken soup. Flexi's eldest son, a kid in his early twenties, pops in a DVD of old punk footage. The cover has a skull-and-bones on front and the title *The Lost Decade: 1985–1995.*

"It was tremendous, the situation," Flexi says, sitting on an armchair next to me as the *consomé* comes out in heavy bowls. "It was tough, *manito.*" We watch grainy footage of boyish punks in mohawks, talking about their ideas of resistance, what being punk means to them. Images of angry moshing mobs, hundreds and hundreds of Mexico City punks pounding their way through the lost decade. Who knows where most of those kids are now, but right here before me I have a family of survivors, originals of punk. One of those moshing punks on the screen, Flexi points out, is her dead husband. He died in a fight, she says.

"They would tell us," Flexi is saying, "that we had to get out of there, because it was no longer ours. But we would say, 'No, the land belongs to those who work it.' We would say, 'They'll have to take us out of here dead.' In that moment, *manito,* we were ready to give our lives for that land."

As tortillas and beer round out the meal, Flexi tells me about an especially terrifying night of battle in Santa Fe with the riot police, two months into the war. Again, she says, the state came in the middle of the night. "We strapped ourselves to gas tanks and said, 'If they come in here, we'll kill ourselves.' We didn't want to lose, so we brawled with those *cabrones,*" those motherfuckers.

Hours pass. Reyes seems happy to be at home. He lives on the exact opposite side of the city, making any visit to see his sister a feat of endurance. He jokes with his nephews and hugs his father. Finally he suggests that we go back to his area, to the remaining slums of Santa Fe, for a daylong *toquín*. He refers to the street concert as a *ruido*. Literally, a "noise." Flexi shows me some of her embroidery work while a baby boy I assume is her nephew or grandchild walks carefully in my direction to hold on to the top of my knees.

"Now I show up at El Chopo, and apparently there are nationalist *pelones*." Flexi shrugs, perplexed. "They are nationalists and they sing the national anthem."

After filling up on beer and *consomé*, we say our good-byes. I remember to ask for a group photo. I capture the happy day out on Flexi's street, the entire family standing in a row, arm in arm, smiling.

Reyes doesn't say specifically where the concert will be, just that it is in an *hoyo fonqui,* just as in the old days of the Mexican counterculture. This *hoyo fonqui,* Reyes says, is happening at a place known as El Garcy, way up in the slum hillsides from the Tacubaya transit hub, in the Santa Fe neighborhoods that were not cleared to make way for the "new Santa Fe" of corporate office buildings and heavily guarded condo complexes. Bands will play, El Reyes says, and we'll meet more original punks.

At this point, around 6:00 p.m. on a Sunday, we have been to the far eastern fringes of the city and are now heading to the city's outskirts on the opposite end, entirely by foot and public transit. Metro Tacubaya is the cavernous westside transfer station that connects three lines. After arriving, we climb aboveground, where Tacubaya is also the hectic and confusing terminus for many bus routes that serve the rising hills of the far west. Taco-stand men call, and where anyone can find space, vendors sells snacks to help ease long commutes. Chocolate-covered marshmallows, peanuts, sugar-coated gumdrops. "I used to live around here," I tell Reyes, who is happy to hear it.

We hop on a microbus. The musky sweat of a damp afternoon in the city lingers on every sidewalk and on every moving body. Reyes briefly chats up the bus driver and scores the tiny navigator seat up front on the dashboard, the barrio way of riding a *micro,* while I hang on to a greasy standing pole. He keeps glancing back toward me, smiling reassuringly. We ride up, up, up, into the dense, graffiti-scarred streets, past shops and stores of every kind, into territory as unfamiliar to me as any I have ever seen in Mexico. By the time we land on pavement, I immediately sense a heightening of the dangers involved in the outsider-insider dynamic that comes with walking the streets of a neighborhood that isn't yours.

This urban rule governs the backways of any dense city, analogous to how I imagine the streets operating in the slums of Bombay or the favelas of Brazil. Yet the gleaming towers of the modern Santa Fe are just a few blocks over the hills to the north of us. We cross a street, and a band of no-good-looking guys standing on a corner whistle at us menacingly. Reyes ignores them and stops before a poster for the *tocada*—yet another term for an underground concert—taped to a public telephone. *Security is all of us,* the flyer says, listing the bands, then reminding rockers, *No violence. No weapons. No glass bottles and no drugs.* Reyes yanks it off and hands it to me as we walk up a steep alley, where more bands of youth are standing around eyeing us.

After greeting a few old-timers he recognizes, Reyes turns to me, steely-eyed. "If someone asks you to go with them, if someone talks to you that I don't talk to, you don't go nowhere," he warns under his breath. "You're with me. *Machín. Machín.*" The word sends me echoing back in time to the streets of Tijuana and inner-city San Diego. *Machín* means to be tough, ready for anything. The threat of violence is a form of mediation or negotiation in the hood, anywhere in the world. It's the only way things are kept cool, if everyone displays equal and balancing levels of *machín.*

At a crest in the hill, a breathtaking urban canyon with a dank reservoir at the bottom opens up before us. Cinder-block houses slouch down the steep hillsides, as if piled atop one another, and still more and more houses pile up on the canyon's opposite side. These meager homes were built during the chaotic expansion of the city in the 1970s and '80s. Many now appear refined with time, painted, neat, as relatively stable as the economic position of their inhabitants. People stare at us from windows and stoops. The streets before Reyes and me now turn into steep cement staircases, diving down into the canyon. From far below, drumbeats and guitar riffs echo upward.

"An *hoyo fonqui*," Reyes says, grinning. "Just what we wanted."

The "hole" is an asphalt basketball court at the very bottom of the hillside, surrounded by trees. It is late dusk now, chilly, the sky inked in brilliant purple. The *ruido* at El Garcy had officially started at 10:00 a.m. and was supposed to have ended at 6:00 p.m. We arrive at seven. A dark-core band called Cicatriz has yet to play. People are hanging out, drinking, holding on to one another. A few mangy dogs keep watch from the edges of the scene. Reyes and I stroll down the steep asphalt road to the basketball court and clearly draw attention to ourselves. Indirect but not indiscreet whistles rise from a row of guys sitting on logs and drinking against a sagging metal fence. Without minding them, Reyes leads me directly to the back of the stage, just a yellow tarp hung over a few elevated wooden planks where the drum set, microphones, and amplifiers stand. "What a miracle!" Reyes's friends holler, throwing their arms around him. "Reyes! Reyes!" There are Mary, Alfredo, La Mouse, Rebeko, Robo, and D'Mon, a graying punk who had put the *ruido* together. They are drinking, smoking, jamming along to the music. They are Reyes's other family, his band of punks. He identifies them all as Santa Fe originals.

They don't look it, I think. No chains, no spikes. Now in their mid-thirties, this *banda* is mellow, pleased with defending their punkness by their actions and not their dress. Someone offers me a cigarette and I decline, a nervous reaction. It is hard getting your bearings in a new place, among new people, trying to figure out who's who and what's what. *No one seems to wear punk out here,* I think. The younger kids out in the crowd appear more influenced by the downtown San Judas aesthetic—white T's, white baseball caps, jeans, and white sneakers. The culture of Santa Fe has, it appears, shifted since the days of Reyes and his crew.

A few guys are stumbling around glassy-eyed, beyond drugged. The smell of marijuana and paint solvent hangs in the crisp air before us. One guy does look like a Santa Fe throwback, lost in 1983. He wears *Top Gun*–style aviator sunglasses, a bright blue bandanna knotted into a headband, and mesh cloth gloves with the fingers cut out. I feel as if he should be break dancing. The guy strolls around the basketball court like a mute, concentrating on something invisible to the rest of us, then suddenly—*POW!*—he is pumping his fists into the air before him or jumping up and down to the music. "Don't mind him," Rebeko says, noticing my mixture of fear and fascination. "He's just crazy."

I am still scanning the *hoyo* when someone thrusts a *caguama* in my face.

"Drink up," D'Mon says. "What, you don't drink?"

D'Mon has the sort of persona that I imagine is made by constant proximity to old *Rolling Stone* magazines, old records, old rock-festival posters, and old leather. His hair is gray, his skin pale, and with a large hooked nose and sad, clear eyes, he has a vaguely witchy air about him. I'm told he used to be in some pretty serious Mexico City punk bands in his day. Today, he plays in a band with Alfredo, Mary, and La Mouse. They call themselves A.C.V., Agudos, Crónicos, y Vegetales.

"Drink!" D'Mon commands.

Cicatriz is bringing the *ruido* down to a suitably somber finish. In front of the bandmates on the drums and guitars, a girl wails into one microphone in a high operatic voice while taking puffs off a cigarette, and a guy on another microphone screams in death-metal style while ravaging his guitar strings. They all wear black boots and long black leather jackets. Behind the stage Reyes's friends pass around the same *caguama*, swigging at it like pirates— an essentially punk activity because it is very punk to swap spit without a care. My guide for the day, the original punk of Santa Fe, is back in what is left of his home turf. He smiles at me broadly from across the way. Reyes looks happy.

And that's when the fight starts. It happens so fast. I am standing behind the sound guy—"I'm beat," he has just exhaled—when in the middle of the basketball court before us a girl appears, arguing loudly with a guy, who knows over what. They are cursing and yelling, and people are gathering around them, moths to the flame. In a snap, the girl delivers a direct closed-fist blow to the guy's chest. The guy bowls over, stumbling back. Someone grabs the girl, someone grabs the guy, and for whatever reasons, in between all of them, six or seven or so people, the pushing and blows begin. It is a rumble swaying this way and that.

Reyes and his crew of older punks look on briefly. The members of Cicatriz begin rushing to pack up their things. "Let's go," I say to

Reyes, who was now beside me, quietly watching the commotion.

Back against the court's fence, against the logs, dozens of Santa Fe kids are now in a rolling brawl—and it is getting bigger by the second. I hear a glass *caguama* shatter on the asphalt. People are whistling, calling new fighters to rush up from the hillsides and down the stepped alleys, ready to rumble. The noise grows. The bassist and drummer in Cicatriz smile at me nervously.

"Well, this is gonna get heavy," D'Mon says flatly.

Mary, who had happily been chatting with me just a few moments earlier, is now corralling her two small children.

"Let's get out of here," someone says. "Where's Rebeko?"

The group explains to me later that a *ruido* in Santa Fe almost always ends in a brawl, usually between rival neighborhoods. It is like an obligation, the event's natural ovation. But this doesn't minimize the fear rising among us. Reyes and D'Mon and La Mouse and Mary and Robo are quickly striking the stage. The *ruido* is over. It is now time for the rumble, but no one around me appears eager to stand around and watch it find its finish.

Old women and small children begin peering out from windows and doorways. We are trapped in the back of the court. Our only way out would be back through an alley and down into a grassy ditch, across the reservoir's dam, to Alfredo and Mary's house on the other side. We begin walking along, carrying instruments and empty beer bottles.

"Where is Rebeko?"

Rebeko had been plenty drunk and is now somehow in the middle of the rumble. Mary goes in after him. "Be careful, Mom!" her little son shouts.

"This is where we walk fast," Robo says.

Mary pulls Rebeko from the rumble and they quickly catch up with us. Everyone in the circle briefly chides Rebeko for straggling.

Reyes leads the way. A neighborhood guy in a white tank top stumbles along behind us, following our crew absently. He is intoxicated to his maximum, unable to keep his balance. We hike down the wet, grassy ditch. The guy following us is sliding and falling on the wet rocks.

"He's gonna fall into the water," Mary's little boy says.

"Let him," someone calls ahead of me.

"Let him die," Robo chuckles. "We'll read about it in the morning."

It is nearly nighttime now. The dying reservoir—the Presa Mixcoac—is filled about a quarter of the way up with still water that smells like putrid filth, and I have only a moment to ponder the state of the water supply in Mexico City, the dehydrated metropolis. We cross the lonely dam's bridge and are now safely on the other side of the *presa*. The rumble in the distance is turning into a riot. Police sirens echo in the canyons. Mary's little boy keeps a frightened watch up the alleys that peel off the desolate road before us. Across the canyon, we hear a few piercing rounds of gunfire. We march more urgently. Up a few more slanting blocks, into a metal doorway, up a flight of crooked stone steps into the darkness, and into the house.

Outside, the muffled sounds of sirens and gunfire filter inward. Safe now, Reyes and his crew and the children are chatting and decompressing. Someone passes around another fresh *caguama*. We would wait for the commotion to die down, for the rumble to end. We'd hail a cab, get on a bus, and make it back to Tacubaya. In the meantime, Reyes throws in a student-made video about D'Mon's life as an original Santa Fe punk. La Mouse turns down the lights. I am past my own point of total exhaustion. Exhaustion of the body and mind. We watch the thirty-minute video from beginning to end: footage of D'Mon talking, remembering, rocking out, staring absently into the leaning camera, a forlorn voice-over. I sit at the dining table, behind the living room couch where Reyes and Rebeko and D'Mon sit. Overcome by nostalgia and other emotions only he could name, D'Mon curls over in the dark. It sounds like he's crying. I see his silhouette in the glow of the television. Reyes takes his friend in his arms and cradles him, holding him tight.

12 | Attack of the Sweat Lodge

Ciudad Nezahualcóyotl. (Photo by the author.)

P resently in Mexico and the world, interest has resurfaced in the ancient bath of sweat still called the Temazcal," the informational booklet declares. The booklet, just a few photocopied pages on plain white letter paper, is awkwardly written. A relative of my roommate drops it off one day back in Tacubaya. She writes *Daniel* in neat cursive on the cover. I should take a look, she says one day in passing. The booklet goes on:

This pueblo considers the temazcal a national institution and with it they leave to other nations and cultures understanding the same spiritual feeling of the sauna baths in the Inapi culture or the Sweat Lodge of the native Americans, or the Japanese *furo*, the Arab *hamam* (obligatory passage for the great events in life: birth, circumcision, and marriage in the Arab communities of north Africa), the Turkish bath.

Without forgetting ancient Europe, the Roman thermals where in antiquity the high authorities gathered to make important political decisions. In our country the practice is well known in the cultures of our ancestors, the pleasure of detoxifying through perspiration, the heat, and water, combined with herbs, in a space that simulates the uterus of Mother Earth.

I am intrigued. The reclaiming of pre-Hispanic traditions is a strong phenomenon on both sides of the border. Friends in California tell me about their devotion to the temazcal bath. In the temazcal as it is practiced today, water is poured over the hot stones and the space fills with a sandy steam. You chant. You listen. You are supposed to pray to be a better person. You sweat in places you never imagined you could sweat. In the ideal scenario, you emerge a new person, metaphorically reborn. In Mexico a lot of people take pride in trying the ritual at least once in their lives, and for others, the ritual *becomes* their lives. In California or in Mexico, the rituals take place in people's backyards or out in ranchland. Back in the States, I never enquired about the possibility of going along or participating.

But here in Mexico City, amid the vestiges of the Aztecs, my curiosity grows. Ruins of Aztec pyramids are a few blocks from my house now in Centro. The pyramidal structure, or subtle signs that it once existed in abundance, dots the city's visual landscape. Fragments of ruins must be buried deep in the ground beneath me. The names of so many places within the capital—Iztacalco, Tultitlán, Iztapalapa, Aztapozalco, Chalco, Xochimilco, Naucalpan, Ecatepec—are reminders that population centers were clustered in this valley for centuries before the Spanish arrived.

Pre-Hispanic history is an omnipresent phantom in Mexico City. In spite of the Conquest, indigenous Mexico still surrounds us. Indians and mestizos and Spanish-dominant criollos still share the same sidewalks. The remaining indigenous Mexicans—nationwide, indigenous peoples number near 10 million—are an almost invisible minority in the slog of the city, but they are here: Náhuatl people, original residents of the valley and surrounding mountains; Huichol, Mazahua, and Otomí from neighboring regions; and indigenous people who have migrated from even farther away, Oaxaca, Chiapas, and the Yucatán. Some communities thrive by selling handcrafts and garments, others live in deep poverty, forced to beg on the streets. They speak among themselves in languages and dialects that are unfamiliar to the colonized ear.

The small interactions we non-Indians make in Mexico City with the indigenous are always tinged with some level of colonial guilt. I think this is why some educated, non-Indian people choose to reclaim our indigenous past in their personal lives. Five hundred years after the contact between Old World and New World, a deep ambivalence remains over the history that gave birth to mestizos today, half-European, half-Indian, sprinkled with traces of African and Asian, racially mixed, speaking in Spanish and English. We are Christians, not sun worshippers. We carry cell phones, not obsidian flints. We passively wait for the weather report to tell us if it will rain, instead of drawing the rain forth in the rite of human sacrifice.

Some mestizos don Aztec garb—or what we imagine Aztec garb must have looked like in the early 1500s—and dance in drum circles near the Zócalo. They burn sage and copal in rituals that are disconnected from their origins—the drum circles take place in the shadows of the Metropolitan Cathedral. The rest of us might dismiss the participants as misguided cultural romantics, but the disdain masks a nagging sense of a fundamental and unsolvable contradiction that exists within every non-Indian.

The divide between recovered indigenous practices and actual indigenous practices is starkly laid by the temazcal of today. The *indigenistas* of Mexico come from the universities, from leftist political groups, from the educated classes, and also from among the working poor. Some are people who have found actual spiritual satisfaction in the subculture they also call *mexicanismo*. But they all still speak Spanish, not Náhuatl. They are not indigenous people in the way we understand indigenous people to be—those who speak native Mexican languages and who generally follow the customs of those untouched by *mestizaje,* not postmodern participants from Mexico City on a weekend retreat. It is controlled indigenism in the age of Walmart and global warming. But not until I see a temazcal in action, then attempt to participate in one myself, do I realize how literal the metaphor of pain is implied in the neo-indigenist movement. The temazcal is no joke. For ardent indigenists—or, below some chuckling breaths, "those hippies"— the direct portal to equilibrium with the world of our ancestors is, apparently, paved by hurt.

One weekend in September 2008, a friend, Julio, is going to be at an indigenist retreat near the great pyramids of Teotihuacán. The so-called City of the Gods is home to the Pyramid of the Sun, the Pyramid of the Moon, the Temple of Quetzalcóatl, and the Street of the Dead. The names are misnomers—the original names for these structures are unknown. The Aztecs gave these ruins nicknames. Teotihuacán's rise and fall as a civilization took place independently of the Aztecs, its apex preceding that of the Aztec Empire by a thousand years. To the Aztecs, Teotihuacán must have been what the Templo Mayor in downtown Mexico City is to us today.

Uriel and I ride up from the city to Teotihuacán, stopping at the nearby town of San Juan Teotihuacán in search of the retreat, which is located at a botanical garden. After a short, intensely nerve-racking wrong turn into a military base, we find the site, and Julio comes out to meet us, his eyes glazed and red, we presume, since Friday.

The botanical garden is a cactus grove of about three or four acres, not very big, fitted with an abandoned greenhouse, a couple of structures with bathrooms, and a natural cave, like an alcove, where people can pitch tents. The setting is beautiful for a weekend away. The air is fresh and damp, the clouds soaring gray, everything lush, with wildly curving cacti reaching into the sky. A few kilometers away, rising in the mist, is the Pyramid of the Sun, majestic and otherworldly. The campsite is set near a clearing behind the cactus grove under a few power lines. Upon our arrival about two dozen *indigenistas* are standing in a circle performing a ritual in the clearing. Above, near the cave, two others are preparing the temazcal, the sweat lodge.

In their hemp clothing and indigenous-printed longpants, beads and necklaces, huipils and serapes, dreadlocks, and piercings and wool sweaters, this indigenist crew is suspicious of Uriel and me. We have arrived on the final day, two guys dressed in jeans and sneakers and wearing dark hoodies. One couple smiles and says hello, but most ignore us or shoot distrusting looks our way. Some seem downright mean, so enveloped in their spiritual journey they are indignant toward outsiders. Others are on drugs and in their own worlds. One guy is so high he sneakily follows behind us as we tour the camp. He is wearing a permanent smile and his eyes are almost completely closed. The *indigenistas* preparing the sweat lodge are heating rocks over a fire and hanging a blue tarp snugly over a low wooden structure, the site of the temazcal, which resembles a flattened teepee. Here, the participants in the ceremony will sit and inhale the hot fumes of *el abuelo humo*—"grandfather smoke."

Julio offers us two pairs of shorts so we can join when it is time, but my instinct tells me right away to politely decline. I am an "urban rat," as the writer Guillermo Fadanelli says, mutated by generations of industrialization and the human-bending forces of modern technology, dislocated. Crawling into a temazcal after a week of frenzied Centro-Roma-Condesa antics and too much red meat seems neither wise nor appealing. Uriel nods vigorously in agreement. I don't think I am ready for a temazcal right now, not physically or mentally in the right place. I wonder if I will ever be. But I am still curious.

"How long will it last?" I ask Julio.

"Man," he says, taking a breath, gently clutching my shoulder, "you can't program yourself. Here it's about *feeling*."

We decide to watch from outside. One by one the *indigenistas* remove most of their clothing and are "cleansed" with burning sage by a guy who takes on the role of spiritual leader. As people enter the temazcal, they kneel and take their head to the earth before the portal into the hut, a form of asking "permission" to enter the sweat lodge. After about fifteen people are inside, the two men who had been preparing the temazcal begin shoveling scorching hot stones into the middle of the lodge.

"Ahí va la medicina!" they holler. "Here comes the medicine!"

The people inside respond with a unified holler sounding like *"Aleh!"*—an unspecific expression of excitement but also possibly some kind of indigenous expression. Who knows? As more people enter, more stones are shoveled in. This pre-ritual lasts for a while. Julio and his girlfriend go in. The superhigh guy goes in. A beautiful girl with freckles goes in and then after a few minutes comes back out, admitting that she will be unable to handle the steam once it really gets started. An old woman with glasses who seems to be passing by asks if she may do the temazcal as well, but is gently rebuffed. "Are you sure, *señora?*" the indigenists outside warn her. "The heat is very intense."

We wait for the last person to crouch into the lodge and the last hot stone to be pitched inside. Many, many people have gone in, maybe thirty, maybe more. The lodge is only about four feet high at its highest point. Where do they all fit? Uriel explains that they would be sitting in rows concentric to the pit dug into the ground in the middle, which would be laced with fragrant herbs. The one time he did a temazcal, Uriel says, he got to sit in the first row, that is, against the wall, so he was able to find a cooler temperature against the temazcal tarp when "the panic" hit him. The panic. People often break into a panic inside the temazcal. Some "ruin" them by insisting on leaving, breaking the ritual and the continuity of the steam for everyone else. There are urban legends galore about "the panic." At dinner one night in Mexico City, an art historian tells me that he knows of someone who died after a temazcal, the man's system unable to handle the stress of extreme heat and steam. How can you concentrate on cleansing yourself of general toxicity inside a temazcal if you are hyperventilating and gasping for air?

The people sitting inside are chanting already—*"They think we're crazy for doing the temazcal! They think we're crazy for doing the temazcal!"*—as if it were a pregame rally for a soccer match.

The tarp is flapped shut. The temazcal now begins. We hear water being poured into the pit inside, followed by an erupting sizzling noise. There are bursts of cheers and chants coming muffled through the skin of the sweat lodge. We watch and listen. Some seconds or so later the front and back flaps are opened to allow a bit of steam to escape. Outside the tent, a guy with a long ponytail stands nearby with an old orange pit bull named Xóchitl. He is watching. I try to snap a couple of photographs of the sweat lodge, but the guy signals at me from afar, *No pictures*, and with his hands asks me to delete the images. I do so right away. The sacred function of the temazcal cannot be compromised by digital photography.

The heat inside the sweat lodge seems to prevent human sounds from escaping. From outside we hear muffled chanting, whispering, people shifting around. A half hour or so later, the people inside the temazcal emerge shivering in the outdoor cold. They give each other deep hugs. They are now bonded by the temazcal, so they are emotional. We leave. Julio is aglow with joy and good vibes as he leads us out. I try to discern in what way this temazcal might have changed him, but Julio does them so regularly, it would be impossible to tell for a first-time observer. To me the people who come out of this temazcal don't seem any different from before they went in. They still have mud on their clothes.

188

———————

Months later, I am back at El Chopo, with friends from Ciudad Nezahualcóyotl who are in a band. After they play at the back of the market, they invite me back to their area. We pile into their van, a beat-up Volkswagen, white, busted, and clearly made for fun. My friend Adonai; César, also known as Pato; Oscar, also known as El Afro; and Oscar's brother, who is also named César but is mostly known as El Chiva or El Venado. Nicknames are a measure of your worth among friends in Mexico City. The more, the better. It is February now. On the ride to Neza, the biggest suburb bordering the D.F., El Chiva, a little more neo-indigenist than his brother, is telling me about the temazcal. Turns out they have plans to do one tonight. It is a full moon.

"I've always wanted to try out a temazcal," I say, almost to myself. "But I've been waiting for one to come to me."

"Well, today is your day," El Chiva says, smiling.

We are heading to an afternoon party at Adonai's house. His parents were putting together a big *pozole* lunch for his birthday. I love going to Neza. I can see why people who live there or were raised there are proud, despite the suburb's reputation. Neza grew in the 1970s and '80s out of the arid plains of the former Lago de Texcoco, unplanned, organically, and by most accounts, painfully. Immigrants who migrated into the Valley of Mexico from outlying states—Guerrero, Oaxaca, Veracruz, Hidalgo—settled in what would become Ciudad Nezahualcóyotl, named after the Texcoco prince-poet whose florid Náhuatl verses to this day adorn the walls of government buildings and cultural centers all over Mexico City. For many years the area was polluted, violent, and overrun by garbage and poor planning. Today, they call it Neza York because so

189

many of its seminative residents relocated to the New York metropolitan region in the late 1990s and early 2000s. To live in New York as an immigrant from Mexico City is to live in Neza York, and to live in Ciudad Nezahualcóyotl as a returning migrant from New York is to live in Neza York as well. At the same time, in a strange cross-continental kind of cultural exchange, a prominent youth look in Neza is the California cholo—shaved heads, crisply pressed Dickies slacks, white T's, etc.

Neza has come into its own. It may not be the most attractive residential landscape in the country, but to me it feels relatively quiet, peaceful, middle-class, and traditional, in that tough barrio sense. By now, it would be one of the biggest cities in Mexico were it not a part of the vast urban swamp of the greater megalopolis. Not much public transit is in Neza besides a metro line that runs along its southern edge, so the culture of the automobile is strong, much like the lifestyle of Southern California. It is a flat grid of roaring, busy avenues and narrow residential side streets. Households are built up in a characteristically postslum improvisational style, a second or third floor added on, a carport, a workshop or shed, new household appendages built on as families improve their economic standing. The homes I've seen tend to have at least a couple of cars in the front yard, a garden, rooftop laundry rooms, large TV sets and stereo systems in the living room, altars to the Virgen de Guadalupe, and pets. In Neza, because it sits on a recent former lake bed, the wind blows stronger than it does in the metropolitan center. It smells worse, too.

Maybe because of its namesake, its history, or maybe something else entirely, Neza has a palpable creative energy. Some of the city's best graffiti artists, rappers, and rockers are from here. A strong sense of a social body and pride in community are in Neza, which remind me of the barrio sensibility in some cities in California. It is an activist bent, a quality to the people and their values that reflects an awareness of a greater cause and a greater community. It makes me feel at home.

Once we get to Adonai's house, I count six cars in the lot, including a truck and a Mustang. Another vehicle is on the way. Adonai and Oscar just put money down for a minivan to use as a *combi*. This is not unusual. In Neza, people often have three or four cars per household. Adonai's home is cozier than most of the ones I've visited in Mexico City. On an outer wall facing the street, the house is decorated with a Southern California–style cholo mural: Emiliano Zapata, an Aztec pyramid, a lowrider car, the words LOS VAGOS—the Wanderers—in old-school cholo block letters. A neighborhood kid who had spent time in California asked if he could use their home's wall to make it, Adonai's dad tells me.

"So he brought that style with him," I say. "That cholo style." They all say yes. *Car culture is cholo culture is Neza culture*, I think to myself. The loop is Los Angeles, New York, and this postslum city named after a prince-poet.

After having *pozole* for Adonai's birthday, and napping a little in his house's middle-floor TV area, watching some of the movie *AI*, it is time to head to the temazcal. It is Adonai, Oscar, and me. We pull away in the white van and gear up for the trip. I look around Neza as we drive, up the long lonely streets, to the facades of the buildings around us, at the carcasses of broken-down vehicles on every block, up at the glowing white moon. Inspired, I send a text message to Ponce: "It's real *Blade Runner*, broke-down postmodernism out here."

Ponce, by now my expert source on Mexican cosmic muta-

191

tion, promptly responds, "The apocalypse is not a metaphor, it is a place full of beauty and we have been there for years. The media mislead us."

Our destination is Ixtapaluca, a faraway suburb also in the state of México that is practically in the neighboring state over, Puebla. I sit in the van's rear with my back to Oscar in the driving seat, watching Neza go by. The busy roads feel alive at night. There are booming nightclubs and places to drink, joints with the rainbow flag hanging out front, churches and funeral homes. The guys are talking and talking, while I drift in and out of sleep. After some time we are out of Neza and nearer to a place that seems even more like *Blade Runner* than Neza does. The roads are busted open and desolate. Dust and dirt mess with our visibility through the headlights.

"Why do we do the temazcal?" I ask Adonai.

"For each person it is different," he says. "I use it to cleanse myself, to cleanse my energy. I think about what I want, about how I want to grow."

We stop at a concrete asphalt barrier and a metal gate that creaks open at the sound of our idling engine. The van lurches into the driveway and into a large, flat yard. There is a fire pit and a tall, dusty tree. It is nearing midnight and the temazcal is about to start. The people mingle. El Chiva has been here since the afternoon preparing the sweat lodge. Most people around me are wearing red bandannas over their foreheads, like crowns. The women have their hair up in wraps, and the men are almost naked in the cold. We arrive out of the blue, so our energy, I feel, is not in sync with the group's. Someone blows into a conch horn.

"They're calling for the temazcal to start," a girl standing nearby says gently to me.

Oscar, Adonai, and I quickly undress in the van and put on swimming trunks. I am so delirious and tired from the long day of travel from Chopo to Neza, and from the afternoon birthday meal, that I just go right along. People are entering the tarp-covered hut, one by one, asking for permission as I had seen them do at the temazcal at the cactus grove near the pyramids. I am dressed, meaning wearing almost nothing, standing in line with those waiting to enter. El Chiva is holding open the portal into the "uterus" of the sweat lodge. He looks at me and asks me to enter. I crouch and crawl inside the small opening in the tarp. The temazcal is like a hut, made on the spot by the people who will participate in it. This one is round like a tepee and made of thick branches tied together to make the shell, then covered in industrial blue tarps. The idea is that the steam not leave the temazcal when it is closed, and that it be pitch-dark.

Adonai follows me in, and luckily we get a spot on the outer ring—up against the cool texture of the tarp. "If you begin to feel the panic," Adonai whispers to me, "crouch down, put your face against the mud, and breathe slow."

We sit on the cold scratchy earth and wait for the temazcal to fill up with the others. You have to enter to the right and you must exit through the left, in the form of the circle. Why? Something about the temazcal being ruined if you enter or exit the wrong way, about the flow of the energies inside being disrupted. People follow in behind Adonai, Oscar, other people. The man who goes in first, the temazcal leader, sits before a single white candle. He begins talking in sage tones about the world around us, our history, our people. "This is a falsehood, this is a lie," he says. It is not clear what he is referring to. The hut fills up to a second and third inner circle of people, those who will sit directly in front of the pit into which the hot rocks will be placed.

We are now all staring at each other by the light of the candle. Children are huddled among us, their eyes wide. This is when I realize I have made a grave mistake. I am already inside the already-stuffy, getting-stuffier hut, listening to this strange man whom I don't know expand on vague mystical topics, and I have not asked myself what the hell I am doing here exactly.

I knew I wanted to try a temazcal, and when I ran into my crew of Neza friends at El Chopo it seemed right at that moment, as if it were meant to happen. But now I am not so sure. I don't know who this man is, the leader of the ritual, and it doesn't seem to me that I should fully trust anything he says. In fact, as he proceeds to tell us some of his wisdom, epigrams, and general thoughts about the ways of the universe, I quickly and perhaps a bit irrationally decide that most of what he is saying is bullshit.

I try to think about friends who see the temazcal as a major element of their spiritual life, people I know who participate in them from Tijuana to Oakland and beyond. I think about Adonai and Oscar and El Chiva, about the affection and trust I feel for them. The temazcal helps them in some way, and I must respect that. I try opening my heart, mind, and body to the ritual. I try, I really do. As they bring the hot rocks on a pitchfork and place them in the temazcal pit, I begin thinking that everyone in here is crazy and I am crazy for having agreed to come in. The rocks look alive, crackling with heat. They had been in the fire all day. I observe tiny dots of burning upon them, microscopic pimples of fire.

"The other day I was passing through a *tianguis*," the leader is saying. He has put out the candle. We are in pitch-darkness. "How wonderful is it that the *tianguis* still exists, on the street, as our *abuelos* had. A man was beating a rhythm on a bottle like the rhythms of our ancestors. It is amazing how many people in the *tianguises* of today make the rhythms of our dead without realizing it."

His incantation sounds like a theatrical climax. "This is for our dead!"—and he splashes water upon the burning rocks. Instantly, my nose and throat burn sore and spicy. My skin feels as if it were catching on fire. I wince out loud, gasping for oxygen. I pinch my eyes as tight as I can to prevent what I feel could be the burning of my cornea.

"Breathe, breathe," Adonai whispers.

It doesn't take long—I feel "the panic." I try to communicate to Adonai with my skin and movements that I will be crouching downward, to bury my face into the dirt. The temazcal leader is saying something but I decide I will just tune him out. Minutes pass. I am now angry at myself. I am not prepared to do this. There is a break. The flaps open. The first round of the ritual has been completed, our first baptism by fire and steam. Light enters the hut from outside, and I see everyone around me is drenched in his or her sweat. The leader has us all introduce ourselves. Everyone is shiny and breathing hard. A peace pipe is being passed from hand to hand, which is strange to me—isn't that a North American Plains Indians tradition? Why are we all wearing red headbands anyway?

"Keep quiet," the leader warns sternly. He is glaring at others who are quietly chatting in the circles, but I feel his scolding is intended for my brain activity. Car alarms are going off just over the yard's walls. The light coming inside the hut is from the sign for an enormous big-box store down the road. *This is not pure,* I think, *because we are no longer pure. This doesn't make sense,* I think again. *I am my own religion. I am my own belief system.*

The leader of the temazcal then calls for our attention and tells everyone gathered, glistening with moisture, shivering now that the flaps are open, that if anyone wishes to leave the temazcal, now is the opportunity to do so. I ponder my options for roughly two seconds. I nudge Adonai and tell him I will see him outside. Adonai nods, without judgment. I stumble out. Thanking the temazcal with my thoughts, I excuse myself and exit to the left.

I clearly didn't learn enough about the temazcal before trying it out, even with a special information booklet squeezed into my stacks of reading material. But then, I find, neither do most other people who enter the sweat lodge for the first time. At the temazcal in Ixtapaluca, I am followed out early by a voluptuous young lady from the nice suburbs in the northwest. We chat in the yard while she reapplies her makeup and sparkly designer eyeglasses. She had gone into the sweat lodge, couldn't handle the heat, and also decided to go out. She didn't seem too tortured by her choice. For her, trying out the temazcal is like trying a dress on in a department-store changing room.

The temazcal just isn't for me. I find urban indigenous practices of today more interesting than those from yesterday. Conquest bred mixture, and mixture implies leaving some ingredients out and adding in new ones, a constant cycle of evolution, a constant stirring. The Indian citizens of Mexico City have created new sets of rituals in five hundreds years in the apocalyptic city. They buy Coca-Cola and cups of Maruchan soup in convenience stores like the rest of us. They ride the metro, which since its inception has been mapped with icons rather than words, so that navigating the system would be possible for non-Spanish-speakers. They sell things on the street like so many others of us. Some of them vote.

The younger generations of urban indigenous gather on Sundays—for many their only day of rest from construction or domestic work—and mingle at the Alameda Central, transforming it every weekend into a festival of modern urban Indianness: music, food, dancing, flirting.

Claiming the Alameda Central as their social space is a significant social coup for these young people, who merge the fashion codes of cholo, ska, and punk. In the viceregal period, Indians were not allowed inside the park. It was strictly the territory of the criollo and his attendant mestizos. In the twenty-first century the Alameda Central is Indian land.

You see them laughing, walking together in pairs, attempting to woo a new romantic interest, boys and girls, young and old, wearing jeans and sneakers and chain necklaces. A young Indian couple—looking like any other Mexico City youth—argue fervently on a corner in a language I cannot understand or identify. A young Indian girl, in supertight jeans, in modern makeup, is gabbing energetically on a public pay phone. The coos, snaps, and scoops of her indigenous words are single-handedly lifting the echoes of Mexico's past to right here, on this street, on a gray corner facing a glowing Oxxo convenience store. She might never have been in a temazcal, but to me she is the true Mexico City indigenist. The mutant metropolis is her inheritance.

13 | Death by Decadence

Potential perdition in Plaza Garibaldi. (Photo by the author.)

O ne of the oldest eateries in Centro," Susana says, pointing to a hole-in-the-wall. It is literally that, a large hole in a white-washed wall on Callejón 57. There is no sign or signal of commerce other than the throng of people who are lunching in the shadows on quesadillas.

"What's it called?" I ask.

"It doesn't have a name. Everyone just knows it as the Quesa-dillas del 57." It opened in the 1930s, Susana says. "But now, who knows how long it will last."

13 | Death by Decadence

There is no time to take a picture of the Quesadillas del 57 or take in its smells. We are on a mission. From the moment Susana and I meet, on the steps of the Torre Latinoamericana, Mexico's first skyscraper, she has a plan. She is determined to show me the corners of the Centro Histórico that she knows and loves. The "real" Centro, she says, the Centro under threat of extinction as the D.F. government implements gradual plans to spruce up the area—a process accelerating with the generous support of a foundation belonging to Carlos Slim, the Mexican magnate and world's richest man. In recent years sidewalks have been cleared of unlicensed vendors, streets have been recobbled, and historic buildings have been refurbished. Police roll around slowly at night in their cruisers, siren lights permanently flashing. Back when I first came to Mexico City, Centro was not like this. The streets were crowded with vendors to the point of making pedestrian and vehicular traffic almost impossible. That summer, almost a decade ago, Mexico City was just entering the early stages of its contemporary sparkle. There were no boutique hotels, no tourist-information booths near major landmarks, no hipster party photoblogs, no Turibus route coursing past the major landmarks. Much of Centro was in decay, with many buildings abandoned or still in ghostly ruins since the 1985 earthquake. Few people of means had dared to venture there since the earthquake and the economic crises of the 1990s. Except the young creatives and misfits of the capital, people like Susana Iglesias.

Leading me up Eje Central, Susana is serious about the task at hand. She has merlot-colored hair and wears green-colored contacts and a black Misfits T-shirt. She carries a bag covered in a black-and-white skull print. Her wide smile communicates pure mischief, the smile of someone who has an eternal hunger for more—and for more after that. As we walk, an abandoned theater with a vertical marquee sign that reads TEATRO FRU FRU catches my eye. "That place won't be there for very long," Susana says. "All of this. All of this won't be here for very long."

Susana lives in the rough-edged north of the city, near metro Consulado. Her nickname is Miss Masturbation after the title of the blog she kept in the early 2000s. It was a period of a great explosion in blogging in Mexico, an exciting time. "I was searching the word *vodka* and I found a blog, Blogger. *¿Qué es esto?*" Susana recalls. "I started looking at blogs in English, in French." She started her own blog, Señorita Masturbación, at some point in 2002. She posted vigorously for a while, about Centro, about her life, about her ideas. But after some time, like so many other bloggers in Mexico City and all over the world in that period, Susana's interest in Web self-publishing withered away. The site died. Then revived. Then died again. In an intriguing mid-twenties transition, Susana has decided to dedicate herself to rescuing stray dogs and to writing fiction. Both pursuits have given her considerable success ever since.

She identifies herself as a former punk, but more than anything else, she is a creature of the night, a *devota* of decadence. We have lunch in a cantina because in cantinas the food is free as long as you're drinking, and at any cantina where Susana goes downtown, she knows the regulars, a few of the waiters, or usually both. Some hearty mushy soup and three beers later, we are back on the streets. Every corner has a story, every mangy dog offers a memory. Susana leads me to Plaza Garibaldi, the traditional meeting point for the city's roving mariachi musicians. It is in active transformation. Near the back, the plaza floor is busted open, workers buzzing about, concrete dust rising in the brisk afternoon breeze, as they replace the floor with new stones.

Around a corner, in a smaller plaza with a dead fountain, the Torre Latinoamericana regal and gray in the distance, we come to a ghostly building of three floors, abandoned. "This is the Acid House," Susana says. The young vagabonds of the Centro used to gather here to do acid and crack and inhale *mona* all day. The cops always knew it was there, Susana explains. Some would even get in on the action. It looks completely abandoned, even for a squat. "They're going to do something new here now," Susana says. "What could it be? A hotel? A housing development?"

Walking more, Susana tells me stories about the Centro's ghosts and about the junkies she knew who are now dead. On one corner, she stops, breathes in and out, smog be damned. "I love living here," she says. "I'd get bored in *provincia*."

From that day on, we start hanging out. A lot.

I never once question why I am here, Friday after Friday, at a new cantina in Centro with Susana. Week after week we stumble into bars we should probably not be found in, in Tepito, the Colonia Guerrero, and in and around the Garibaldi area. I rarely ever turn down her invitations to get together. Somewhere along the way, I guess, in Mexico or in California, I had decided that this kind of ritual isn't just my right, it is my duty. The world stinks, the thinking goes. Go out, rub up against some trouble, and drink until it's not there anymore.

In Susana I find a partner in leisurely nihilism who sees things just the way I do. And eventually, as always tends to happen when athlete drinkers find themselves, Susana and I find an untouched watering hole and make it our own.

The bar is tucked in an alley off a forgotten plaza near Garibaldi. The square is fitted with a fountain and a crumbling structure that appears as though it once functioned as a small chapel, veering wildly into the soft earth. The little building looks both dead and drunk, unused, and at least two hundred years old. Around the corner, next to a permanent mound of fresh garbage and behind a metal grate, with no sign and no fixed name, sits our spot.

It is just one room big and the bathroom is revolting. Nothing decorates the walls but a sticky film best left uninvestigated. Roaches the size of small rodents sometimes amble across the tile floor, giving me the frightening impression that they have large and complex brains. Old prostitutes, gangly old gay men, transvestites or transgendered ladies with saggy chins, gangsters, women with only a few precious bits of teeth hanging from their gums, dealers—it's their spot, too. We get to know the "owners" and become quite acquainted with the running melodramas of the place. It is never certain when we will end up here, never planned. Sometimes Susana calls or texts me late in the night, informing me she is in the area and headed to the bar. I'm at home writing, trying to, stuck on a sentence or a complex thought. Resistance is futile.

Inside the bar, on any given night, customers drink and dance to the *cumbias* and Mexican pop standards blasting on the juke. Midnight turns into 2:00 a.m., and 2:00 a.m. then turns into 3:00, then 4:00, then time dissolves into a slimy toxic pulp. One night we meet an older black woman from the state of Guerrero who can balance a full *caguama* on her head while dancing, gyrating her hips to the African beat that thumps behind every true *cumbia* jam. She writes down her name and address on a small scrap of paper for me, insisting I come visit her, and possibly marry her, so that she can move to the United States. Her breath is spicy and metallic, like sea salt. On another night we meet a young Mexican air force officer with a cropped haircut and plenty of military-related tattoos to show off. Rascally and belligerent, the officer seems to be spending all of his bimonthly salary on beer and dances. He wants to go home with one of us, either of us—it probably doesn't matter who.

13 | Death by Decadence

Every night at our nameless ditch, the last bar on the last crawl, Susana and I have our beers and our dances and our new flirtations. I turn to Susana, who is busy passionately kissing a guy in a tank top and baggy jeans. She orders another beer. We sit around and ask ourselves, *What's next? What's next?* Nothing is next, it turns out. Nothing but the ritual pour.

"How much do you think this cell phone is worth?" the cabdriver asks Uriel and me, passing the device over his shoulder. Uriel examines it. The cabbie, a young guy with glasses, tells us that he just had sex with a fare, a woman who presented him with the cell phone in exchange for five hundred pesos. Uriel says it was an okay exchange, that the cell phone is probably worth a thousand pesos or more.

"Yeah, I just fucked her," the cabbie says. "Took her to a hotel."

He tells us the story as casually as can be. When he picks up the fare, she is "all hot and bothered" and gets into the front seat by his side. She tells him she wants to have sex with him. So the cabbie takes her to a hotel. She was all "torn up," the cabbie says, and incoherent. He says he knew she was a *"prosti,"* so he used a condom. Then he takes her to meet some "scary dudes" in Zona Rosa, at a club. They were probably her pimps. The cabbie says that in all his years as a cabdriver, sex with a fare has happened to him only a few times. Most times, he says, it's the *jotos*—the fags—who try to pick up their drivers.

The cabbie, a young guy, shows us a picture of the girl. She left an image of herself on the screen of the bartered phone. She looks pretty tragic: dyed-red hair, a dramatic pose. *Poor girl,* I think. So bored and lost in her life, she is a prostitute and gets wasted and screws cabdrivers for fun. The Mexico City night is fast and lonely.

People get drunk, do lots of drugs, lots of pills, lots of cocaine, screw around, and screw each other over. The excesses of decadence and self-destruction as they are practiced in Mexico get to me sometimes. The stories I hear. The overdoses, the sexually transmitted diseases, the senseless deaths. Happening all over the place, upstairs, next door, right around the corner.

I can try to rationalize it. In Mexico City the everyday existential urban threats are mediated by partying—hard, extravagantly, with drama and often violence. In this atmosphere, self-destruction itself becomes a threat. Or a goal. It's the idea that if you don't do yourself in first, eventually the city will. Why relinquish control over your demise? This attitude dominated among upper-middle-class globally minded youth of Mexico City in the 1990s and early 2000s. Not yet on the world's cultural map, the city's young artists, designers, writers, pushed the limits of sobriety and safety in the overall cultural darkness of the period. Many wound up in rehab. Some went sober. Some moved away from the city to avoid the parade of temptations. Some did not survive.

After the cabbie leaves us at Cuba Street and Eje Central, back in the Centro, I show Uriel the little dive Susana and I frequent. We walk in and greet the owners and the usual mix of hoodlums, dirty old men, hookers in their fifties, and kids sniffing paint solvent.

A stumbling old woman comes up to us and says, "My respects to you both." A *cumbia* comes on and she asks me to dance. I tower over the old lady but I feel good, happy to be dancing, step-back-step, step-back-step. I love her jacked-up teeth and her green coat with puffy shoulders, and her little grandma shoes. Her name is Chavela. She starts telling us how hard it is to get approved for a conjugal visit in the Mexico City jail system. She has to bring her marriage certificate and all kinds of other papers. "Just so you can go in and fuck your husband!" Chavela says her husband is held in the Reclusorio del Norte and her son is in the Reclusorio del Oriente.

"So your husband is in jail in one place and your son is in jail in the other?"

"Yes." Chavela starts to cry. She put her hands over her face and cries.

"*Ánimo,*" Uriel tells her. "Be strong. You will see them."

From across the room another older lady with premature teeth loss hollers, "Oh, no, Chavela is crying again." She seems indifferent to Chavela's pain. "A lot of us have that problem."

My friend Quetzal, the young fashion designer, dies on a Friday the following September. He is just twenty-three years old. We are not sure what happened. I am home alone, taking a nap. I get a phone call from a friend.

"Quetzal is dead," Gabriela tells me over the line. "We're looking for his parents' phone number."

He is discovered in the narrow inner well of his building, crumpled against the ground from a four-story fall. At the time of his death, Quetzal had been drinking for three days, since that Wednesday. A magazine party. That afternoon is the last time I see him. I am walking down Veracruz Street in Condesa and pass Marvin's building. Quetzal's familiar voice yells his usual hello for me from a waiting cab.

"Hey, *BIOTCH!*"

We haven't seen each other in weeks. We chat happily and say we should finally get together again. He is waiting for Marvin to come down, and when he does and they drive off, they seem happy.

That day, Quetzal wears dark sunglasses and seems out of it, maybe hungover. This is not unusual for him. Quetzal's binges are now becoming legendary. He'd drink all day and all night, for several days straight. He'd wind up in dangerous places, disoriented, alone, sometimes without money and sometimes without any of his clothes. His friends know well that Quetzal would take on a wild and obscene persona under the influence of alcohol or drugs, and when this happened, it meant Quetzal the fashion designer and charming friend would lose three or four days of his normal self to the blur of the bottle.

Some of us believed that Quetzal would eventually grow out of it, find a way. Quetzal, with all his talents, at his tender age, would go to rehab and retreats to attempt to curb his problem. He'd show signs of improvement, then return to the same cycle. Friends tried to remain tolerant and helpful, but many of us, over time, shut him out. Although I had known Quetzal for less than a year, I too found his problem too much handle. I tell him so one day, chatting online. He apologized and promised to do better.

It is sad. Quetzal was talented, committed to his visions and to his loves. But he also carried a demon, which so many countless numbers of people all over the city carry. It proves to be a demon he could not overcome.

Quetzal's death confused many of us. It seems beyond surreal or unfair. It is a nightmare. In a community that values fashion, exclusivity, and money; in a world defined by competition, superficiality, and decadence, the death of an up-and-coming fashion designer in a megacity didn't make everyone stop in their tracks. Even in his stomping grounds, the chic parties, the Mexico City fashion scene, life was essentially unchanged after Quetzal's sudden death. It all happened so fast. His passing was too close for comfort, too violent, too dark.

But I know a lot of us were deeply affected by the loss of Quetzal. His death put in stark terms the dangers we all bring upon ourselves to some degree in the big, bad city. His death—I'd like to hope—forced many of those of us who knew him to question how far we take those risks that Quetzal took to the extreme, the dance with decadence, the dance with death.

I think about him often. I feel for his family. To me, the spirit of the feathered serpent is still strong. Sometimes he comes to friends in a passing thought on a street we had walked together, dancing somewhere, or in a dream. I think about what we could have done to help him. I think about what he'd be wearing these days.

El Internet is shut down right now, *clausurado,* by the authorities. I walk past it and remember the night there that ended poorly, and other nights that did not. I think about all the risks we take in the pursuit of fun in a violent world, and all the other strangers in Mexico City who commit death by decadence, and those who dance around it for years and years, somehow surviving. *Could I be next? What are the chances?*

A call at 3:00 a.m. I am in my study, writing. It's almost Christmas.

"Are you asleep or awake?" It is Susana.

"Well, awake." I am on deadline for a story.

"Can we come over?"

There had been a party, near the south. Susana is heading back to Centro, with a crew of friends and a few *caguamas.* "Can we come over?"

I look at my screen. I look out at the street.

"Well . . . yes."

Part IV | MUTATIONS

14 | At Home

A barrio warrior's essential armor. (Photo by Federico Gama.)

With great reluctance one cool winter morning, not long after moving here, I finally march to the U.S. embassy to renew my American passport. It feels like a defeat even before I get there. Having to renew a passport means reminding myself of the rigidity of national borders and national pretensions, and this is especially true when it comes to border attitudes in the United States. Starting in early 2008, a U.S. passport is required of citizens wishing to reenter their country. My American passport was set to expire. All the warnings from the State Department suggest that if I dare return to America—and *dare* I think is the correct word to use here—I had better be prepared to prove I belong. Visual indicators automatically work against me. In most situations related to U.S. security or sovereignty, my Arab-Andalusian Mexican features ensure I am regarded with extra scrutiny. I am brown, male, of working age, and often confused, ambivalently, as an "alien."

I wake up earlier than usual this morning and dress in the most serious-looking outfit I can muster, careful to make sure it doesn't look too "official" or forced. Dark jeans, a tucked in, buttoned-up shirt, a modest jacket, and glasses. I disembark from metro Insurgentes and walk briskly north through the Zona Rosa, cross Paseo de la Reforma, and arrive at a scene straight out of the frightening panoramas of the film *Children of Men.* Military-style barricades and fencing surround the stout marble embassy. Every few meters along the perimeter, imposing Mexican guards stand wearing cocked berets, navy trousers tucked into laced-up combat boots, and heavy fatigue vests. They hold firearms and I imagine them ready to shoot anything even hinting to be a potential threat.

The whole complex is fortified to withstand the kind of attack that happens mostly in movies—spectacular explosions, apocalyptic endgames—but also in small-scale Mexican real-life. Angry, sometimes violent protests are common at the U.S. embassy in Mexico City. Here fed-up Mexican kids always up for a decently rowdy demonstration come to fling their contempt at the policies of empire they see as inflicting harm upon the society, or perpetuating the sad polarity of Mexican subjugation to American dominance. And here, as in many U.S. bodies in foreign lands, you can witness the full force of official American paranoia, loathing and nasty.

I approach from the sidewalk, gulping unconsciously. "I have to renew my passport," I say in polite Spanish to the first guard I see.

212

"Over there," he grunts. "There, at the corner."

I wait at the corner, looking at others like me. They shuffle nervously through their papers and manila folders. The airborne virus of official paranoia is affecting my sense of reasoning. I don't have anything on me but a book, my passport, and my driver's license. *Did I forget something?* I shift through the book pages, pretending to have important business on my mind. When I am f to the gate, I feel a cold sweat coming on.

"Passports," the guard at the gate says, in Spanish. "Go ahead."

Just inside, another guard meets me, asking, "Cell phone? Electronic devices?"

"Yes, yes," I mumble. He opens a small, worn plastic bag and indicates I have to put all my little gadgets inside. "Open your bag for me, please." I do. "The front pocket." I do. The guard grunts me forward, to have my backpack X-rayed, and to wait to file through a metal detector.

At the other end of the steps, on the other side of a railing, I watch as three tart young American diplomats, women in skirts and stockings and heels, skip into the building with their State Department badges, chirping away in American English. They look alien to me, to the place, to the bizarreness of the scenario. At the third guard, after the metal detector, I am led into another kind of outdoor holding pen, this time with two sections of plastic chairs, set in six rows, watched over by another guard, an American. He directs me to the back row of chairs on the left and without a word motions to the man sitting beside me to move over and make room.

Now we are entering a twilight zone. It is suddenly chilly and brisk, in the shade. The deadline for certain forms of business at the embassy, 10:30 a.m., has passed. Every few minutes the front row is allowed to go to the supergate, a window that looks bomb-proof, where some kind of attendant studies your face and forms and gives you a visitor pass to enter the embassy building. Every time the front row goes in, the row directly behind it has to get up and move one row forward, a cruel game of musical chairs.

The inspections so far have been conducted in Spanish, by Mexicans, and most of the people seeking to enter the embassy appear to be Mexican as well. Besides the young American ladies darting inside without a stop, I haven't seen a single "all-American" type around. Except for the man sitting next to me. He is as American as you could possibly get, wearing a crisp shirt and tie, tan trousers, and brown dress shoes. His facial complexion is unnaturally red. When I sit down next to the American, we look at one other with expressions that say, *What are you in for?*

"I just need to notarize something," the American says. "Not a good time to be refinancing your house."

The American is a midlevel manager for a multinational tele-communications company. Mindful of whatever looming financial catastrophe is brewing in the United States at the moment, he says he is attempting to refinance his home in a suburb of Dallas. His mother is living there now, the American says. Casual conversation between Americans in recent years, anywhere in the world, must include the question that follows: "You looking to buy?"

"Oh, no," I tell him.

"Where are you from?"

"San Diego."

"Nice place," the American replies. "If I could pick a place to live, it'd be San Diego."

I nod. San Diego seems about three continents and four or five dimensions of sanity away. For a few seconds I fantasize about its glimmering waterfront skyline, that auburn Pacific sunset that bounces golden and lazy off the cool dark waters of the San Diego Bay, up past the rolling hills of inner San Diego, past its bungalows and palm trees, into the barrios of my childhood. I sigh and ask the American, "So what do you think about Mexico?"

"Interesting place. A lot of classism. Even in the business world."

"Oh, yeah?"

The man is pleased to have his opinion solicited on the topic. "Oh, yeah. Certain jobs here are done by certain classes." He uses himself as an example. Here he is, a manager for a big telecom company, living with his wife and kids in a company-paid mansion in Lomas Altas. If he were born Mexican, he says, this would not be his reality. In the States, his mother was a waitress and his father "worked for a railroad."

The American says, "I would have never made management. The only exception I see are women who are gorgeous and beautiful, who can date above their class."

I like this all-American American. He knows what he's talking about, and he talks about it in that Southwestern U.S. horizontal *swang* that I know how to turn on and utilize just like him. The American asks me what I do for a living, and I say, speciously, that I write about art, mostly younger artists. The American has an opinion about that, too. He's been to some art events, he says, and he and his wife had come upon some amazing "Mexican folk art" during a weekend out to Taxco, "something authentic." But overall he isn't too impressed with what he has seen by young artists in Mexico. "They're all just trying to be American or European. People here try too hard."

The American goes on, "A lot of what I see is really derivative, which doesn't make sense. They have a huge culture here to work out of. It's a very interesting place. Lots of potential. Think we'll get in there before noon?"

The embassy security apparatus appears to have passed its rush hour. No musical-chairs rows were being replaced behind us as we trudged forward. "We're going to get in right when they go to lunch," the American says fatalistically. "You should see the cafés around here. By twelve thirty, they're packed with all the Americans. And then they empty out by one thirty. And at two, they fill up again with all the Mexicans."

Our turn is coming up, causing a new anxiety to rise in my throat. When it's my turn to approach the security window, the final barrier between me and my country's bureaucrats, I have to decide, will I speak to the pretty receptionist lady in Spanish or in English? This is the *American* embassy, but I am *in* Mexico. Our row is called up. Panic sets it. The receptionist, who appears to be Mexican, calmly and politely deals with the people in line ahead of me in clean Spanish, a reassuring sign. A series of possible sentences in both languages scroll quickly through my head. I want to appear as cool and collected as possible before this first-responding emissary of the United States of America.

And under that, of course, I feel a wave of self-loathing. As Americans, have we grown accustomed to fearing our own government? Even with nothing to hide, we cower before our bureaucrats, our *own employees*. The thoughts roll through my head as I try suppressing a darker sort of fear. It is that feeling I get in the moments before I approach the United States as a pedestrian at the border between Tijuana and San Ysidro. The wild, pitted fear that just this time, out of so many hundreds throughout my life, something could go inexplicably wrong, and a pack of men in black will silently march at me and I will be disappeared forever into the monster-machine of the U.S. government.

My turn. Behind the heavy glass, the receptionist smiles at me brightly and asks what sort of business I hope to attend to at the

U.S. embassy. It is all happening so fast. I hand over my expiring passport and blurt nervously, *"Es que tengo que hacer* renew *mi pasaporte."*

It rolls down my brain and off my tongue without warning, as Spanglish as me, as California as me, perfectly incorrect on multiple levels: *Es que tengo que hacer* renew *mi pasaporte.*

The graffiti writer in Colonia del Valle has a few central interests: tagging, dogs, hip-hop, and maintaining anonymity. He is suspicious of any phone call and prefers that his name—even his tag—not be used in public. His insistence makes him a bona fide graffiti fundamentalist, those who see tagging as vandalism and vandalism as a form of anarchic resistance, those who move about the city like phantoms, leaving their markings furtively in the night.

The graffiti writer kicks back in his living room overlooking a busy lateral avenue, night after night with his homies, listening to Mexican and U.S. MCs on his two-turntable sound system, admiring the easygoing strength of his potbellied Rottweiler. A West African wooden mask hangs near the door, and in a corner a large fish tank houses two large turtles. Sometimes the graffiti writer brings the turtles out of the fish tank so they can get some exercise on the carpet. When his friends drop in and gather, they flip through magazines—about dogs, about weed, porn catalogs—and talk about music, skating, and the North. The Rottweiler lies about, inhaling a cloud of sweet marijuana smoke. The guys' girlfriends sit around the place, at ease, enjoying the company.

Andrew, one of the graffiti writer's friends, has lived in Santa Ana, in California's Orange County, working for six months. He made money at various odd jobs and at a Japanese restaurant. He also went North to skate. "The skating over there!" he exclaims.

Andrew, wearing a 2005 Dodgers opening-day T-shirt (bought at a *tianguis* in Mexico City, not in Los Angeles), said he liked it up there all right, but he didn't love it. He's glad to be back in Mexico. One time, Andrew says, he bought a pack of weed from someone on the street and a black dude in the neighborhood noticed. The guy wanted to know what Andrew was doing in his neighborhood, saying he would shoot him. Andrew says he handled the situation all right. He just took off. The graffiti writer, citing other examples in his head, brazenly declares, "Black dudes are scared of Mexican dudes. A black dude will talk and talk, and a Mexican dude will just start shooting."

I laugh nervously. The boys at the graffiti writer's house don't hear much from me on this night. Like the other nights that I am over, I mostly listen. Yet each time they include me in the conversation, they refer to me as *vato* or *loco* or *ese*, terms used among Mexican Americans or their acculturated counterparts up and down California, both North and Baja.

"No, *vato*, it's crazy over there!" . . . "*Loco*, you like Sublime, *loco*?" (At this question, I admit that I do.)

These are cholo diminutives, terms of endearment and respect in California's barrios. Obviously, I think to myself, I am not a cholo. But I am a Mexican American. My heritage is something people can almost smell on me here in Mexico City. It is a skin I cannot shed.

There's a guy I run into a lot in the Centro, for example, who says he was in the gang Florencia 13, in L.A. He used to live in Compton, specifically. He spent six years locked up, up in Chino. He lost his girl and his kids. His *jefita* lives in the state of México. He lives over here, "in la Guerrero." He lives there with his "lady." He doesn't want to "fuck it up again." Some "fools" who get deported after serving time in California, as he did, get here and just get right back into it. They start "banging" in Mexico, becoming transnationalized gangsters.

Let's call him Joe. He has a single teardrop tattoo below his right eye, signaling in some barrio symbologies that he has killed someone in his days banging. For a few months I see Joe work the entrance at a cantina where I often meet Susana. He holds the doors open for people entering and leaving, making sure no one takes off without paying. He breaks up fights when necessary. Joe doesn't want to get back into the gang culture, even south of the border, so he goes looking for work. Everywhere he goes, he tells me, he is turned away. He walks into businesses in the Centro, asking to speak with the owner or manager, and workers respond with fear upon their faces, asking, "What do you want?" Life in Mexico City is hard for Joe. People are afraid of him. Because of his shaved head and tattoos. Because he looks like a Southwestern U.S. cholo.

Talking with Joe outside the door of the cantina, the one place that does offer to hire him, I tell him I had lived in L.A., and that I know his area, Compton, Inglewood, Long Beach. "Cool, cool," Joe says. He wears a long, gray sweatshirt with a fat blue LA on his chest. I tell him I am going back inside to my table with Susana. We do *the* handshake. Two hands clap, knuckles lock, one arm grabs the opposite elbow, opposite shoulders meet in a friendly bump.

I run into guys like Joe all the time. They wear close fade haircuts and baggy jeans and LA caps and sweatshirts. Tattoos are often visible. They are *güeros* found suddenly in Mexico City because they've been booted from their native country—the United States—into Mexico, a place where they might have been born but which has become entirely foreign to them. Deportations from U.S. prisons have risen sharply in recent years. The repatriated and "rehabilitated" often wind up here because Mexico City is a big place. There is money, and hustle, and maybe they can find some kind of work—if people are willing to give them a chance. Joe's case indicates that's probably rare. Sometimes these guys end up selling candy on the metro.

Their presence in D.F. is not exactly new. The photography and essay book *Cholos a la Neza: Another Identity of Migration,* by Pablo Hernández Sánchez and Federico Gama, says the source of the cholo look in Mexico City predates the present wave of U.S. prison deportations. Beginning in the 1980s, young guys in the outskirts of the city were drawn to the styles and cultures represented in popular U.S. movies about pachucos, gangsters, and life in the barrio: *Zoot Suit, Colors, American Me, Mi Vida Loca, Blood In Blood Out.* The cholo subculture then flourished in Ciudad Nezahualcóyotl in the 1990s, when migrants began returning home after time spent in California, bringing that influence directly to the streets of Mexico City. They formed Mexican copycat versions of some of the most fearsome *pandillas* from the North: Barrio Logan, the Mara Salvatrucha, Sur 13, the Latin Kings, and Florencia 13.

Federico Gama's images in *Cholos a la Neza* show a self-contained world populated by guys who look exactly like guys in California barrios—gang tattoos, Dickies slacks, tough poses, flashing gang signs—in settings that appear completely transplanted from north of the border—Chicano murals, like the one on Adonai's wall, lowriders, tricked-out bikes. "These guys are responding to the binationality we are living in Mexico," Gama tells me one day. "The border is no longer Chihuahua, Tijuana, Reynosa, the border is now all of Mexico. The border arrived to Mexico City, the heart of the country, and now from there is a strong relationship with Los Angeles, with New York, with Chicago."

Cholos in Mexico, Gama says, are living a U.S. achievement narrative that is sharply different from most.

220

"For them the American dream is not the same as you guys understand the American dream to be. The American dream is coming back with Nikes, Dickies pants, jerseys, with caps, with tattoos. When they see someone like that, they go, '*Órale,* that's a real gringo.'"

In Mexico City, I am a real gringo, too. After three years of living here, I am still referred to as *güero*—white boy—by strangers on the street. To *capitalinos* who know enough about what a U.S. upbringing produces—our manner of walking, for one, quick and exasperated, our tentative Spanish, that starting *pocho* accent—I am a gringo regardless of how dark my skin might be. I am a Mexican gringo, if you will.

We are still regarded with some level of suspicion in Mexico City. Native *capitalinos* might see *pochos* as cultural bastards. In the city of swindlers, people might also presume *pochos* pose an easy opportunity to squeeze some extra pesos out of the day. But mostly people in Mexico City these days just want to make connections.

"What part of the U.S. are you from?" a girl asks me plaintively one night.

She is making a deep and accurate assumption; not a word has yet been shared. I am with Susana, at our bar on the downtown alley near the mound of garbage. Again. I tell the girl where I am from, and she just starts crying on me, there in the middle of the cantina, by the jukebox. She cries about how she misses her man on the other side. She holds on to me tight, clutching my shoulders, feeling for my California skin.

"There, there," I say, holding her. For a moment, I am her transmitter, connecting her to her migrant husband, the man who left her behind.

A drunk guy on López Street comes up to me as I'm walking home one night. He is stumbling, lost and intoxicated on a Sunday evening. Without thinking it through, he starts talking to me in a slurring English.

"Hey, man, do you know where this bar is, man?"

I tell him.

"All right, cool," he says, in that California drawl.

It happens all the time, a reading of my *pocho* exterior at first glance, a presumption comfortable enough for the strangers who skip the questions and just dive right into English when addressing me.

"Where are you from?" they ask up front, sizing me up and down at scenester parties. "You have this *onda* Chicana all over you ..."

"Hey, man." A guy at Cultural Roots, a reggae club downtown, leans in to me, indicating my instinctive pose of toughness, *machín*, as my punk friend Reyes would say. "What are you so mad at?"

For those of us who are back-and-forth in our cultural stance and worldview, we can *feel* each other when our paths cross on the streets of D.F. No words are necessary. We move about Neza, Iztapalapa, Tepito. We sense and spot each other at a market, on the metro. We share a mutual regard, less amicable than respectful, vaguely competitive. Anywhere in Mexico, I know another barrio guy from the U.S. Southwest when I see one, even from behind. This is how Mexico City is making me more instinctively aware of my Californianess.

At African Star one night, a reggae club in Neza, dancing, free, I'm thinking about my aural influences, the sounds I was raised on. In other words, what my older siblings fed me. My older sisters, Lisa and Sandra, were cholas back in the day. In the eighties we were surrounded by Latin freestyle and early hip-hop, electro, and R&B. From San Francisco, the Central Valley, and New Orleans, Ernesto brought us ska, postpunk, and new funk. From Tijuana and the barrios of San Diego, Luis Gaston introduced

us to Chicano hip-hop and the most quality subterranean reggae. Through Sergio I absorbed classic rock—Santana, Jimi Hendrix, the Doors—and pure nineties' hip-hop—Dr. Dre, Too Short,
Snoop, Ice Cube, Notorious B.I.G., Wu-Tang Clan, the Fugees,
De La Soul, Rakim, Nas.

This was my true cultural formation, the sounds in the car on
the way to school, in the driveway, in our rooms, BET on blast every
afternoon after school. In Mexico City, in certain worlds, the beats
come back to me. They echo through the clubs, parties, *toquines*,
through the haze of Oaxacan weed. They belong to the archaeology
of the moment, the fluidity that exists between North and South,
the unifying thump. I reside in those in-between spaces, the rip-
ples, the intersections.

One day I go to Calle República de Argentina deep in the back
of Centro, Tepito territory. I come upon a stretch of the street that
is lined primarily with stores that sell baseball caps. I find a spot
with a stand outside lined with straight-billed caps that are in plain
colors, from black to pink, with the elaborate skull-and-flower Ed
Hardy–esque designs that are in style right now among some of the
tepiteños, and knockoff caps for certain American teams: NY, LA,
AZ, and SD, the insignia used by the San Diego Padres. It is block
letters, the *S* placed slightly above the *D,* both symbols knitted in
heavy white.

Does this mean a critical mass of San Diego barrio exiles is in
Mexico City? What about Arizonans? Nah, I decide, these must
just be popular pairings of letters. I ponder the SD cap. This is not
a piece of attire I would ever feel comfortable wearing in actual
San Diego, but here, the insignia calls to me. I go for the straight-
bill SD cap, in dark brown. I pay my fifty pesos for it, slap it on,
cock it to the right, and walk back into the energy and noise of
the street.

Shortly after I move into my apartment in the Centro, I go next door to meet the neighbor, Osvaldo, an architect. I knock on Osvaldo's door and see the inside of his house, a cozy, Catholic apartment. With a simple hello he walks past me and heads to my apartment, just to check it out. It is empty except for my bed and desk. I ask Osvaldo, "How do you deal with the noise, from the *ambulantes*?"

Osvaldo looks at me flatly. He says he read a book and took a course on how to disconnect himself from it.

The *ambulantes* on my block, the street vendors, play music from their special little enclosed market on blast all day, from eleven in the morning to about nine at night. Every day. The speakers are on the concrete, on the sidewalk, facing the open air. Early on, I debate whether I should go down to the guys who sell Shania Twain and Beyoncé, *cumbias* and reggaeton, Vicente Fernández, and an audio English-learning program, and tell them, "Yo, guys, can you turn it down a little?" This is one option. My other option, I think, is to complain to my borough government, a very American gentrifier thing to do. But then, at the *delegación* they'd probably ask for my name, my address, and who knows what they might do with that information. I picture it somehow getting back to the mafias that run the street vendors—the D.F. government negotiated to get them into their new indoor spaces, off the sidewalks—and then somehow, in a not so nice way, its getting back to me.

My third option, the most winsome of all, would be to write them a clear, direct handwritten note calmly explaining how the noise from their stage-grade speakers is perfectly crisp and sound in my apartment, and probably all the apartments above and to the sides of me, and if they would please not play their music at full blast all the time, maybe just downgrade it a bit, even a quarter down. I would sign the letter and slip it under the grates of their market in the middle of the night and wait for something to happen. It's like something I would do if I were thirteen years old, but I'm desperate.

The noise comes in every day as I settle in, invasive, unapologetic, mocking me. I ask the landlord, the *licenciado*, what he thinks about the noise problem from the *ambulantes* when I go downstairs to pay my first full month of rent. Well, he tells me, he's tried to go over there, tell the guys there's a lady in the building who is sick, and they don't care. They just say they have to play it loud or else they don't sell anything.

I ask Osvaldo if talking to the vendors would be effective, and he said it wouldn't, they wouldn't care.

"It's just the way it is," he says.

Uriel concurs. "It would be like talking to a window."

It's noisy, he admits, but at least it's good noise. At least it's decent music most of the time. I mean, music that when it comes on, you don't mind 100 percent having to listen to it. Even "Feel Like a Woman." At least it's not nineties' high-energy Mexican techno on loop or something awful like that. "And Dance with the Devil," or something like that. Uriel is right. I have to learn to live with the noise. I have to embrace it. I have to realize that something about the racket is nourishing.

After smog, noise is the most prevalent pollutant in Mexico City's air. Both have their obvious drawbacks but both also have their magic. When I lived in Los Angeles, the toxic coastal smog created some of the most spectacular and psychedelic sunsets I have ever seen. Here, in the high landlocked capital, the smog sits on you but it also makes for dazzling skyspaces. Neon orange, electric gray, brilliant purples, and slanting pinks. I begin to listen to the noise as a blanket of security. Noise, like smog, means people, commerce, signs of life. There is safety in noise, as there is safety in numbers. Silence is not to be trusted because in Mexico City silence is insincere. The city never wants to be quiet.

There is peace to be made with the noise. I now try to picture my square, little apartment as a magical urban tree house—without a tree—hidden above a really exciting river of people and energy. There is magic on the streets, I tell myself. *The hustle! The raw kernel of big-city life!* Listening to Beyoncé or Wisin y Yandel blast through my bathroom window every day reminds me, ultimately and of all things, that I live in Mexico City. That means a place in the world with too many people, too much pollution, and too much noise. It is a place, like so many others in the world, that runs on illegal street commerce, on pirated content, on pirates, like my fantasies of cities in Africa and India and the Middle East, and the borderless barrios that those places share with neighborhoods in London and New York and Chicago. It is a truly cosmopolitan place because here, in the orbit of Tepito, every kind of film, concert video, or album, no matter how obscure, is potentially within grasp, expanding our boundaries and influences.

More than extravagant parties or roaming mariachis, life in Mexico City means an English lesson on fruits and vegetables booming in my ears, supersized and out of my control during my morning shower.

It takes a tall Scandinavian woman with lanky features and a rough tenor of a voice to break down to me, finally, what it means for me to be living here in Mexico City.

It is early 2008. I'm wandering the desolate gloomy streets of Colonia Roma hoping to fight the wave of depression that comes with the dusk of Sunday, every Sunday, without fail, no matter what city I'm in. I meet up with Josh, a twenty-one-year-old student from Louisiana, and we talk about home, about graffiti, and our parents. We sit down for tacos on Álvaro Obregón, then find our way to an apartment of a friend of his, to sit around on leather couches and watch the TV show *Dexter* with subtitles on, except on the parts where the Cuban police officer throws Spanish into the dialogue.

We sip tequila and have popcorn and packaged *chicharrón* chips doused in lime and chili. When I'm sufficiently certain that dusk has passed, and that I can walk home without too much Sunday gloom, I thank the hosts and get up to leave.

"And what's with the English?" the tall Scandinavian woman, Josh's friend, asks suddenly.

"The English?"

"It's very good," she says.

"Oh," I respond, getting it. "I'm from California."

"You're not Mexican?"

She is genuinely confused.

"No, no, I'm Mexican American."

"Ah! Well, you've come home," she concludes happily.

"Well, no one in my family has been here," I reply. "I'm the only one who's made it here."

Made it here. The words roll together and fly away. The girl smiles big and is truly pleased to meet and greet. Our cheeks meet in the customary good-bye kiss. "Welcome home."

Back I go to the sidewalks, toward metro Hospital General. The night is chilly, crisp, and still for January. I listen to the streets and walk steadily. I had been trying to communicate to Josh's friend that I am not "home" because my family is not native to central Mexico, but to her it doesn't matter. To her I am in my epicenter, the belly button of my ancestral homeland. She is proud, for me. I stroll down busy Cuauhtémoc, past the door at number 226, where

I lived for a few weeks in summer 2002, three stories above the roaring boulevard, with two Scots and a Mexican from Torreón.

I peer in. It looks the same, the heavy glass-and-metal door, the tiled art deco passageway, the box elevator and narrow staircase. I'd go up every night and sit on the porch and watch the river of traffic below and wonder what I was doing here. Tonight everything is the same. The Scotiabank branch downstairs, the Sanborns café down the block, the stark hotel across the street, the Benidorm, still somehow in operation. The city has miles and miles of "passing-through" hotels. For lonely businessmen, hapless tourists, lunch-time trysts between married men and their mistresses, married men and their male lovers, drug deals, for dying.

Walking to the station, I feel the flash of familiarity. The *torta* and taco stands, the homeless people begging for small coins, the reeking steam rising from vents leading to a subterranean nowhere. This is home, the impossible megacity. Some find it in New York, some in Los Angeles, for some it is in Europe or East Asia. For some it is Mexico City. Walking here, I could be anywhere. Streets and people and sounds and bad smells. Sidewalk obstacles and sex shops. A new jetliner cruising down to earth on the established pathway overhead. Megacities do not pretend to be pretty or picturesque, do not pretend to deny that ours is now a planet overrun by humans, and that humans are filthy and destructive creatures but are also prone to romancing one another. The megacity is the perfect place for romance. Romance between two people, between strangers exchanging quick looks on a platform. Romance for the tenuous proposal that is a global society.

On the platform at metro Hospital General, two teenage couples are ravenously making out. On the train, an African man in hip-hop gear who must have teleported onto Mexico City's Line 3 from the subway in New York or in Paris nods in my direction.

Easy-listening is playing softly from a few strategic speakers in the transfer corridors of metro Centro Médico. Then, in the Tacubaya station's main transfer passage, three deaf people, one man and two women, are happily chatting in Mexican sign language. They have found each other.

It is Sunday, so more love, more couples making out on the escalators up. Back on the surface, a fully costumed clown, in full makeup, heading home after a long day's work. Clowns work parties, then drum up extra earnings performing wacky skits on the trains. The clown and I nod to one another when our paths cross. Everyone leaving the metro tonight is going along to the humid little boxes that we call our bedrooms, home, aware that in the modern megacity the walls that separate our homes are membranes that only temporarily keep apart the millions and millions of people who must, at all times, breathe the same city air, eat the same city food, share the same treacherous city sidewalks, and greet the same city clowns heading home on Sundays in red plastic noses and long flappy shoes.

15 | The Seven Muses of Mexico City

El Águila Ciega, 2010. (Painting by Daniel Lezama.)

From the Associated Press:

> 12:48 PM PDT, April 27, 2009
> MEXICO CITY—A strong earthquake struck central Mexico on Monday, swaying tall buildings in the capital and sending office workers into the

streets. The quake rattled nerves in a city already tense from a swine flu outbreak suspected of killing as many as 149 people nationwide.

"I'm scared," said Sarai Luna Pajas, a 22-year-old social services worker standing outside her office building moments after it hit. "We Mexicans are not used to living with so much fear, but all that is happening—the economic crisis, the illnesses, and now this—it feels like the Apocalypse."

Co-worker Harold Gutiérrez, 21, said the country was taking comfort from its religious faith, but he too was gripped by the sensation that the world might be coming to an end. "If it is, it is God's plan," Gutiérrez said, speaking over a green mask he wore to ward off swine flu.

People are standing in rows around the center of the Zócalo, held back by an invisible line made by soldiers from the presidential guard, placed a few meters apart. The soldiers stand at attention, their boots gleaming in their white laces, their white gloves spotless, their green helmets covering faces marked by the severe glare shared by sentries guarding only the most solemn of totems. Around the plaza traffic moves as usual, people and cars and buses and trucks. But in the center something important is about to happen, the lowering of the enormous national flag that is hoisted to the top of a towering pole in Mexico's preeminent central square. Everyone, the soldiers, the people, stand silently, waiting for the drum detail to emerge from the National Palace.

It is not every day you stumble upon the flag ceremony at the Zócalo. When you do, for Mexicans and foreigners alike, it is important that you wait and watch. The ritual is dazzling, and it has been a particularly significant week in the story of the nation's sense of self. Barack Obama has made his first visit to Mexico as head of state. It is spring 2009. The U.S. president's visit was intended as a display of solidarity with the southern neighbor at its most trying historical juncture in almost a century. The political class, the infrastructure, the entire social contract, were being held hostage by the threat of the stateless narco cartels. Could Mexico survive the orgy of drug-related violence? And if it could emerge intact, would Mexico ever be the same state again?

The two presidents met in an almost baroque welcoming ritual at Los Pinos, with bleachers full of rosy-cheeked schoolchildren from a few surrounding academies joyously waving tiny American and Mexican flags. Felipe Calderón spoke, Obama spoke, their words instantly translated between English and Spanish by unseen voices that sounded extravagantly worldly and well educated. The two nations would be friends, *compadres* against the threats that challenged them both: organized criminal syndicates, climate change, the global economic recession. Obama promised that undocumented immigrants would no longer be subjected to humiliating racial profiling in the United States. To be a Mexican in the United States, Obama assured, would now be A-OK. A year later, Arizona would pass a law that allows police officers to ask to see someone's immigration papers if "reasonable suspicion" exists they are in the country illegally, and Mexico's government goes up in arms. But at the moment, the salutations appear genuine.

"All across America, all across the United States, we have benefited from the culture, the language, the food, the insights, the literature, the energy, the ambitions of people who have migrated from our southern neighbor," the American president declared.

Mexico, wounded but proud as ever, needed the reassurance. Mexico needed the gringo country's money to fight the cartels.

So how did Mexico articulate its needs to the U.S. executive and his delegation of diplomats and business leaders? By inviting them over for a drink. At the National Museum of Anthropology, the grand repository of Mexico's archaeological skeletons, Obama and Calderón and legions of dignitaries from both countries clinked glasses together in a toast of goodwill. It was tequila. They toasted twice.

Barack Obama spent less than twenty-four hours in Mexico City during his visit. One commentator in the United States warned—without any sense of satire—that sending Obama to D.F., even for less than a day, would be a matter of serious national risk. We wouldn't want the emissary of empire to get *too* infected with the toxicity of the Mexican way of doing things. Or infected literally, with the swine flu virus that had by then already been surfacing in the country, unknown to most of the population. Air Force One delivered Obama to the Benito Juárez International Airport and military helicopters shuttled him to the comforts of Polanco and Chapultepec Park. The Beast, the Cadillac-made fortress-on-wheels that Obama commutes in at home, drove him between meetings and the Presidente InterContinental hotel, although word eventually leaked that the president did not in fact ride in the Beast but in another less ostentatious vehicle hidden within his caravan. The presidential car had been flown from Washington, D.C., to be used simply as a decoy, an imperial extravagance. One local newspaper noted that the visiting president did not set foot upon a Mexican sidewalk during his twenty-hour visit.

Obama nonetheless promised to return. Both parties agreed to work together more closely in the future—just as every other president visiting Mexico has said since John F. Kennedy. Calderón emphasized that Obama was most welcome. Warm salutations poured endlessly in both directions. To me, a sadness hung over the affair. Inviting Obama into the most intimate spaces of Mexican nationhood—Los Pinos, the anthropology museum—implied a kind of defeat, an indistinct lameness.

Yes, we're good enough to host and pamper the American president, the pageant said. *He really likes us.*

On the Friday after Barack Obama departed Mexico City, I am among the many faces of Mexican society who intersect daily on and around the Zócalo. We find ourselves facing an especially buoyant and proud Mexican flag. It really billows and flaps majestically, I think. Its enormous panels of white, green, and red are glowing in the neon-poison sunset. I sit against the municipal-government palace and watch as the drumming detail of the presidential guard march solemnly out from the Palacio Nacional. A tension rises from the ground, the *beat, ba-beat, ba-beat,* of the military drums. People stop and stare, then join others along the edges of the long rectangle made by the line of standing guards, ready to join in the salute.

The soldiers' white gloves give me a bit of the creeps. At Tlatelolco in 1968, white gloves were the signal of evil. Government agents donned them to identify themselves once the order was sent to fire upon the unarmed masses. White gloves, the clean, pure call of state control, now worn by the guardians of the most sacred national totem. As the soldiers lower the flag, the drumming intensifies. Above me I notice that Mexican flags flap at attention on all the surrounding palaces, including the Metropolitan Cathedral. More people who are passing through the plaza stop and gather in silence. Many raise their right arm straight across their chest, the right palm straight, facing downward. It is the salute Mexicans are taught since kindergarten.

The guards roll the enormous flag into a long tube, ensuring with a total religiosity that the fabric never once touches the brown floor of the Zócalo. They march back in lockstep to the Palacio Nacional, and the drumming ends. Silence, then activity once more. The people who had gathered seem to release a collective heave of fervor. They now spread apart, move along, crisscrossing one another on the Zócalo as if nothing had happened. Back to normal.

Across the way, near the open-wound ruins of the Templo Mayor of Tenochtitlan, a temporary digital-clock installation marks the time that remains until celebrations begin for the bicentennial of independence and the centennial of the Revolution. Its digits tick backward, more terminal than celebratory: *516 days, 05 hours, 54 minutes, 01 seconds.*

Dropping into a cab on Victoria Street. We are soaked. Delirious and giddy from the rain. Too much rain. Pouring angrily, sloshing in pools and streams on the street. The driver can barely see through his windshield. He looks a little frightened. The rain seems *alive.*

"This rain," someone in the car says, as if speaking to it and not us. We sit in silence, listening to the downpour drum upon the roof of the car as we inch along. "What's up with the rain?" someone asks.

"It doesn't matter," comes a reply inside the car. "In 2012, this will all become a lake again anyway."

For days one July it won't stop raining. It rains all day. In the morning, during the lunch hour, during rush hour, all night. It is unusual summer rain for Mexico City because it is a cold rain, where the rain feels as if it is seeping under your skin, chilling your marrow. Hustling around, people wear scarves and navy coats and buy easily breakable umbrellas at the entrances to metro stations. On Sunday nights, I sit in the cold living room of an empty apartment, covered in a blanket, shivering. I listen to the raindrops dance down the building's inner well. Its tiny splashes echo upward. Alone, I think, rain in the well of a building is one of the most depressing sounds there is.

You can't escape the rain even in the subway. Water drips in through the heavy layers of asphalt, concrete, and pipework above the tunnels and crowded passageways. Many of the metro lines go aboveground when they radiate away from the center, so trains return to the core dusted in raindrops. The seats nearest open windows are drenched. Nastily, the showers almost always hit during the afternoon and evening rush hour, spreading misery and respiratory bugs among millions. Whenever Mexico City experiences a rainier than usual streak in the rainy season, a curious urban legend resurfaces. So the saying goes, ever since the National Anthropology Museum obtained a massive pre-Hispanic statue of Tlaloc and placed it at the museum's entrance, it has rained more and more violently in the D.F. They say Tlaloc, the god who supervises rain, must be restless. One of the two sanctuaries that sat atop the Templo Mayor in the ceremonial heart of Tenochtitlan was dedicated to Tlaloc. The other was for Huitzilopochtli, the god of the sun and of war.

Who is to know? All I know is that rain here has its own personality. Sometimes it is hard and mean, making people slip and fall in the puddles or on steps, cruelly. Sometimes it is gentle and sad, pattering away on thirsty plants and cracking sidewalks. It rains and rains, yet Mexico City is officially running out of water. With too many people here, potable water must be imported from surrounding regions to keep the thumping urban jungle alive and running. Reservoirs are drying up. Tensions over the water supply are growing between the D.F. and its neighboring states, between neighborhoods, and inevitably, between people. They're saying that soon the price of water will skyrocket in the Valley of Mexico. They're saying the lack of potable water in Mexico City could potentially, in the bleakest scenario, spark urban warfare. Jorge Legoretta, a prominent water expert and a former borough chief in Mexico City's Cuauhtémoc *delegación*, is predicting that within the next few years we could also have a "great flood," as extreme and catastrophic as the flood of 1629, which nearly destroyed the city.

What does that do to the psyche, I've been wondering, living in an extremely rainy place that is at the same time running out of potable water? A place that was once an enormous lake? That could return to lake form someday, by the will of the gods? I can't wrap my brain around it. Is this the beginning of the spiral? The end of it?

Everything is thrilling in Mexico City because everything is out of whack. There is a sense of delirious rupture, everywhere. The video game arcades are packed. I'm looking at male stripper clubs for women in Iztapalapa, extremely open public displays of affection on the metro, between men and women, children, and men and men, at political propaganda calling for the death penalty for kidnappers. A man without legs is begging on the sidewalks, just a human stump riding on a skateboard. A little girl is stricken with panic, screaming in an indigenous language, as she gets off a metro car before her mother can reach the closing doors. On the platforms, the blind are walking the blind. How, I wonder, can we mediate the doom?

We forget to ask it. We are watching out for ourselves, like true urban rats, wondering, *What is it that I want?* I fall into the same mind-frame, thinking lecherously, *I want it all.* I want clothes. I want the Hustle. I'm a Mexico City mutant eating sidewalk hamburgers for dinner under a pounding brown rain. I want cactus juice to flow through my veins. I want to dance upon the pyramids. I want to sweat droplets of jade. I want acid.

Will we make it to the harmonic convergence of 2012, when the Mayan calendar supposedly "ends"? What will Mexico City throw at us then? Sometimes I pass the bicentennial clock near the Zócalo and imagine it's a lift-off count. I imagine the moment when the clock reaches its row of zeros. *Five . . . four . . . three . . . two . . . one.* I imagine the Zócalo flagpole rumbling and breaking away from the ground, revealing a gargantuan Aztec spaceship that had been hidden inside the earth, shaped like an inverted pyramid. The spaceship is made of obsidian, jade, quetzal feathers, and volcanic *tezontle* stone. Its exhaust smells like burning sage. I imagine every person in Mexico City rushing to the noise and light of the plaza as the spaceship prepares to lift off. The people are peeling their clothes off and emitting primal human screams while fighting one another with their bare hands, each one of the many millions clamoring to get on board, desperate to leave the impossible city, to new uncharted planes. I march myself home, microwave some popcorn, and lie back on my bed, listless. I stare at the white ceiling and watch a neighborly cockroach scurry to his destination upside down, defying gravity. There is nothing left to do, I think, but rejoice in the thrill of the coming unknown.

No one can know what's going to happen near the end of 2012, the end of the Fifth Sun in Mayan cosmology. Astronomers tell us there is nothing to worry about. The planet will not shift its poles and send us into oblivion, the experts say. Wild theories, however, are abundant. Neo-indigenist mystics believe there will be a massive realignment of time and space, that the world as we know it will cease to exist. Others believe we will have a "rebirth" that is unimaginable to us until we see it. I know with certainty that there will be an election in the United States, an election in Mexico, and a lot more anxiety and madness than we've ever seen—and we've seen plenty of both already.

One night in Condesa, I meet two travelers from Norway who are living in some kind of commune a couple of hours outside D.F. They looked like magical Burning Man graduates, but a little more hard-core about it, with dreads and garments in muted browns and pastel blues and greens, and weird piercings. We are talking about a "light show" being planned at the Mayan ruins in Palenque. A notable trend among regional governments in Mexico is the mounting of concerts and "light shows" at pre-Hispanic archaeological sites. The spectacles are intended above all to generate tourist revenue but are seen by archaeologists and their admirers as desecrations. The pyramids of Mexico may be unknown to us in so many ways, yet we are deeply aware that, as Paz wrote, they are our "geometric metaphor for the cosmos," "the point of convergence of the human world and the divine." The Norwegian women and I sit together and bemoan the phenomenon. I ask one of them what she thinks will happen in 2012. Something *big* will happen, she replies, but not in the form of a cataclysmic end to the world, more like a "shift in consciousness."

"It's already happening," the Norwegian girl says excitedly. "It's already started."

I never know when Denise is going to call. Sometimes she falls off from the busy grids of modern communication for weeks at a time.

Sometimes she is in Guadalajara, where she is from, but sometimes she is in Puerto Vallarta or Los Angeles, where she was born. When Denise is in D.F., sometimes I see her, sometimes I don't. One day I spot her on her bike in Centro. She is pedaling in wildly high heels. We stop for some quality street-stall seafood near my apartment and a scoop of ice cream, Denise's idea. She has little impulses, expressing them by starting off with a lulling "I don't know why, but I feel like a . . ." and then going for what she feels like. This day it is ice cream. She doesn't know why. We sit in the Michoacana shop and watch the Centro *chaka* teens playing the arcade games and the large Great Dane, the mascot of the block, lounge on her favorite corner. I ask Denise, trained as a fashion designer, for an interview. It starts with her birthplace.

"*Nací en* Monterey Park in Los Angeles, California, *y crecí* in Hollywood," Denise says, speaking Spanglish. She often mixes her prepositions, switching an *at* or an *on* for an *in*. "Where the Chinese Theater is . . . like, five blocks . . . in Sunset. I went to elementary in Blessed Sacrament."

Denise left L.A. early on. She was ten when her mother moved them back to Guadalajara. That's where Denise went to middle school and high school. "I had no choice to go back to Mexico. I just felt weird, a little bit paranoid, because of my way of dressing . . . and going to Guadalajara. . . . Even though I was ten, I was wearing Doc Martens and little booty shorts. I was hard-core at, like, ten, eleven. Actually, I think I'm very timid. I don't know. And I think clothes had an effect for me . . . to express myself."

Denise has yellow and orange shoulder-length hair, a wide, sensual mouth, and spacey green eyes. Her legs are long and lean. She is not a daughter of privilege. In her late twenties, she still dresses "hard-core." Fashionable, but fashionably punk, with touches of *Party Monster* glam. One day it might be tiny jean shorts not worth more than twenty pesos and barely even there, paired with shiny gold designer heels worth ten times that. Before going out at night, she might draw white squares around her eyes and mouth with makeup, or do her eyes to recall the classic manner of women cholas in Southern California. The clothes she designs reflect her personal style: sexy, eccentric, a kind of classic barrio futurism. In the four years I've known Denise, I have never looked at her and not instinctually thought, *Denise is gorgeous.* No matter where she walks, heads turn. It doesn't matter what she is wearing or what time of day it is, she radiates a quality that is both welcoming and intimidating, an almost awkwardly pure grace. She oozes natural style, one of those rare alchemical arts, handed down from muse to muse. Denise Marchebout, to me, is one of the city's muses.

She was eager to get out of Mexico after her mother passed away, a victim of a long illness. At just twenty-one years old, Denise had no other family in her life but her maternal grandparents. She was aware of her father but only as a distant figure, unavailable, in another city. And she had her friend Enrique González, another style misfit from Guadalajara. Restless after high school, they decided to check out London. Denise worked odd jobs and submerged herself into the underground nightlife of the turn-of-the-century city. She was living, it sounds like, just as I was living in Mexico City at the same moment, one unknown to the other. Day to day, led by instinct and the will to survive, led by inspiration.

"You meet people there that you'd never imagine," Denise says, now in Spanish. "There are English people, but mostly you meet people from other places. What I loved was that all those people who have that restlessness, from every country, make it to London. So if you are a restless person, London is the city for you. The honey for the bees."

London life was not easy, though. "I was a squatter, we went from place to place," Denise goes on, back in English. "We didn't have that much money, actually, to live in one place. I met someone, I'd go, 'Look, I don't have a place to stay, can I live with you for a week?' At first, I stayed in one place for two months, then a month here, a week there, with my luggage. With all my luggage."

She found work tending bar.

"I remember the images of myself, walking at five in the morning, walking the Thames at five in the morning, with my huge coat and just looking at the river, for minutes, going . . . 'I'm tired.'"

We laugh.

"Once I slept in the bus and woke up in the end, at the end of the bus. The driver was like, 'Miss, this is the last stop.' I go, 'Where am I?' I was so tired."

Denise studied fashion design at St. Martins. Then, after her journey in London, she and Enrique brought all the influences of the contemporary club scene in the U.K. back to Mexico. It was 2005. They started an electroclash night in Mexico City. "That period was when Quetzal got here, all the fashion kids," Denise said, switching back and forth now between English and Spanish. "It was the first time this was happening in Mexico. There were parties, but not electro like this, from London. We wanted to push people to dress up and go out. There weren't any blogs back then. Nothing of what we have now."

Denise speaks in an esoteric and liberating way about style. The alchemy of fashion, you might say.

"I think people should be themselves, you should love it, if you love it, it's something that's in it," she says, pressing her hand into her chest and heart. "But to be authentic, that's the key. And be legendary a little bit, to have your own look is being legendary."

We find our way to a Starbucks. Denise wants a latte and carrot cake—she doesn't "know why." It is raining again. Enrique and Denise decided to open a boutique in Mexico City for their budding fashion lines. They called it Clinica. They were among the first to bring a globalized, underground style sense to D.F., just as they had planned. "I think money should never be a limitation for what you want to do," Denise explains passionately now. "You can never limit yourself. Do it. *Do it. . . . Find a way. . . .* If you really want it, you'll find a way."

"Do you like living in Mexico?" I ask.

"I'm always inspired by Mexico, more than Europe. When I was in St. Martins, and they'd send me to the library, I'd take out books about Orozco. I'm from Guadalajara, and I had never seen an Orozco. But you look at the paintings, the colors, and you could do a whole collection inspired by Orozco. So I was drawn to the Latino, the Latin American. It's going back to your roots, going back to basics."

What about the decadence?

"That's what can happen in a big city. So often we feel alone. You're looking for fame, you're looking for everything, and there is access to drugs there, too. Some people say, 'I need to be high to be creative.' But I don't. I think about a person like Quetzal, who I think was . . . naturally insane."

We both laugh.

"Like, naturally insane," Denise goes on. "When you're naturally insane, I don't think you need all that, because I think it clutters your vision and ideas. And that's what I think was interesting about him, he was one of those special human beings that . . . you know . . . they have something."

We pause for a moment, remembering.

"And I think it's just a loss, what happened to him. People should do less drugs and be more creative, or . . . do more than drugs. Because in the end, you die, you wanna leave something. You wanna be remembered. 'Oh, she did this,' you know? That's what I think. You want to leave your grain of sand. Lots of people have kids. But some people don't have ambition to have kids. Some people have more ambition to show their work, or their own personal thinking. It's like leaving their grain of sand to another person. It's passing on their own restlessness."

We are having tall glasses of white sangria at a bistro sort of place in the Centro. Two other appointments come and go. I am not looking at my watch. Around Denise, time becomes a playground for inspired indecision. Eventually she decides she needs to get somewhere she should have been three hours ago, and I walk out with Denise to frenetic Madero Street. She asks if I can hail a cab for her. I spring into action. We meet our cheeks in good-byes. I stick my head inside the taxi and tell the driver, "Take care of this one."

I walk home, refreshed, almost high. Denise is one of those figures a life in Mexico City so often breeds, a woman walking with pure creative force, an agent of energy not just a figure to be admired, channeling in every word and deed the four continents and five centuries that form the base of Mexico's invisible cosmic pyramid. A few, I think, making my way through the multitudes, become internationally famous or historicized, such as Frida Kahlo, Tina Modotti, or Leonora Carrington. For each of those, however, many other muses in Mexico City reveal themselves only to a few.

I think about this some more, until the idea spawns its own vision. It is evening. I am wrapped in foreboding and loneliness when, peering out to the street from my study, through the smog and rain, peering into the future, I see the Seven Muses of Mexico City walking among us.

We do not locate them but instead they find one another. It is a December in the distance of the new century. The scheduled harmonic convergence has passed. For the past year everyone has been talking about pyramids, potentiality, and a pyramid-shaped Aztec spaceship that never comes. The city is drowning in water it cannot drink. There are three self-declared presidents and four "autonomous" regions governed peacefully by new drug cartels that are named after saints. Cocaine is sold clean and fresh on street corners and sprinkled over coffee and tea. Marijuana fumes are pumped into the metro in the morning, hashish during the evening commute. The twin volcanoes overlooking the Valley of Mexico have been glowing mysteriously in the color orange, pulsating with an inner anger. The sky is either pink or purple, never blue. We speak in tongues—Spanish, English, Spanglish, Náhuatl, Korean, emoticons.

The Seven Muses bump into each other on the street. One is a striking young designer with long legs and yellow hair. One is a powerful but inconspicuous old medicine woman from Oaxaca. One is a graffiti artist with dreadlocks to her knees and green fingernails. Another has black skin, a billowing orange Afro, and sings in four languages. One is a transgendered kabbalist and neo-indigenist with Asian features, slanting eyes and arching cheekbones. The other is a sign-language interpreter with no arms and purple plastic hair who draws comic books out of brain waves. The last of the Seven Muses is a gothic queen, in black leather and black lace from head to toe, and a trench coat long enough to hide an obsidian sword. She reads the Torah, Koran, New Testament, Popol Vuh, Bhagavad Gita, Bataille, Artaud, *The Catcher in the Rye*, and June Singer.

The muses bump into each other on the Zócalo and freeze and stare. They begin weeping in joy. They join hands. There is chaos everywhere. Thunder and lightning, sheets of rain. Pulque—the maguey-plant "drink of the gods"—begins spouting from the city's fountains and cracks in the concrete. The valley is returning to its lake form, restoring the equilibrium. We climb to our rooftops. Buildings crumble, revealing buried pyramids. Joined together, the Seven Muses of Mexico City sing and dance awash in a divine light, lifting into the sky, the *boom ka-chi ka-chi boom* of a *cumbia* rhythm echoing down from the heavens. The Seven Muses are levitating. A shimmering red egg appears before them. They bow in unison and prepare to herald our rebirth.

| Notes on the Chapters

As I wrote *Down and Delirious in Mexico City* I practiced what might be called incidental research. I looked at sources sent to me, books or films recommended, stuff passed my way, and in many cases I picked up books or magazines from markets or temporary stalls on the street. The following is a selective and subjective compilation of notes on sources and inspirations.

1 | Guadalupe's Test

The primary source for the historical references here is *Mongrels, Bastards, Orphans, and Vagabonds: Mexican Immigration and the Future of Race in America,* by Gregory Rodriguez (Vintage Books, 2007). In Chapter 2, Rodriguez examines the central role played by the Virgen de Guadalupe in the formation of mestizo mixed-race identity in the land that would become Mexico. Rodriguez emphasizes that the Tepeyac hill had served as a sacred space for Tonantzin, where sacrifices and feasts were held in honor of the feminine deity, and also that the "origins of the holy image . . . are contested." But in any case, the image's power was undeniable from the very beginning. She "became a symbol of an emerging mestizo nation."

"The private flag of Mexicans" is a quote from Richard Rodriguez, in his 1973 collection of essays *Days of Obligation,* as cited in *Mexico in Mind: An Anthology* (Vintage Departures, 2006).

"La Morenita" is Spanish for "The Little Dark One," in feminine form; one of many nicknames for the Virgen de Guadalupe.

"*Órale*" is such a great slang word. It is used to mean "Right on" or as an especially affirmative "Yes."

Mota is slang for marijuana, weed.

As for *pocho,* I cite the current definition on UrbanDictionary.com: "It is a derogatory term that can be someone who's trying to 'act white' but it has been largely embraced by Chicanos with a sense of defeatist humor—We're pochos, *y qué*?—so that it's actually becoming more playful than bitter."

2 | Points of Arrival

I'd like to cite two texts that helped influence my move to Mexico City. First, a pulpy short novel titled *Nada que ver,* by Jorge Dorantes (Era, 2001), about the exploits of a crew of hard-partying, apocalyptic *chilangos,* and, second, *The Other Side: Notes from the New L.A., Mexico City, and Beyond,* by Ruben Martinez (Vintage, 1993). Other sources that capture the gritty allure of Mexico City in the early part of the decade and century include the films *Sexo, Pudor, y Lágrimas* (1999), directed by Antonio Serrano; *Amores Perros* (2000), directed by Alejandro González Iñárritu; and *Y Tu Mamá También* (2001), directed by Alfonso Cuarón.

Later, I found great insights in *First Stop in the New World,* by David Lida (Riverhead Books, 2008), and *El Monstruo: Dread and*

Redemption in Mexico City, by John Ross (Nation Books, 2009). For looking at D.F. through the lens of texts on architecture, urbanism, and visual culture, I enjoyed consulting *Citámbulos: Guía de asombros de la Ciudad de México* (Oceano, 2006), by Ana Álvarez Velasco, Valentina Rojas Loa Salazar, and Christian von Wissel; as well as the book *ZMVM,* by Fernando Romero (LCM Laboratorio de la Ciudad de México, 2000).

From Lida: "Despite her role in the Conquest, for much of Mexican history La Malinche was a highly revered figure, nearly as exalted as the Virgen de Guadalupe."

The term *mexica* is the Náhuatl word for Aztecs.

Regarding the reference to the Central de Abastos as the "largest in the world," I turn to the blog Edible Geography ("The Axis of Food," June 28, 2010), by Nicola Twilley, who writes that the market "sprawls across a 327-hectare site on the eastern edge of the D.F., dwarfing fellow wholesale food markets such as Hunt's Point (24 hectares), Tsukiji, or even the massive Rungis, outside Paris (232 hectares)."

The Sad Night, *Noche Triste,* occurred on June 30, 1520. Cortés's forces were nearly vanquished by the Aztecs, who ambushed the invading army from canoes under the cover of night as the conquistadors were moving across Tenochtitlan's western causeway to Tacuba. Hundreds of Spaniards and their Indian allies were killed. For Cortés, it was a sad night.

Mexico City's population is difficult to measure with precision because, like other megacities, its functional boundary is open to interpretation. I've seen Internet and official sources with population estimates ranging from 17 million to 23 million. Nearly 9 million people live in the Federal District and some 14 million live in the state of Mexico, but not all commute to or interact with the city core. Twenty million is a comfortable median between 17 million and 23 million, and it is the figure many journalists have used since the start of the 2000s. The Valley of Mexico, which includes the Federal District and portions of the states of Mexico and Hidalgo, is now generally said to have a population of 20 million, making metropolitan Mexico City the second or third largest in the world.

Mexico City sinks at different speeds in different parts. During a talk at Postopolis, a week of talks and presentations related to urbanism, at the Museo Experimental el Eco, on June 10, 2010, water expert Jorge Legorreta said D.F. sinks about seven centimeters a year.

Regarding boxing, everything I know is oral history, provided by my father, Sergio Hernandez, and my maternal biological grandfather, Abel "El Tiburón" Rojas. One source that I read for an introductory history is *Pasión por los guantes: Historia del box mexicano I, 1895– 1960*.

3 | *La Banda*

My primary sources for the history of the Chopo market and alternative youth subcultures in Mexico City include: the independently published history cited in the chapter text *Tianguis Cultural del Chopo: Una larga jornada,* by Abraham Ríos Manzano (Ediciones AB, 1999); *¡Qué Onda Ése . . . ! De contracultura y otros rollos,* by Merced Belén Valdés Cruz (independently published, 2008); *Rock Mexicano,* also by Valdés Cruz (independently published, 2002); *¿Qué transa con las bandas?,* by Jorge García-Robles (Editorial Posada, 1985); relevent sections of *Los rituales de caos* (Era, 1995) and *Amor perdido,* both by Carlos Monsiváis (Era, 1977); relevant chapters in *Refried Elvis: The Rise of the Mexican Counterculture,* by Eric Zolov (University of California Press, 1999); and small magazine articles, news stories, and video clips too numerous to mention. I found *¿Qué transa con las bandas?* most illuminating.

The book is a collection of oral histories of members of the early *chavos banda* gangs.

For the history of the 1968 Tlatelolco massacre, the 1971 Jueves de Corpus massacre, and the Avándaro festival, I consulted the sources listed above as well as *La Noche de Tlatelolco,* by Elena Poniatowska (Era, 1971); *El 68: La tradición de la resistencia,* by Monsiváis (Era, 2008); *Tragicomedia Mexicana 1,* by José Agustín (Espejo de México, 1990); the archival exhibit on 1968 at the Centro Cultural Universitario at Tlatelolco; and the fictionalized film version of the night of October 2, 1968, *Rojo Amanecer,* directed by Jorge Fons and released in 1989. I also read the essays and consulted images and text in *The Age of Discrepancies: Art and Visual Culture in Mexico, 1968–1997* (Turner, 2007), the catalog for the UNAM exhibit of the same name, edited by curators Cuauhtémoc Medina and Olivier Debroise. I collected many flyers, magazines, brochures, and other prized print ephemera in my frequent visits to El Chopo.

"Perfect dictatorship" is the phrase coined by Peruvian novelist Mario Vargas Llosa, who, in 1990, accepted an invitation from Octavio Paz to visit Mexico and discuss "liberty" in eastern Europe. Live on Televisa, according to the next-day story in *El País,* Vargas Llosa drifted off-script during the discussion and said: "*México es la dictadura perfecta. La dictadura perfecta no es el comunismo. No es la URSS. No es Fidel Castro. La dictadura perfecta es México.*" ("Mexico is the perfect dictatorship. The perfect dictatorship is not Communism. It is not the U.S.S.R. It is not Fidel Castro. The perfect dictatorship is Mexico.")

A crucial recent text on the "Dirty War" is *México armado,* by Laura Castellanos (Era, 2007). Castellanos charts the history of all armed rebel movements in Mexico in the period of 1943–1981, and lays out the still murky events of urban warfare and targeted repression that characterized the "Dirty War" years in Mexico.

Foreign bands barred from playing in Mexico at the height of the PRI is mentioned in Zolov, in his conclusions in *Refried Elvis*: "At a 1980 Johnny Winter performance in Pachuca, for instance, the concert 'ended in police repression against the audience.' Two years later, at a Mexico City opening of *Ladies and Gentlemen, the Rolling Stones,* police entered the theater and prevented the screening. These were among scores of similar incidents that affected foreign rock performance in Mexico and characterized to an even greater degree native rock."

4 | Fashion & Facsimile

This chapter appeared in Spanish translation in the March 2010 issue of *Gatopardo* magazine, which is produced in Mexico City and distributed across Latin America. Gratitude is due to the editors and staff there.

There is a robust fashion blog community in Mexico City and a burgeoning local fashion press and several other outlets online. In addition, major style chain publications have Mexican editions, including *Elle, Harper's Bazaar, Vogue, Nylon, GQ, Playboy, Maxim,* and *Vice.* Plenty of people labor in the fomenting of a fashion consciousness in Mexico, which, despite my critique of the scene at large, is an encouraging recent development in Mexico City culture.

On the gentrification of the Condesa, I consulted two primary text sources. First, the chapter on the Condesa in Lida, *First Stop in the New World,* offers a neat summary of the neighborhood's transformation between 2004 and 2007. Second, I looked at a tangential document of the early formation of the "scene" in the Condesa through activities at the independent art space La Panadería, in the art book *La Panadería: 1994–2002* (Turner, 2005), edited by Alex Dorfsman and Yoshua Okon, who cofounded La Panadería with Miguel Calderón. An interview

Dorfsman conducts with Calderón for the book is telling. Dorfsman asks Calderón to contrast the international scene, which they had just absorbed while studying abroad, and Mexico City in 1994, when La Panadería was founded in the Condesa. Calderón responds: "Even though Mexico City is one of the biggest metropolitan areas in the world, in 1994 it was full of limitations: you had to wait for days to go to a party; there were hardly any concerts; bars were really hard to get into, if you weren't there with a date or if you were wearing sneakers they wouldn't let you in; cantinas always closed early, drinks were really expensive and the music was always the same top 40 crap."

5 | The Warriors

"The Warriors" is based primarily on first-person accounts in interviews; news reports in print, radio, and online; and on loads of Web chatter, as cited throughout the chapter itself. I also consulted other sources for general overviews of the anti-emo violence in Mexico and the emo culture at large. The book *Nothing Feels Good: Punk Rock, Teenagers, and Emo,* by Andy Greenwald (St. Martin's Griffin, 2003), is the best study of this wide subcultural genre as it grew in the United States. A strange book, *Emos, darketos, rockeros: ¿Cuál de ellos es su hijo?,* by Argentine writer Constana Caffarelli (Lumen Mexico, 2008), is worth looking at purely to see how such cultures are superficially distilled for worried parents of teenagers. On this note, *Chilango* magazine published an entertaining cover story on parents and their emo kids in June 2008 ("*Mi hijo es emo,*" by Caroline Vera). I actively reported on the anti-emo violence as it developed on my personal blog.

A version of this chapter appeared in the May 2008 issue of *Gatopardo* in Spanish ("*La* flower *sin el* power"), and another version, with added material, appeared in English in issue 95 of *Flaunt* ("The

Emo Wars: Dispatch from Mexico City"). I also commented on the anti-emo violence for a radio piece for NPR by Michael Scott O'Boyle ("The Mexican Emo Wars," April 16, 2008) and for a video piece for Current TV by Ioan Grillo ("Mexico City Emos," July 18, 2008).

I'd also like to acknowledge the work done by the Federal District Human Rights Commission on the violence among youth groups, particularly the November 2008 issue of *DFensor,* the commission's magazine.

Regarding the use of *naco* by one of the teens I interviewed in Querétaro, a wonderful essay on the term and its sociocultural implications by Claudio Lomnitz, "Fissures in Contemporary Mexican Nationalism," was published in *Deep Mexico, Silent Mexico: An Anthropology of Nationalism* (University of Minnesota Press, 2001).

Sergay.com.mx extensively covered the anti-emo riots, signaling early on an alliance of gay activists with emo youth.

The Multiforo Alicia on Cuauhtémoc Avenue, headed by Ignacio Pineda, is an essential meeting place for the many subgroups that constitute the "urban tribes" of Mexico City. I've attended many concerts and events there in the course of my work. Héctor Castillo Berthier, a researcher at the UNAM, is the go-to voice for youth-related issues for most mainstream news outlets in Mexico City. He is chief organizer behind Circo Volador, a youth-oriented alternative arts and music space in the Jamaica area of the Venustiano Carranza borough.

In the May 2008 issue of *Eres,* a Televisa pop culture magazine, Kristoff explains his heritage as such: "I was born in Poland and I arrived here in '82, when I was eight years old. . . . My father is my hero because at 43 years old and without speaking Spanish he decided to take his wife and kids and move to a place that had nothing in common with Poland. It was either that or starving to death."

Emo, despite what its detractors say, emerged in Mexico as a defined subculture with defined characteristics. It might not ever have an ideological or "tribal" foundation but it does imply a specific sound in rock, a specific look, and adherents who are transient, of a specific age, and self-define as "hard-core." Most of the emo teens I interviewed for this chapter have since moved on from emo, adopting even less defined markers of any specific group, but still making rock. For insight into this, and insight into how emo is relentlessly marketed at teens, I looked at a couple of issues of *Mundo Emo* magazine, a sort of generic cultural fanzine published by a company called Mina Editores.

6 | The Lake of Fire

There is no greater influence on my conception of the cosmic violence of the Valley of Mexico than the major archaeological sites that stand as living historical emblems amid the urban density: the Templo Mayor, Teotihuacán, Tlatelolco, and Cuicuilco. The sites' related museums offer illuminating examples of how native groups lived, helping me understand the centrality of ritual human sacrifice in cosmologies and sociopolitical orders in Mesoamerica, which can make the imagination run wild. I was also inspired in this chapter by Rodrigo Betancourt and conversations with Mariana Botey, whose knowledge of, first, the cultures of violence in Mesoamerica and, second, Georges Bataille, gave me unmatched insights into intersections over distant philosophies. Then I read *Queer* by William S. Burroughs, and it rattled those pathways even more.

Historical review of the Conquest crucial to my understanding: *Mongrels, Bastards, Orphans, and Vagabonds,* by Gregory Rodriguez (where I drew the "die like brutes" reference); a standard textbook history *The Course of Mexican History,* by Michael C. Meyer and William L. Sherman (Oxford University Press, 1979; fifth edition);

and *Death and the Idea of Mexico,* by Claudio Lomnitz (Zone Books, 2005), a thought-provoking guide to understanding the ways in which death and structures of violence have helped shape Mexico's identity since the point of contact between Mesoamerica and Europe. The quote "foundational holocaust" is from *Death and the Idea of Mexico* (Chapter 1).

Thanks to the D.F. natives who shared with me personal stories about the 1985 earthquake.

It's important to note that air quality has improved steadily in Mexico City since the 1990s and start of the 2000s. It has probably improved even more since this chapter was written. The chapter's narrative basis is two higher-than-normal smoggy periods I experienced early after moving here. The *Washington Post* and Agence France Presse reported in 2010 that Mexico City no longer belongs to the list of the ten most polluted cities on the planet, thanks in large part to systematic efforts to reduce pollutants in vehicle emissions, manufacturing, and by building more public transit, which includes shared public bike programs ("Mexico City drastically reduced air pollutants since 1990s," by Anne-Marie O'Connor, Thursday, April 1, 2010, and "Clean-up efforts pay off in Mexico City," by Sofia Miselem, March 17, 2010).

Other sources guided and inspired me here. First, the photography of newspaperman Enrique Metinides, whom I interviewed in Mexico City in October 2006 and October 2010. His work basically functions as a decades-long catalog of the most gory and grisly crime and accident scenes in Mexico City. The interview appears in edited form in Los Angeles–based *Journal of Aesthetics & Protest,* No. 5.

Mexico compares favorably to other countries in homicide rates per 100,000 inhabitants, according to a 2009 study by the Centro de Investigación para el Desarollo (CIDAC) entitled "Índice de Incidencia Delictiva y Violencia." El Salvador tops that list, followed by fourteen other countries including Venezuela, Colombia, Belize, Jamaica, Ecuador, Brazil, the Dominican Republic, and Paraguay before reaching Mexico at number sixteen.

The painting that is mentioned at the end of the chapter is *Erupción del Volcán Xitle, Destrucción de Cuicuilco,* by Jorge González Camarena, 1962.

7 | Kidnapped

This chapter was based almost entirely on media reports that I clipped and consulted daily on the Silvia Vargas and Fernando Martí kidnappings in the following sources: *La Jornada, Excelsior, La Prensa, Reforma, Crónica, Milenio,* and *El Universal.*

Data differs on kidnapping statistics in Mexico because a uniform definition of what constitutes kidnapping does not exist and because a vast majority of such cases are said to go unreported. Additionally, according to a 2010 study by the Instituto Ciudadano de Estudios Sobre la Inseguridad (ICESI), states report different kidnapping data than the federal government. Another degree of ambiguity is added with the question of whether the kidnappings of migrants traveling through Mexico should be counted as opposed to merely those of Mexican citizens. In a 2008 study by the Netherlands-based organization IKV Pax Christi ("Kidnapping Is Booming Business"), in 2006 Mexico was the worldwide leader in the "estimate of the absolute number of kidnappings," followed by Iraq. Citing ICESI, the report estimates that only 29 percent of kidnappings in Mexico are not reported to authorities.

ICESI also says that among express kidnappings alone, which usually occur in taxi cabs, corrupt police participate in about 12 percent of such cases. The group provided no such figure on more sophisticated ransom kidnappings such as those of Silvia Vargas and

Fernando Martí. At the height of the kidnapping hysteria, the *L.A. Times* reported ("Fear of kidnapping grips Mexico," by Ken Ellingwood, September 1, 2008): "A report by the daily *Milenio* newspaper said a review of federal statistics showed that only 1 in 8 kidnapping victims was a business executive. About half were in the middle class or below, the newspaper reported." This piece is also where I gathered the figure of approximately seventy kidnappings a month being more realistically a figure of five hundred.

The march against *"inseguridad"* in 2008 was the second such march in Mexico City since 2000; the first occurred in 2004 during the administration of Mayor Andrés Manuel López Obrador, who claimed the demonstration was a political plot against him cooked up by the right.

8 | The Delinquent Is Us

Numerous sources informed my understanding of corruption in Mexico, first among them news accounts of lynchings or attempted lynchings of both police officers and suspected "delinquents," in addition to archival articles and John Ross, in his comprehensive descriptions of illicit political acts in each post-Revolutionary presidency, in *El Monstruo*.

I looked at several issues of *Proceso*, though the magazine has a somewhat shoddy reputation of making factual errors on small points of information. But *Proceso* remains an influential running screenplay of the drama that is Mexican graft, extortion, money laundering, illicit and unethical political activities, violence, and the drug-trafficking organizations' operations and conflicts. People read it. Two particular issues were crucial here: The *Proceso* of November 16, 2008, published an excerpt of *Los cómplices del presidente;* and the November 1, 2009, issue, which revisited the federal government's questionable investigation into the Learjet crash that killed Juan Camilo Mouriño.

The CIA World Factbook sets Mexico's poverty rate this way: "18.2% using food-based definition of poverty; asset-based poverty amounted to more than 47% (2008)." It's been getting worse. Reuters says ("Rising poverty weakens Mexico conservatives," by Jason Lange, April 14, 2009): "A slowing economy has probably pushed 4 million or 5 million Mexicans into poverty in the two years through August 2008."

Regarding the reach of the cartels into non-drug-trafficking enterprises, I source the *L.A. Times* ("Mexico drug cartels thrive despite Calderón's offensive," by Tracy Wilkinson and Ken Ellingwood, August 8, 2010): "The groups also are expanding their ambitions far beyond the drug trade, transforming themselves into broad criminal empires deeply involved in migrant smuggling, extortion, kidnapping and trafficking in contraband such as pirated DVDs."

9 | A Feathered Serpent in Burberry Shades

Sexuality in Mexico is a complex issue that demands further research. I would like to acknowledge some sources that have helped me understand it to this point. First, the photography book *Flesh Life: Sex in Mexico City,* by Joseph Rodriguez (PowerHouse Books, 2006), with an introduction by Ruben Martinez, who writes of his time in here: "I was swept up by what I experienced, initially, as the incredible eroticism of having all that's hidden and forbidden suddenly laid out before you . . ."; Lida's chapter on sexuality in *First Stop in the New World,* "Sex Capital"; the July-August 2010 edition of *Arqueología Mexicana,* a special issue on sexuality in Mesoamerica; the unforgettable novel *El Vampiro de la Colonia Roma,* by Luis Zapata (Grijalbo, 1979); and one book by Salvador Novo, Mexico's earliest modern gay writer, *Las locas, el sexo y los burdeles* (Diana, 1979).

For my understanding of gender and sexual identity, including transgender identity, a strong influence is the work of June Singer in *Androgyny: Toward a New Theory of Sexuality* (Anchor Books, 1976).

10 | Negotiating Saints

The story of Jonathan Legaria was reported extensively in the newspapers in Mexico City, and I contributed my own reporting in several visits to the Santa Muerte altar in Tultitlán, partly for a video report for Current TV, produced by Grillo ("Mexican Death Saint," November 25, 2008). *Death and the Idea of Mexico* by Lomnitz informed the writing here as well. The destruction of Santa Muerte altars in Tijuana occurred in March 2009 and prompted protests in Mexico City (see Intersections, "Messing with the Santa Muerte . . . ," April 14, 2009).

Regarding Tepito, it's important to note that its myths are often more powerful than its realities, and acquiring real data on how Tepito operates is a difficult task that few foreign or national researchers have undertaken. Most news reports related to Tepito usually cover police operations and arrests of pirate vendors. In November 2007, the magazine *Letras Libres* published a reporter's exploration of Tepito ("*Bienvenidos a Tepito*," by Cynthia Ramírez) that gave a population figure of 38,000 residents and at least 10,000 "floating" residents, or vendors. The story says Tepito's official languages are Spanish and Korean "if you want to establish commercial relationships in the zone," but makes no reference on whether any native to the barrio actually speaks it. Seven of ten pirated items sold and consumed in Mexico pass through Tepito, *Letras Libres* said. The Monsiváis quote—"a cemetery of ambitions, a congregation of thieves"—is from the chapter on Tepito in *Días de guardar* (Era, 1970).

Regarding the cult of San Judas Tadeo, it is relatively new, so research or journalism is scarce. In June 2010, the *New York Times* produced a video report on the subculture ("Streetwise Saint Joins Mexico Drug War," by Greg Brosnan and Jennifer Szymaszek) that focuses mostly on the crime and addiction connection between the cult and its adherents. The *sonidero* culture is closely tied to the San Judas and Santa Muerte cults, but my understanding is limited compared to the work of others, including Mariana Delgado and the team behind the Proyecto Sonidero, ethnomusicologist Cathy Ragland (see "Under the Musical Spell of the Sonidero; Mexican D.J's Relay Messages, on Dance Floor and to the Homeland," *New York Times*, November 22, 2003), and the work of *tepiteño* cultural producers and local historians.

11 | Originals of Punk

There is plenty of documentary and historical work on Mexican punk. The work of Mexico City filmmaker Sarah Minter was vital to my understanding of the general geography of punk in Mexico City. Minter produced a documentary/drama chronicling the lives of punks in Ciudad Nezahualcóyotl called *Nadie es inocente* (1987), then returned two decades later to seek out her original subjects for another film called *Nadie es inocente 20 años después* (2010), which she kindly allowed me to view before its release. For an understanding of contemporary punk, I just spent a lot of time at Chopo, again, and attended punk shows and events. The photographs of New York–based William Dunleavy and D.F's Federico Gama are a strong window into the geography of punks and related subcultures in recent years.

I found research or journalism on the history of the razing and development of Santa Fe lacking, but did look in newspaper archives and niche articles to get a general sense of how Santa Fe became what it is today. Lida's take on Santa Fe in *First Stop in the New World* is also very illuminating. He sums it up this way: "There are no parks, no gardens, and there is nowhere to walk."

I also consulted a few academic sources to get a sense on how punk is read by researchers, including "Punk and globalization: Spain and Mexico," by Alan O'Connor at Trent University in Canada (International Journal of Cultural Studies, 2004).

12 | Attack of the Sweat Lodge

The temazcal is part of a curious resurgence or reclamation of pre-Hispanic cultural practices that operates awkwardly in the context of the social stratification, urbanization, and globalization that defines everyday life for many Mexicans, and certainly most of those who live in the capital. It's also increasingly used as an "immersion" or "relaxation" spectacle for foreign tourists who congregate in Mexico's coastal resorts and officially tagged "*pueblos mágicos*" such as Tepoztlán. Nonetheless, its practice is taken seriously by a segment of educated modern Mexicans and Mesoamerican descendants. What's not clear to me still is how prevalent the temazcal remains among indigenous communities in Mexico, and whether its use has changed in any measurable way since pre-Hispanic times. For now, the question is another future area of inquiry.

The Neza portion of this chapter appeared first as raw notes on Intersections, then in an expanded form in the inaugural issue of *Slake* magazine in Los Angeles, as "Tripping Out in Neza York." Neza is fertile territory for studies of urbanism and built space, and has many researchers and historians who work on chronicling the *municipio*. A recent easy-to-digest account in English is found at the site Geo-Mexico.com ("Nezahualcóyotl, an irregular settlement which grew into a monster," July 2, 2010), which describes the area in part: "By 2000, Nezahualcóyotl had essentially joined the mainstream. Nearly all residents had electricity and TVs, over 80% had refrigerators, 60% had telephones, nearly one in three had access to an automobile, and almost one in five had a computer. While Nezahualcóyotl has slums, gangs, and crime, it also has tree-lined boulevards, parks, a zoo, banks, shopping centers, offices, libraries, hospitals, universities, cinemas, and apartment buildings."

In a documentary project called *Mazahuacholoskatopunk,* Mexico City photographer Federico Gama looks at the lives of urban Indian young people who come to the city from the outer highlands to find work. Gama gives the subculture a term—*Mazahuacholoskatopunk*— that amalgamates those urban cultural subgroups and adds a reference to the Mazahua nation. Their style is a shield in the urban jungle, a way to identify and defend themselves against other city natives, Gama argues. The photos have been exhibited extensively and were published in book form (IMJuve, 2009).

13 | Death by Decadence

This discussion of the culture of excess and "decadence" is based mostly on anecdotal stories, which run aplenty if you spend enough time among people who survived the anecdotes. One tragic case of note is the death in 2005 of Natasha Fuentes, a daughter of the celebrated writer Carlos Fuentes, under mysterious circumstances in Tepito. Fuentes was reportedly scoring drugs and pregnant at the time of her death, but the incident has never been conclusively reported. Rumor and myth, once more, may be colliding with fact here.

Quetzal is sadly one of those noteworthy deaths of a young person in Mexico City, a death that as time goes on also becomes subject to rumor and mythologizing. The December 2008 issue of *Chilango* features a long article reported by César L. Balan on Quetzal's formation as a young designer, his relationship with Marvin Duran, and his death, including interviews with his family. My rendering here is purposefully not peppered with too many details. My intent is to frankly and thoughtfully address a loss that affected me, many friends, and the "scene" at large. I'd like to acknowledge once more Quetzal's survivors, his family, whom I had the pleasure of meeting during a Sunday celebration after a successful Fashion Week for Marvin y Quetzal.

Regarding addiction, I consulted directly with anthropologist Angela Garcia, author of *The Pastoral Clinic: Addiction and Dispossession Along the Rio Grande* (University of California Press, 2010). She writes to me in an e-mail: "Even the wealthy, with decent access to rehab (only about 20% of Mexican addicts receive some kind of care), relapse. Rates of relapse are estimated at 70–90%. So quitting is super hard, even when the desire/access is there. Folks I've talked to say the poorest Mexicans are experiencing the steepest rise in addiction rates (esp. crack), but are often not included in these studies because they're 'outside the system.'"

Marvin Duran continues working on the Marvin y Quetzal label with friends and collaborators. In 2009, Susana Iglesias won the first international Aura Estrada Prize, honoring young Spanish-language women writers, which author Francisco Goldman established in honor of his wife, Aura Estrada (Q.D.E.P.). El Internet, meanwhile, is open again as of early 2010—for now.

14 | At Home

There are active and historical graffiti and hip-hop communities in Mexico City with strong ties to similar scenes in other cities in Mexico, the U.S., the rest of Latin America, and Europe. A recent significant documentary on the scene is a 2005 title *Otros Nosotros*, produced by Mexico's Canal 22. A book of interviews with Mexico City MCs is

Ciudad Rap, compiled by Alan R. Ramírez and published in 2010; it's available at hip-hop stalls and shops at various points in the city. I also looked at many editions of several Mexico graffiti magazines, most prominently *Rayarte,* and attended several hip-hop or graffiti events in different areas of the city.

Regarding the deportation of prison inmates without proper U.S. documents, I cite the *Washington Post,* which reported that in 2008 the U.S. government deported 117,000 "criminal aliens" from prisons and jails ("U.S. to Expand Immigration Checks to All Local Jails," by Spencer S. Hsu, May 19, 2009). In an Obama administration pilot program expanding efforts started by George W. Bush, the government hopes to expand a fingerprint database to search for illegal residents in prison populations to all local jails by the end of 2012, the *Post* says.

15 | The Seven Muses of Mexico City

The opening excerpt is reprinted with permission of the Associated Press, 2010. This chapter is inspired by the work of Alejandro Jodorowsky, Pedro Friedeberg, the Surrealists movement, and by conversations with various friends, mentors, and muses.

The quote by Legorreta is from a talk at the Postopolis events cited earlier. An important and cutting satire documentary on the culture of fear during the swine flu crisis of 2009 is *Love in Times of Swine Flu,* by filmmaker Gregory Berger, of The Revolutionary Tourist Project (www.gringoyo.com). The Paz quote is from *The Other Mexico: Critique of the Pyramid* (Grove Press, 1972).

How to delve into the contemporary mythology of the end of the Fifth Sun in Mayan cosmology when Hollywood does it for you in a blockbuster summer film (see *2012,* directed by Roland Emmerich)? An intriguing recent article on the topic is by Castellanos, in the February 2010 issue of *Gatopardo,* titled "2012, adiós al materialismo").

The piece is a profile on a mystic and pseudo-prophet named José Argüelles. Castellanos writes (in my translation): "Argüelles presumes the role of preacher and prophet of the message that the 'galactic maya' of the Pleiades left us five thousand years in their calendars, and contradicts the film. In the year 2012 a cycle ends for humanity but will not be the end of the world. The planet will align with the center of the galaxy and from there a new vibrating frequency will take us to a superior dimension, which will have profound effects on the collective consciousness and will succumb the materialistic system that rules today. In this year, on top of that, the cosmic maya could return to Earth. Their spaceships will sweep our skies to take 144,000 terrestrial humans more spiritually evolved than others and carry them to another planet or dimension to continue their learning."

| Acknowledgments

The genesis for this book, and its title, starts at the *LA Weekly* in 2006. Editor Laurie Ochoa gave me one of the weekly's last-ever foreign assignments, to cover the presidential race in Mexico between Andrés Manuel López Obrador and Felipe Calderón. I wrote a story (with edits from Ochoa, Tom Christie, and Joe Donnelly) that used the turmoil of the election as a backdrop for a tale about the culture and moment in Mexico City. It discussed a maturing art scene, a maturing sophistication in Mexico absorbing foreign influences, and a sense of foreboding about the future. The headline for the piece was "Down and Delirious in Mexico City." When it came time to choose this book's title, the winning choice was also the most serendipitous. So thank you Laurie, Joe, and Tom.

Thank you, Colin Robinson, for being the first to spot this book lurking inside me. Thank you, Paul Whitlatch, for helping me see it through with skill and persistence. Thank you, Katherine Fausset, for being a tireless and genuine advocate.

To all the *chilangos* whom I've met along the way, who went with me on phases of this journey, thank you for your generosity, openness, encouragement, and trust. I hope that you find I've rendered your city faithfully and with the love we and so many people around the world share for it. Thank you Familia Uruzquieta. Thank you Familia Mejía Urbán. Thank you Familia Flores Magón Bustamante. Thank you Familia Botey. Thank you Familia Rangel Sánchez. Thank you Mom and Dad, Sergio and Norma Hernandez. Dad, thank you for always being in my corner.

The following lists are long because I feel compelled to thank all the people who have given me a hand along the way.

Thank you, sincerely, in Mexico: Umair Khan, Elka Morgado, Rodrigo "Ponce" Betancourt, Miguel Calderón, Gabriela Jauregui, James Young, Caroline MacKinnon, Jason Lange, Guillermo Osorno, Froylan Enciso, Yoshua Okon, Francisco Goldman, Armando Miguelez, Cristal Ortiz, Savlan Hauser, Alfredo Villareal, Enrique González Rangel, Nuria Hoyer, Mario Ballesteros, Susana Iglesias, Ioan Grillo, Victor Jaramillo, Juan Carlos Bautista, Valerio Gámez, Trisha Ziff, Cindy Hawes, Carine Zinat, Yvonne Dávalos Dunnig, Galia García-Palafox, Andrea Aragón, Cynthia Gonzalez, Rafael Breart de Boisanger, Tatiana Lipkes, Avril Ceballos, Marvin Duran, César Arellano, Carlos Temores, Naomi Palovits, Guillermo Fadanelli, Yolanda M. Guadarrama, Daffodil Altan, Marco Villalobos, Abe Atri, Ana Karla Escobar, Anne-Marie O'Conner, Sumer Susanne Carlos, Ryan Warmuth, Morgan-Lovely N'gouda, Jim Fitches, Rodrigo Hernández, Liliana Carpinteyro, Arturo Mizrahi, Héctor Mauricio Cadena Ainslie, Gabrielle Civil, Adam Saytanides, Elizabeth Flores, Leslie Diego, Carina Guzmán, Niki Nakazawa, Gustavo Abascal, David Lida, Federico Gama, Jorge Arguello, Sarah Minter, Pablo "El Podrido" Hernandez, Maru Aguzzi, Claudio Lomnitz, Michael Scott O'Boyle, Monica Campbell, Livia Radwanski, Jesus Chairez, Lesley Tellez, Anita Khashu,

| Acknowledgments

Diego Jiménez, John Ross, Ali Gardoki, Yasmine Dubois, Florent Ruppert, Rafael Uriegas, Mariana Delgado, Catalina Morales, Anibal Gámez, Tracy Wilkinson, Ken Ellingwood, Natalia "Galletas" Ruíz, Oscar Sánchez Gómez, Diego Flores Magón, Carlos Alvarez Montero, Pablo Chemor, Romeo Guzmán, Pia Camil, Cuauhtémoc Medina, Eréndira Cruzvillegas, Jerónimo "Dr. Lakra" López Ramírez, Laura Castellanos, the crew at Mercado Negro, all my neighbors, and Patrick Corcoran.

Thank you to the crews: the homies in Neza, Reyes and the band in Santa Fe, "Gomita" and the guys in Murder for a Lover, the guys from the tollbooth to Cuernavaca, Señor Arturo and all the friends at Las Duelistas.

Thank you to the artists and photographers who shared their work with me. Your images are golden and indispensable in these pages.

In the United States and elsewhere, thank you Pilar Perez, Adam Jacobson, Richard Fausset, Gustavo Arellano, Alexis Rivera, Ruben Martinez, Alexandro Gradilla, Daniel Alarcon, Aura Bogado, Douglas Foster, Margarita Florez, Juan Maya, Ángel Marcel Porras, Francisco Dueñas, Josh Kun, Andy Greenwald, Gregory Rodriguez, Jonathan Gold, Rita Gonzalez, Mandalit del Barco, Pedro Ciriano Perez, Sandra de la Loza, Ky-Phong Tran, Adolfo Guzman Lopez, Erin Gallagher, William Dunleavy, Eamon Ore-giron, Adam Teicholz, Jessica Sanders, Vincent Valdez, Ashland Mines, Wu Tsang, Ector Garcia, Jose Luis Lopez, Nick Morrow, Valmiki Reyes, Mark Mauer, Nina Mehta, Harry Gamboa Jr., Shizu Saldamando, Jordan Long, Alma Ruiz, Raul Pacheco, Elizebeta Betiniski, Lyn Kienholz, Abel Salas, Melissa Sanchez, Macarena Hernandez, Emi Fontana, Marco Antonio Prado, Sarvia Jasso, Leilah Weinraub, Natalie Rodgers, Mehammed Mack, Eric Zolov, Carolina Hernandez, Alan Mittelstaedt, Sarah Ball, Jorge Neal, Natalia Linares, Elisa

Sol Garcia, Neil Rivas, Rebecca Kahlenberg, Richard Kahlenberg, Erika Hayasaki, Marc Cooper, Cheech Marín, Sasha Anawalt, Reed Johnson, Marla Dickerson, Ben Gertner, Carribean Fragoza, Matthew Fleischer, Erin Blakemore, Richard Lidinksy, Suzi Weissman, Kathy Ochoa, Michelle Neely, Adrienne Crew, Luca Martinazzoli, Nadia Ahmad, Joshua Glenn, Joy Hepp, Ana Castillo, William Nericcio, Alan Minksy, Ernest Hardy, Conrad Starr, Darrel Ng, Samuel Vasquez, Gabriel San Roman, and the esteemed members of the H.C.

Thank you to those whose names do not appear here and who deserve my gratitude.

Thank you, Uriel Urbán, for always being down.

Thank you to my inspirations, the baddest women I know: Susana Chavez-Silverman, Mariana Botey, Andrea Daugirdas, Denise Marchebout, Nina Tahash, Jazmin Ochoa, my sister Erika Hernandez, and Kathryn Garcia. This book is dedicated to those for whom it is primarily written, for the enjoyment of Erika, Sergio, Ernesto, Gaston, Lisa, Sandra, Victor, Michi, Christian, Ángel, Alan, Brian, all our cousins far and wide, for Tía Martha and for all the nieces and nephews.

And in the memory of Anna Andrade, and Dash Snow, and Quetzalcóatl Rangel Sánchez.

Finally, thank you, K. Bandell, a reader in Norwalk, California, who in August 2007 sent me in the post a short note of encouragement and congratulations, the kindest and most sensitive I've ever received.

Postscript

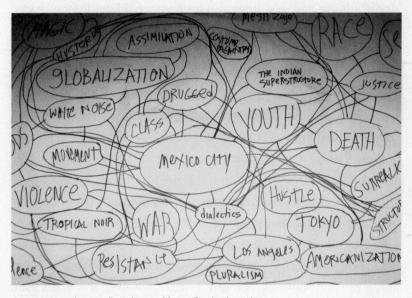

A spontaneous thematic flow chart on Mexico City, by the author.

The Mexico City streets are calling, pulling me away from the keyboard. I pinch my cheeks and step outside.

It is a carnival every day. Food, music, sounds, faces, and clothing of every sort, around every corner. It is a cosmopolitan feast. Cultural riches both fresh and old purr at me from inside museums, theaters, galleries, plazas, cafés, and the ruins of glorious past

271

civilizations. I can enter in a single day a market that's been in the same place since before the Conquest and an IMAX movie theater after checking into the Office Depot. I wait for the next trendy cult, or seek grace in the presence of Xochipilli, the Aztec god of song, dance, queers, male prostitutes, and psychedelic plants.

Life here is good and getting better. The air is clearer. The city is adding new bus lines and a new metro line. Public shared bicycle programs are popular. I look up. Modern new structures reach elegantly into the sky, under construction. I look down. The sidewalks are older than in most U.S. cities. A tag catches the eye that makes me smile. The city is becoming a haven of rights and simple rewards. Same-sex marriage is legal and everywhere I look couples across gender lines express their love for all to see. No one bothers them. Love and freedom conquer hate and demagoguery.

But there is always another side to this place. I have a rule about cities: I don't trust any that all people love unconditionally. You have to hate what you love every once in a while for it to be a healthy affair, especially when it comes with the place where you live. Despite all its gems, there are things I still dislike about D.F. and its culture. I can find a zone of comfort and expression among friends, loves, the families you chose. Yet I've found over the past three years that my social worldview remains constantly at odds with the strict class stratification many Mexicans regard as something like the natural order of things. Class strata makes people fearful of whole regions of their own city, preventing them from opening their experiences to other systems or cultures. The family structure remains strong and insular in society at large. Circles are difficult to penetrate. These realities have brought me many moments of conflict, isolation, and doubt.

I look back at these pages and see a person different from the person I am today. This writer is already becoming a stranger.

Youth ends. At some point I have to take those painful and lonely steps required for the evolution of the psyche. Everyone around me is doing it, too. I am at home here, but I could never say I wouldn't move on. I have visions of Istanbul or Shanghai, a nameless coastal paradise, a dark nightmare in the sort of world we haven't seen yet. Sometimes I see a future back in Los Angeles or on the border. The border is the only place in the world I know that is a metaphor we all live.

—D.H., September 2010